SOCIAL CONFLICT AND THE CITY

Enzo Mingione

Social Conflict and the City

St. Martin's Press · New York

© Enzo Mingione 1981

All rights reserved. For information write:
St. Martin's Press, Inc
175 Fifth Avenue
New York, NY 10010
First published in the United States in 1981
Printed in Great Britain

ISBN 0–312–73163–9

Library of Congress Catalog Card No. LCCC No. 81–1393

Contents

Preface 7

CHAPTER ONE
A Marxist Critical Approach to Urban and Regional Development 9

The theoretical-methodological problems of a Marxist interpretation of modern societies 9
The foundations of a critical approach to the urban and regional question 18
Class conflict and urban development 30
The capitalist state, the fiscal crisis and territorial policies 40
The new structure of the labour market and the crisis of urbanism 55
Recent urban and regional studies 63

CHAPTER TWO
Territorial Division of Labour and Capitalist Development 72

Mode of production and transition 72
Patterns of capital accumulation and urban development 73
Primary accumulation and industrial 'take-off' 75
Role of rural classes: primary accumulation and urbanization 76
Primary accumulation and urbanization in Italy 81
Final thoughts on the comparative analysis of primary accumulation and urbanization 89
Mechanisms of capital accumulation and their complex effect on territory 95
From the city as a factory to the imperialist metropolis 99
Urbanization and economic development in Italy 106
Monopolistic development in Italy, and urban structures 112

CHAPTER THREE
Uneven Territorial Development and the Crisis of
Advanced Capitalism   124

- Introduction   124
- The industrialization process and its territorial logic   126
- Monopolistic accumulation and territorial typologies: the industrial areas   128
- Accumulation and typologies of underdevelopment   134
- Over-urbanization and the underdevelopment cycle   137
- The crisis of capitalism and territorial contradictions   144
- Uneven development within the Italian economic structure   148
- Congestion and dualism in north and central Italy   150
- The question of the south and the poles of growth   154

CHAPTER FOUR
Socialism, Class Conflict, and Land-Use   159

- From socialist theory to socialist experience   159
- The theoretical debate on socialist territorial development   163
- The socialist characteristics of the Chinese experience   172
- Decentralization as a socialist issue   180

Notes   188

Name Index   204

Subject Index   206

Preface

In the late sixties I became engaged in a research and political project on urban renewal and social conflict in central Milan. Many of the ideas which I develop here arise directly from this research and from the experience of working within this city. These and other notions in the book have matured, too, in the context of the critical debate on the 'new' urban studies which has taken place among sociologists, economists, planners and geographers in France, Great Britain, the United States, West Germany, Spain and Italy, and been promoted in particular by the International Sociological Association's Research Committee on Urban and Regional Research and in the *International Journal of Urban and Regional Research.*

I am only too aware that this book is by no means the final word on the pressing problems of our cities. Many points raised here reflect an early stage of theory and practice and the need both for considerable research and, I feel, for new conditions of political and intellectual debate. In Chapter 1, for example, in discussing the links between the theory of political power and the theory of class structure, I suggest the redevelopment of the Gramscian concept of hegemony as a class-based theory of the legitimization of power. I hope this goes some way towards countering the weakness of Marxist theoretical accounts of the relative autonomy of the political sphere from productive relations, but I am nevertheless conscious of deficiencies in hegemonic theory which have significant and unwanted implications for the political praxis of the working class.

In Chapter 4 I discuss questions and problems arising out of a consideration of socialist theory and practice. Here we are in the dark – for can we really award any present regime a properly 'socialist' status? Can we, and should we, argue that socialism will emerge as a world strategy for the solution of problems and injustices? If so, then what would be its main characteristics? When and where will it emerge? How, too, shall we be able to detect true socialist tendencies and to distinguish these from the symptoms of capitalist decay and decline? The contrast between the aspirations and the achievements of the socialist revolutions indicates the need for caution. I hope the reader will forgive the tentative nature of the answers I provide.

The four chapters of this book began life at different times and for different purposes. They have been rewritten and restructured for this book and I have been particularly helped in this by the editorial efforts of my friend Stefano Magistretti and by the publishers' editors.

Chapter 2 is based on an article in *Current Sociology* (volume 23, 1977) and I am grateful to the International Sociological Association for allowing me to reproduce it with relatively few modifications. Chapter 3 was written originally as a paper for the Ninth World Congress of Sociology, Uppsala, Sweden in 1978 but has been entirely rewritten. It now fully reflects my views concerning the main characteristics of the current capitalist crisis. Chapter 4 is a reshaping of several papers written between 1976 and 1977. I would like to have felt more satisfied with it, but feel, firstly, that at present I am unable to do any better yet, secondly, that the problems of socialist development must be raised and examined even if no easy solutions to them are thus revealed. I expect that some of my readers will find the ideas presented here controversial. If they do, I look forward to and welcome debate and criticism of them.

June 1980   Enzo Mingione

CHAPTER ONE
A Marxist Critical Approach to Urban and Regional Development

THE THEORETICAL–METHODOLOGICAL PROBLEMS OF A MARXIST
INTERPRETATION OF MODERN SOCIETIES

Social scientists studying modern societies have encountered certain serious problems which have impaired the validity of traditional systems of interpretation, and necessitated a major redefinition of their theoretical approach. The world has seen the progressive development of a socio-economic order founded on elements and processes which the traditional interpretations of capitalist societies, whether neo-classical, neo-Keynesian, monetary, marginalistic or orthodox Marxist, cannot easily take into account. The new problems, briefly, are these:

(1) The production of goods has become a secondary activity in comparison with the provision of services and other activities lying outside the cycle of production of goods in the strict sense, activities such as advertising, marketing, technological research outside the factory, management and bureaucratic control of companies, etc.

(2) Both the production of goods and these other economic activities occur within an increasing variety of situations: large, technologically very advanced factories where labour productivity has reached very high levels; small units of the informal economy where lower labour productivity is compensated for by lower salaries, by a lower susceptibility of workers to political and trade union influence and thus by a greater elasticity and mobility of the labour-force; the public sectors in which labour productivity counts for little while policy agreement with the elites in power and clientistic connections are favoured.

(3) The complexity of socio-economic organization has favoured a re-ordering of the international economic situation. American hegemony has diminished and ground has been gained by those industrialized economies favoured by particularly advantageous

circumstances (West Germany and Japan), and by some economies of the Third World which are rich in energy resources and raw materials (above all the OPEC countries and South Africa). Concurrent with this there is an increasing tendency towards economic stagnation, in a constantly diminishing rate of growth. This results from continual recessions, government policies, the prospects of energy crises and especially from the combined control exercised by large companies and governments.

(4) State intervention in the organization of economy and society has increased considerably but has become increasingly problematical owing to the incompatibility of the two different types of objective present. On the one hand, the state attempts to ensure constant economic growth and therefore the profitability of public and private economic activities. On the other hand it endeavours to reproduce a social consensus based on full employment and the elimination of the more notable inequalities of income. These objectives are contradictory because the conditions of the former, technological progress and the concentration of capital and expertise, lead to a shrinking employment base and a widening inequality of incomes.

(5) This contradiction has led to the failure of social democratic policies in Europe and the end of the myth of 'welfare' in the United States. In the absence of alternative strategies a serious political void has developed. The large popular movements are still dominated by reformist and social democratic political forces, whilst the elites in power have failed to find a third way apart from the strategy of repression and authoritarian control, and that of reforms, based on a selective redistribution of the excess profits deriving from unequal exchanges with the Third World, towards certain classes of workers.

(6) The experience of the so-called socialist countries has been similarly problematic. These countries, driven by the need to promote an accelerated industrial development in relatively backward economies, and in conditions of partial but increasing integration in the world capitalistic market, have developed a socio-economic organization very similar to the capitalist one. The mass of workers is deprived of any possibility of participating in or influencing political decisions and an authoritarian bureaucracy has developed which exercises a strict control over all aspects of social and individual life. The intellectual competition between capitalist ideals and socialist ones has been replaced by a series of inter-capitalistic contradictions, and international struggles for supremacy

between the great powers and between large economic and financial groups.

The result of these new conditions in modern societies is a very complex process of social 'disgregation' (the term is too vague and indefinable to be appropriate but it is the only one that gives an idea of the phenomenon). Within this process of disgregation a number of different elements can be distinguished. The main social classes fragment into numerous components which, at least at the moment, favour the particular interests of the group rather than the general interests of the class (for example, the success of sectarian impulses in the trade unions). The progressive increase of social margination on a wide range of bases, which give rise to new lines of division and discrimination within society (there are many examples: the development of an informal economy which exploits labour in terms very different from those of the official economy; discrimination against women, young people, old people; the continuous diminution of the capacity to employ the potential labour-force, which clearly differentiates the social positions of the 'favoured' minority, who at least work, from those of the majority of the unemployed). An increasingly disgregated territorial structure has developed, which favours local interests rather than general interests (the main example is the revival of regional autonomistic movements, another is the mobilization of city or district populations to protect local interests threatened by national tendencies).

These social structures are contradictory and incompatible but the focal points of the contradictions are so diffuse and differentiated that it is increasingly difficult to generalize about either the shape or the future of social conflict. Furthermore, the main axis of the contradictions of modern societies is progressively shifting from the economic sphere of production relationships to the social sphere of complex reproduction relationships, as will be explained more fully below.

The result of this is that modern societies seem to be characterized by very complex and differentiated elements which cannot easily be accounted for using the traditional interpretative instruments of the various social theories. Social scientists thus find themselves faced by an important choice: they can either emphasize the importance of complexity and specificity by abandoning any attempt to reconstruct a general theory of society and an interpretative methodology suitable to all the different situations; or, alternatively, they can try to construct, or reconstruct, a methodology capable of explaining and interpreting contemporary social processes.

The first alternative is not of great interest to us because, explicitly or implicitly, it undermines the scientific dignity of the study of society. If generalizations are excluded because the complexities and particularities are far more significant than the elements of comparison and common tendencies, no scientific interpretation of social facts is possible, only a disconnected series of episodic observations.[1]

With regard to the second alternative, there exist a number of approaches which differ both from a methodological and from an ideological point of view. Here I want to mention the important reformulations and revisions which are being elaborated on the basis of the Marxist theory of capitalistic societies, primarily because my own analysis falls into this field. Orthodox Marxist analysis is founded on a number of closely interconnected elements such as the theory of labour-value and exploitation, the theory of accumulation of capital, the theory of classes and of the class struggle. This theoretical approach emphasizes the social relationships of production rather than the other elements of social life and permits the immediate translation into social and political theory of the structural data of economic analysis. These fundamental theoretical elements reveal considerable shortcomings when applied to the new conditions existing in modern societies.

The theory of labour-value and exploitation is based on the belief that all exchange values (which in capitalistic society are fundamental, because production is based on the exchange of goods for money in a prevalently competitive market, and not on use-values, that is, the final importance for the consumer)[2] have their origin in man's working activity. The exchange values developed in the working process are correlated with the average working time necessary to produce a particular good, irrespective of the ability or alacrity of the individual workers. There is exploitation in this social relationship in that the capitalist, who is the owner of the means of production, disposes of the total value created (goods produced) and pays the workers a salary which constitutes only a part of the value they have created. The other part, that is, the surplus value, remains at the disposal of the capitalist. The theories of capital accumulation, of classes, and of the class struggle are based on the theory of labour-value. According to Marx, a significant part of the surplus value produced by the workers is reinvested in order to increase production. This is the central feature of the process of the accumulation of capital. Individual capitalist economic units are obliged to embark on the process of accumulation because they are competing with each other and therefore have to employ their income (profit, that is, the part of the surplus value remaining to the capitalist after he has remunerated other, non-productive, social strata) in order to remain competitive on the market, which means increasing labour productivity and exploitation margins and reducing the production costs of goods. Accumulation is thus a long-established historical process whereby capital continues to increase, creating new productive sectors, replacing traditional productive systems, constantly increasing labour productivity and the exploitation margins of the workers.

A system based on this type of social relationship with regard to production is characterized by the division of society into two fundamental classes with contrasting interests: the capitalists, who aim at increasing the margin of exploitation of the workers in order to be able to reproduce themselves as such and, on the other hand, the productive workers whose interest is not only to oppose increases in the exploitation of labour but also to abolish the system that permits such exploitation.

The conflict between capital and labour is the main dialectical characteristic of all capitalistic social formations because the two parts are complementary and yet have inevitably contrasting interests; a situation which gives rise to a continuous reproduction of the class struggle. The capitalistic mode of production is characterized, furthermore, by a series of contradictions deriving fundamentally from the anarchic character of market-competition relationships. Competing producers regulate their productive capacity with a view to the maximization of profits without taking into account the maximum potential of absorption of the goods on the part of the intermediate and final consumers. As a result overproduction, under-consumption and disjunction between productive sectors lead to economic crises which, as capitalism develops, become increasingly serious and increasingly difficult to resolve. Further, their devastating effects are augmented by those of the class struggle, in which the workers tend to increase their bargaining and political power and develop class consciousness, and an organization capable of disrupting the social order and replacing it with a different social order no longer based on that exploitation of labour which is characteristic of capitalism. This theoretical framework enabled Marxists to establish an immediate connection between the economic factors of production, social factors and the general organization of society. The concepts of value, of labour, of accumulation are not merely elements of economic analysis; they have the more general significance of interpretative elements of society in general.

14   A Marxist Approach

The theory of labour-value, and with it the whole of the Marxist theoretical approach, has been called into question for two different types of reasons. In the first place, many economists say that it is impossible to use the theory of labour-value in the analysis of specific economic situations. It is in fact impossible to translate into terms of value-quantities (average times required to produce a given product) the economic data available: salaries, profits, production costs, prices, which are always expressed in monetary terms. This impossibility of translation becomes even more evident in late-capitalistic societies, where labour productivity differs greatly from one economic sector to another and even from one company to another. This means that in each productive unit the equation between the working time required to produce a good and the monetary expression of the value of that good is different. Moreover, in view of the notable interdependence which has always characterized the productive cycle (from the extraction or production of the raw materials to the final marketing of the product), the calculation of the values is too complicated, even where a limited and detached economic situation is concerned. Such criticisms are justified, but they are also unacceptable because they ignore the methodological-theoretical content of the labour-value theory, which is not proposed as a means of economic calculation but is, rather, a general theoretical instrument for the interpretation of economic issues as parts of a complex social reality. Salaries and profits are not quantities that can be translated into monetary terms so much as general variables, permitting the identification of social classes and of general social relationships. Marx himself[3] was aware of the impossibility of using the labour-value theory for economic calculations. This is demonstrated by the fact that, in his analysis of nineteenth-century capitalism, he never made use of specific monetary data but detailed other macro-social data, such as the level of unemployment, the living conditions of the workers, the long-term trends of prices and salaries, and so on. The emphasis on economic calculation, in the strict sense of the term, leads, on the other hand, to profound segmentation of the study of society, for the very reason that singular monetary data lose all macro-social significance and are completely divorced from an overall theory, which is thus repudiated.

The second series of criticisms is much more interesting and lies at the root of all neo-Marxist theory. I shall mention briefly some aspects of this revised theory which seem to have a particular relevance here. The most complex and general problem derives from the new importance acquired by social reproduction relationships, as opposed to production relationships in the strict sense, in modern societies. The number of workers and capitalists involved in industry characterized by the increasing productivity of labour has become a minority and is tending to diminish. If the exploitation of capital is understood in a restricted sense, as a process taking place only in the economic sectors producing goods for the market, it has to be admitted that this process today involves only a minority of the population, in continuous relative diminution. It would follow that, likewise, the production of surplus value, exploitation relationships, and the class contrast between capital and labour, concern an ever smaller part of society. It is for this reason that it is necessary to interpret the theory of labour-value in very extensive terms and to correlate it with a theory of general social reproduction. Contributions in this area have been made by the Frankfurt school, and above all by Habermas,[4] by the neo-Marxist 'surplus' theoreticians,[5] and by neo-Marxist urban sociology.[6] The theoretical re-elaboration to which these contributions have given rise is founded on two series of arguments.

The process of capital accumulation cannot be interpreted in a restricted sense as an exclusive relationship between capitalists and workers engaged in the production of goods, for it also directly involves various other social groups which have a collective role in the reproduction of capital. Furthermore, capital is also accumulated in the service industry and non-material goods sector. Secondly, the process of capital accumulation is closely linked by a series of complementary social relationships of subordination and exploitation to all the remaining social sectors. Through these takes place the general reproduction of a society founded on exploitation. But this wider view of the matter is also to be found in the classic works;[7] Marx considered that surplus value was produced by all collective labour in economic activities organized for purposes of profit, irrespective of the quality of the work and product or of the result or specific content of the work. It is possible to find already present in the nineteenth century various elements of a theory of social reproduction as a complementary factor necessary for the extensive reproduction of capitalism. The problem is thus fundamentally different: that is, it concerns the articulation of general and specific social relationships in a society which we presume has remained fundamentally capitalistic but in which the productive basis is constituted by a diminishing minority of the population, while the majority is either unemployed or works for social reproduction in general, and the state intervenes with great force in order to ensure this reproduction. The theoretical revision called for by the new social situation is an attempt to conserve the theoretical-methodological presuppositions of Marxist interpretation by integrating and adapting them so that they can take into account two fundamental variations of late-capitalistic societies: the new importance of social reproduction relationships and the part played by the state in the economy and in society.

The process of theoretical redefinition is far from complete and reveals a number of contradictions and weaknesses, but also some clarificatory elements which should briefly be mentioned.

(1) The accumulation of capital in the strict sense, deriving from the fact that it is in the interest of capitalists to make the maximum profit, always has an immediately complementary relationship with the need for general social reproduction. That is, the continuous reproduction, and, if possible, extension, of conditions permitting further capital accumulation in successive economic cycles is a requirement of capital.

(2) Social reproduction tends to become more complex and important as labour productivity increases and the percentage of workers employed in agriculture and industry[8] diminishes. General social reproduction means not only the maintenance of a labour force able to satisfy the capitalistic demand for workers but also the reproduction of a consumption structure capable of absorbing the production without too much waste, thus permitting the realization of surplus value; and the conservation of the social, economic and political balances that permit the realization of the exploitation relationship in the productive sectors.

(3) As the mass of produced surplus value increases and the number of directly productive workers diminishes, the late-capitalistic societies encounter growing difficulties with regard to general social reproduction. To be kept under control this must be directed in an authoritarian and oppressive way and based on various types of social margination.

(4) The result is a very complex process of social restratification, founded on the differentiated social relationships which the various classes have in the general reproduction of society. On the one hand there remains the exploitation relationship necessary for the immediate accumulation of capital, but it takes different forms in the concentrated sectors of the economy and in the sectors which are little concentrated, a large part of the so-called informal economy. On the other hand there is a series of margination, oppression and control relationships between the classes directing

the general reproduction (in particular the state bureaucracy) and the very diversified complex of subordinate classes, which have different potentialities as regards resistance and access to instruments of self-defence and political bargaining.

(5) The process of capital accumulation is increasingly characterized by the fundamental contradiction between its two driving forces, the need to maximize profits and the need to reproduce a social organization in which the capitalist production relationships are not too easily affected by the social contradictions which it brings into being, such as unemployment, margination, overproduction, economic waste, etc.

(6) The intervention of the state is concerned both with the immediate interest of capital accumulation and general social reproduction. However, this second field of intervention has recently come to be the main one and has come to condition the whole work of redistribution of surplus value on the part of the state. The fiscal crisis[9] of the late-capitalistic state is the expression of the impossibility of maintaining levels of accumulation of capital which are rational and compatible with the levels of general social reproduction necessary for the realization of such levels of accumulation.

(7) The various contradictions of modern societies lead to a disarticulation of social conflict. Apart from the traditional political and trade-union antagonism between the workers and concentrated capital, we have the development of conflicts within the informal economy and above all social struggles against social reproduction in general. Here the strata of the working class which are better organized and have a greater bargaining power (also called the 'guaranteed' strata because they enjoy stable employment) are in a far better position to protect their interests than the marginated strata of the population.

A theoretical revision founded on these elements poses two very important methodological problems, which are the subject of neo-Marxist intellectual debate. The first concerns the redefinition of the classes and of class conflict, the second relates to the significance of the mechanisms of the capitalistic market in societies where a number of economic concerns have become veritable monopolies and where the state intervenes in the economy with a weight capable of subverting market laws.

Since I shall revert to these questions later, I shall here confine myself to giving a provisional outline of the solution I prefer. The process of social restratification does not significantly modify the division of society into two antagonistic parts, the strata that manage capitalism and those that undergo it in its various forms of oppressive organization. Instead, both in the capitalist and the working class (using the term in a wide sense so as to include all the oppressed classes), there has been a process of differentiation which has given rise to highly composite and differentiated groups with different and interwoven reasons for conflict. It is not, however, impossible to presuppose the existence of an impulse towards unification. In the capitalist sector this derives from the need to defend the social organization and the hegemony of the class when this is endangered by the development of social crisis and the anti-capitalist struggle. In the working-class sector the unification tendency is a result of the diffusion of a relatively lower standard of living, of the fundamentally anti-capitalist nature of numerous different conflicts and of the need to unify the class in order to be in a position to propose an alternative social system when this appears to be the only strategic solution, given the permanent state of crisis of capitalist society.

The mechanisms of the market continue to characterize late-capitalistic societies even though they now operate on two different levels, international competition and local competition between small non-concentrated units, and are increasingly integrated (but not replaced) in a complex manner by the intervention of the state.

This rapid survey of the elements of a Marxist theoretical redefinition certainly does not take stock of all the contributions to a debate which is not only very wide and highly differentiated but is still largely inconclusive. As we shall see, in the field of analysis of socio-territorial problems some major divergences still remain. It seemed, above all, important here to explain certain theoretical-methodological elements which will constitute the implicit presuppositions of our analysis of the socio-territorial problems of late-capitalistic societies. In fact nearly all the more important recent contributions to an understanding of the urban and regional problems of modern societies have been the result of this Marxist re-theorization.

THE FOUNDATIONS OF A CRITICAL APPROACH TO THE URBAN AND REGIONAL QUESTION

Since the middle sixties, social scientists have expressed a renewed interest in urban and regional questions, especially in connection with the exploding social struggles in many Western countries and with the general crisis which struck the world economy in the seventies. Contemporary capitalist societies have proved able to survive for a long time on the ideology of welfare, to develop an extremely divided and concentrated territorial structure and to sponsor a monstrous urbanization process. At the same time, however, they have proved unable to guarantee social justice, to provide lasting solutions to the housing question or the problem of regional underdevelopment, to diffuse wealth among different social strata, to promote independent industrialization in the Third World, and so on. The critical condition of capitalist societies became evident with the Vietnam war, the social unrest which began in 1968, the economic crisis of the seventies, the clear failure of the American welfare myth. These same events, and the Chinese cultural revolution, upset the dogmas of both Marxist and bourgeois social scientists. This was the background for the development of a new 'urban sociology', a neo-Marxist political economy, and various new methodologies of class analysis, in several Western countries.

It is difficult to say how much this renewed scientific interest in certain important social questions has contributed to a better understanding of today's societies. Some basic objective limits have always negatively affected the work of social scientists. The division of scientific knowledge, the integration of intellectuals in a capitalist society through academic or bureaucratic research organizations, the difficulties of linking scientific analysis with a working class praxis, which is itself increasingly divided and complex, are unavoidable obstacles to the difficult task of a better understanding of current societies. Recent social studies have raised important questions, but they remain largely unsatisfactory from the methodological point of view. I believe that one of the greatest weaknesses of most recent studies on urban and regional problems and on the capitalist state is the lack of consciousness of the objective limits of a social scientist in a late capitalist society, i.e. the autocritical sense. It remains extremely difficult to achieve a comprehensive understanding of the current social crisis – which should be the ambition of any good social scientist today. But it may be useful to contribute a specific critical and autocritical view. In any case I shall take into account that my own social knowledge is as abstract, fragmented and remote from the immediate needs of the large majority of the population, as that of other scientists I am criticizing.

Four important points characteristic of my methodology should be outlined in anticipation, in order to indicate my approach to the social problems of urban and regional development. On pp. 63–71 outline the main points of criticism on the different methodological solutions adopted by other neo-Marxist scholars who have contributed to the renewal of urban theory.

(1) It is neither convenient nor feasible to build a general theory of urban and regional questions, as these are only partial, non-autonomous aspects of a more general social process, which cannot be broken down to isolated urban or regional problems. This point can be extended to attempts to create a general theory of the capitalist state: the state being an expression of the general process of capitalist accumulation and of a specific social formation at a certain stage of development, any attempt to isolate the study of the state from the analysis of capital accumulation at both general and particular levels will prove to be a methodological mistake.

(2) Urban and regional problems should be studied in connection with the social reproduction processes of specific capitalist societies under a strictly dialectical, materialist, historical, comprehensive methodology. This approach is certainly very difficult and, in certain cases, almost impossible – given the limits of contemporary social scientists – but it is the only effective methodology for an understanding of contemporary societies.

(3) The different levels of abstraction used by Marxist scholars to study capitalist societies appear also in the analysis of urban and regional social problems. The most abstract one refers to the mode of production as such and to its general laws of reproduction, and is the closest approach we have to a general theory. It is, however, very imprecise on the specific features of urbanization and regional processes within individual capitalist situations. In any case, to be acceptable, this abstract level should have serious historical references, since it is deduced from the long term development trends of specific capitalist experiences. The second level studies specific social formations, dominantly capitalistic, in an historically precise dimension – long, medium or short term. The third level consists of individual case studies. These three levels are strictly interconnected among themselves: no author can produce knowledge at a specific level of abstraction without a good deal of reference to the other two.

(4) The choice of this methodological option excludes any return to alternative methodologies, such as functionalism or historicism. I deal with this more fully later in the chapter.

A few years ago, when I first tried to find a methodological-theoretical basis for a Marxist approach to urban and regional development problems I elaborated the following sociological definition of territory:

(a) territory is a map of social relationships of production because it is fundamental to all these relationships;
(b) territory is itself a means of production;
(c) territory is a consumer good in short supply.[10]

Although this approach achieved the goal of connecting urban and regional problems with accumulation processes without limiting or autonomizing complex social relations, it was unsatisfactory for terminological and substantial reasons. The means of production and the consumer good aspects of territory cannot be separated from the general and specific features of capitalist accumulation; on the contrary, the first part of the definition remains a very vague and trivial assessment if we cannot explain the specific articulation of territorial features within capitalist development. But my main point is that I would now consider any kind of definition of socio-territorial relations a mistake, since they are only partial aspects of a more general and complex social process. Any definition will create an artificial segmentation of social reality and prevent a more scientific knowledge of contemporary societies. Our efforts would be more usefully employed in suggesting a descriptive synthetic pattern for studying these phenomena. On this basis I am prepared to suggest three subsets of problems which are strongly interconnected among themselves and result from different perspectives which may be useful in the study of territorial features of capital accumulation.

(1) The immediate territorial feature of capital accumulation and its exploitative and contradictory nature is an uneven and contradictory distribution of social relationships over a territory. This subset of problems includes regional underdevelopment, over-urbanization, suburbanization, urban congestion, urban diseconomies, etc.

(2) Since the land is an essential means of production, it has a particularly contradictory role in the capital accumulation process, further complicated by the fact that land ownership is essentially a 'surviving' precapitalist relationship, conditioning capitalist development in a specific way. The main problem here is the role of various forms of land rent and speculation within the capital accumulation process.

(3) Land is also a consumer good in short supply, which can be consumed in very different ways: for industrial or agricultural activities, for service settlements, or for housing and infrastructures for different social strata. The alternative competitive utilizations of land are another important contradiction within the capital accumulation process.

Some important territorial social problems, like housing, would not fit into this tripartition because they are connected with all three aspects at the same time. In fact housing reflects the uneven contradictory features of capitalist accumulation. It is a productive utilization of land and it is a form of land consumption. I want to stress that production and consumption are two indivisible aspects of the same, fundamentally indivisible process, as Marx often pointed out.

Territorial social relations are fundamental aspects of both the process of capital accumulation, intended in a strict sense, and of the process of general social reproduction. I shall develop this point when criticizing other recent works where the authors underline overmuch either one or the other of these two aspects.

In this framework we can also understand the limits of the Marxist concept of the dialectic opposition between city and countryside. This contradiction was an important territorial feature of early capital accumulation but it has progressively disappeared as a general class contradiction. Very few Marxist scholars have been able to make use of it, and then only in historical studies of the industrial take-off period. The territorial features of late capitalist accumulation are much more complicated and quite different from the dialectic relation between urban and rural social settlements. Only primitive accumulation systematically drains resources and manpower from the countryside into cities to establish the conditions for an industrial take-off. I also doubt very much whether, in class terms, this opposition can be classified as an aspect of the confrontation between capital and labour. It appears to me mainly as a conflict between the old precapitalist societies, based on rural agricultural social formations, and the new capitalist order, exploiting and destroying the old ones in order to establish itself definitively. With the development of capitalist agriculture and the diffusion of industrial ways of life, the relationship between rural and urban is progressively reduced to one between different production sectors.

The opposition between imperialistic capital and underdeveloped exploited societies cannot be reduced to a confrontation between city and countryside. The exploitation of underdeveloped regions (see Figure 1.2, p. 29 and Figures 3.1, 3.2, 3.3, pp. 139, 141, 142) occurs through unequal exchange and surplus profits[11] in both the urban and rural milieux of the Third World. It is in part true that cities have a different role from that of the countryside, and that the agriculture of underdeveloped areas remains the area of maximum exploitation, but even this does not justify the adoption of a city/countryside approach to the study of territorial problems in contemporary societies.

The territorial features of advanced capitalist societies can be interpreted in a dialectical sense only as a possible expression of the confrontation between capital and the working class. Capital accumulation creates and reproduces a territorial social order which is contradictory in itself and incompatible with the interests of the large majority of the population. Generally, class conflict is the confrontation between two opposed principles of social organization: the capitalist one is exploitative and contradictory, but remains very clearcut and maintains – up to a point – hegemony over specific societies. The socialist one is, on the positive side, only a vague social project, but negatively it is also a permanent challenge to the contradictions of capitalist society. As is demonstrated more clearly in the last chapter, it is almost impossible to describe what a socialist society should be in positive terms, while it is not very difficult to say what it should not be in negative terms.

Capitalism, while seeking maximum profit and reproducing the exploitative contradictory order, is trying to force the working class – understood, in an enlarged sense, as the great majority of the population – to pay as many economic and social costs as possible, including those involved in the process of shaping the territorial order. For instance, the working class will be asked to bear increasingly longer, unpaid commuting times, and to accept increases in income taxes to pay for the re-establishment of the ecological equilibrium damaged by industrial development. It will have to tolerate environmentally dangerous but capitalistically convenient settlements, be obliged to move into suburban segregated areas which happen to be more expensive and less comfortable than the central ones, and so on.

The working class has two main areas of conflict in which to oppose the patterns of capital accumulation: the factory and the community. A great number of social conflicts arise from the contradictions of late-capitalist societies. Different social movements struggle on different grounds against capitalism. Within the factories the workers struggle to recuperate in terms of real wages what they have lost in terms of costs of labour-force reproduction. Through the factory struggle they also try to gain control of the patterns of production processes, to channel investment in their favour rather than to their exploitation, to compel individual capitalists to pay directly the additional costs of the reproduction of their labour-force. I might suggest various examples: the factory struggles to obtain from management free transportation for the workers, or subventioned housing, or leisure and education facilities; the workers' opposition to decentralized investments in the Third World in favour of the development of national depressed areas; the struggles against capital-intensive and superconcentrated investments in favour of a less exploitative and better distributed industrial development.

It is more difficult to evaluate in class terms the anti-capitalist struggles which take place in the community and in politics generally because these are more differentiated, partial and very poorly organized. Various social and political movements oppose in different ways the patterns of general reproduction of capitalist societies: left wing parties, community groups, ecological organizations, women and youth movements, and various organizations of marginated and unemployed people.

On some occasions the class may win radical social reforms which challenge and endanger the rhythm and the possibility of the accumulation process itself. On other occasions the class gets only social democratic reforms, which share the additional costs of social reproduction between the two classes, preventing a dramatic worsening of the conditions of life of the large majority of the population. As I shall elaborate later on, it is extremely difficult to evaluate, either in scientific or political terms (which are strictly linked together), the contents and the results of these social struggles. This is because of the complexity, variety and disunity of anti-capitalist movements, because of the different significance they assume in different social contexts, and because the relation between short-run impact and the long-term historical confrontation between the two classes is complex.[12]

So far as land use is concerned, the working class struggles against general capitalist reproduction processes to utilize land in an alternative way. To understand the real content of urban class struggles we must consider the general class controversy over the reproduction of capitalist societies.

Urban conflicts to get better housing or transport are only a part of a much more comprehensive conflictual movement to establish an alternative social system. They can be interpreted and evaluated only within this more comprehensive dialectical process. If we isolate them, we may be able to establish a specific branch of our knowledge of society but we completely distort social reality and, methodologically, we have to return to a functionalist option. So, according to any approach which isolates urban realities from the general class context, urban struggles result in achieving the goals of the most powerful branches of capital. In fact it is absolutely impossible to give a class evaluation of specific social events if we ignore the general accumulation process. All individual urban and regional developments are functional to capital reproduction and accumulation if we do not consider them as aspects of the complex contradictions characterizing capitalism: the class struggle, the opposition between different capitalist units, and the resulting generalized anarchy.

Starting from a very abstract – and consequently general and vague – level of analysis, I shall try to understand the connections between capital accumulation and the reproduction of capitalist societies on the one hand, and urbanization and other territorial processes on the other.

I shall not deal with the experiences of underdeveloped countries except in Chapter 3, when I refer to the over-urbanization process in connection with the underdevelopment cycle. Thus, the whole first part of the book is about cases of classical accumulation in Western capitalism (the countries which are now more or less advanced and industrialized). My frequent references to the specific Italian experience may, however, also help in the understanding of underdevelopment processes; Italy is an exceptional mixture of advanced industrialized areas and underdeveloped backward ones. The capital accumulation processes (both primitive and strictly capitalist accumulations) have fairly clear territorial features: division of labour over the territory, urbanization processes and their complex social consequences, regional specialization and uneven development; centralization and decentralization; the combination of both economic policies and market interrelations.

We shall first consider the territorial consequences of capitalist take-off and early development, when primitive accumulation of capital is still predominant as compared with strictly capitalist accumulation. Figure 1.1. tries to summarize this situation roughly. In the first part of Chapter 2 primitive accumulation is extensively studied, while in the second part of the same chapter I try to describe further developments of capitalism. The most important territorial effects of initial capital accumulation are located in the urban sector. When capitalist production leaves the initial stage of cottage-

26 A Marxist Approach

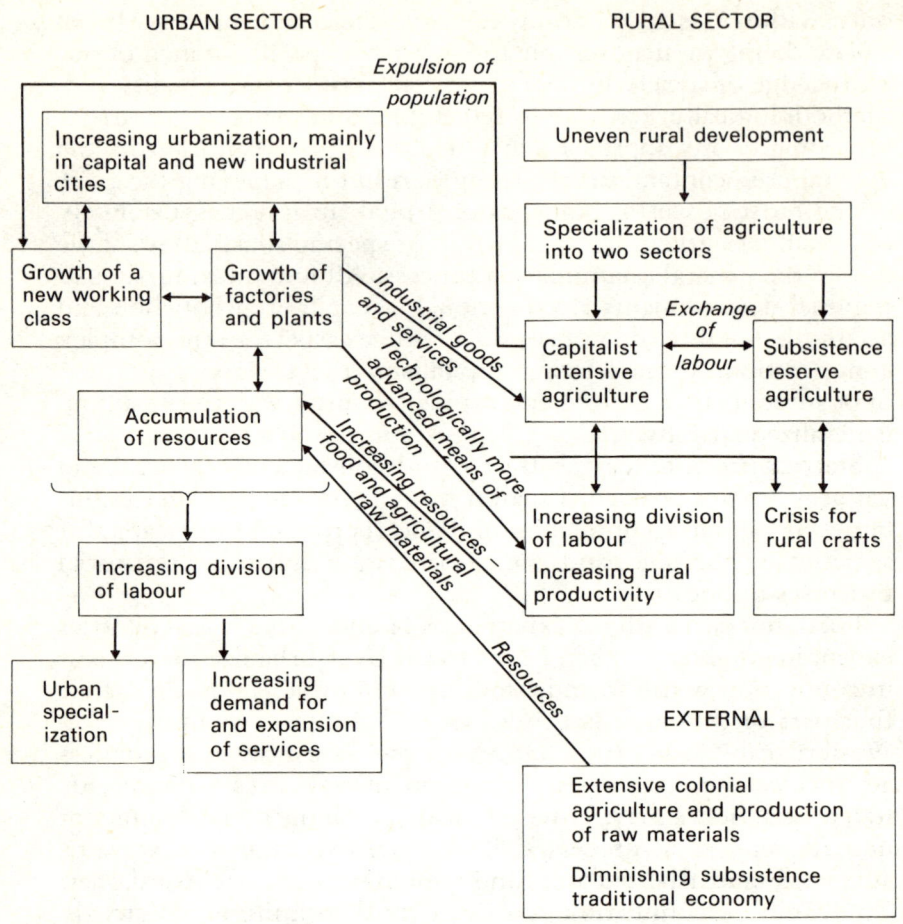

FIGURE 1.1 Urbanization under early capitalist accumulation.

decentralized organization, it becomes, by definition, concentrated and urban, being organized in increasingly large factories which presuppose both the existence of an urbanized labour force and the progressive creation of concentrated markets where the increasing industrial production can easily be sold. Capital accumulation encourages further urbanization and uses precapitalist urbanization for economic expansion.

The major processes at this stage are:

(a) urbanization, i.e. a wave of rural to urban migration, either

from developing new capitalist agricultural areas or from declining rural subsistence areas;
(b) uneven rural development;
(c) progressive urban specialization and new forms of territorial division of labour;
(d) underdevelopment processes in colonized countries and in other backward regions through the expansion of extensive colonial agriculture at the expense of traditional subsistence economy and the exploitation of the backward areas' raw materials and labour force.

In any specific experience, the rhythm, intensity and quality of these processes are related to the quality of capitalist accumulation itself, especially to the degree of concentration and centralization of capital, to its ability to exploit non-capitalist societies, to its rate of growth, to the possibility of expanding production of relative surplus value through increasing labour productivity, and to the role and position of any individual society in the international division of labour.

These territorial processes are highly contradictory just because they are part and parcel of the capital accumulation process. They reflect in territorial terms the internal contradiction of capital (competition among units of individual capital and a general incapacity to fully realize the produced surplus value) and the external contradiction of capitalism (the class confrontation between capital and labour). Territorial processes are further complicated by a number of contradictions created by the survival of land ownership and absolute and relative rent.

Urbanization is the most complex and comprehensive of these processes. It is characterized by several important social contradictions. One of the most important and persistent among these is the housing question, whilst other serious problems are urban unemployment, periodical shortages of labour in the metropolitan development areas, commuting and transport issues, urban renewal, etc. These contradictions are not mainly urban features, but rather aspects of the accumulation process which have great importance in the shaping of the capitalist territorial structure. This can be exemplified by the housing and rent question. Capital accumulation requires an appropriate increase in urban population in order to reproduce and enlarge the working class employed in the expanding industries and in urban services. Once the unoccupied precapitalist residences have been transformed and utilized to house the new working class, the housing demand grows at an increasing rate, and the building sector becomes fundamental, both for accumulation and for the production of subsistence goods. These two aspects cannot be split but are often mutually incompatible. The high income extracted by rentiers in this sector contributes to fix prices, qualities and quantities of housing, at a level which does not meet the requirements of housing demand, or the necessity to keep labour costs as low as possible and urban migrations high enough to obtain the additional labour force required by capitalist expansion. Land rent plays an additional contradictory role, as a speculation and as an independent factor of economic stagnation.

In parallel with the industrialization/capital accumulation process, capitalist cities grow anarchically to new dimensions, determined by contradictory interests. The intervention of the state or local authorities, being subject to prevalent class interests, is able merely to recognize the contradictions and find short-term compromise solutions. These favour the specific needs of short-term capital accumulation. In times of rapid accumulation and economic growth, the state and local authorities promote cheap housing and transport in order to settle an additional and more efficient labour force in the cities. In times of slow accumulation and economic stagnation, they favour land and building speculation to freeze a part of the non-accumulable capital or alternatively to promote a new accumulation wave through a high occupation rate and a strong increase in the demand for industrial goods in the building sector. But these interventions cannot solve the radical opposition of different class interests and of incompatible individual units' behaviour within the housing sector. We will come back to this problem in the second part of the chapter and again later in the book.

The urbanization process in classical terms tends to stop when a very large proportion (about ninety percent or even more) of the population of industrialized countries lives in urban or suburban environments. In the meantime capital concentration and the quality of accumulation (based on oil technologies, car lobbies, individual transportation, etc.) determines an increasingly devastating process of urban gigantism and congestion. The combined effects of concentration, congestion and new technologies on the one hand, and of the traditional 'popular' anti-urban feeling on the other (particularly developed in Anglo-Saxon countries) – for various reasons[13] pushes people to move their residences out of the city centres – if they can afford it – thereby creating a vast suburbanization movement. The new situation of the present phase of accumulation is synthesized in Figure 1.2.

A Marxist Approach   29

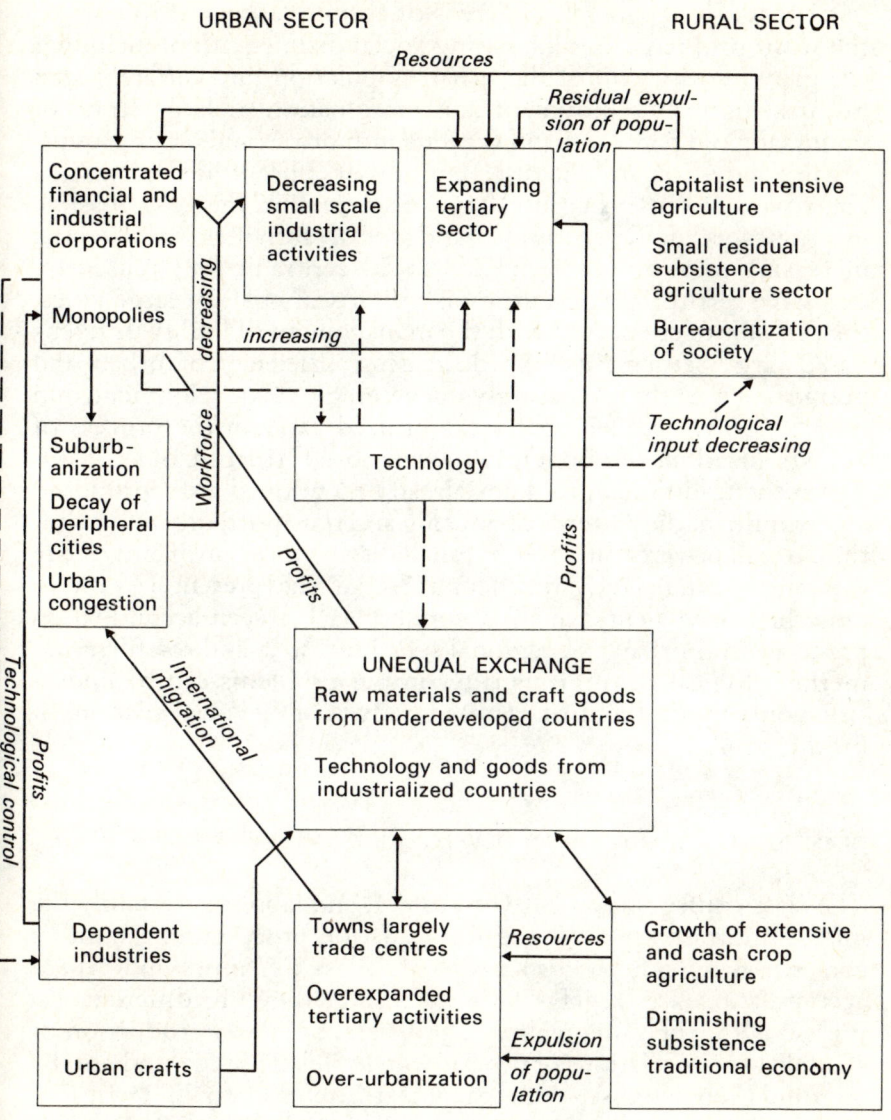

FIGURE 1.2 Urban and regional processes under late capitalist accumulation.

The territorial structure of late capitalism enters into a major persistent crisis, parallel to a crisis of accumulation. At this stage, the main problems are: increasing social disintegration, including the growing division of the urban population into differentiated groups; high unemployment and margination of large strata of young and old people, women, ethnic minorities and other groups; urban congestion and the diseconomies of concentrated cities (in a controversial sense, because large cities remain the best possible location for many economic and social activities, despite the increasing location costs and the social contradictions caused by excessive territorial concentration); the fiscal crisis of large cities; the difficulties connected with the management of highly differentiated large settlements; the decreasing efficiency of urban and public services; the increasingly uneven regional development, and the economic decadence of areas utilized early in the process of industrialization. Moreover, in the territorial structure of late capitalism the traditional problems already mentioned are reproduced and amplified: the patterns of housing and transport, urban segregation, urban poverty, and so on. I shall discuss these problems of late capitalism extensively in Chapter 3. For the present I want to underline once again the strict connection between accumulation processes and urban and regional social features, and re-affirm my methodological commitment: territorial problems can be understood only by starting from a broad analysis of the social relations of production.

CLASS CONFLICT AND URBAN DEVELOPMENT

The class confrontation between capital and labour is certainly the most important aspect of the accumulation process and cannot be considered outside the process itself. Class dynamics and capital accumulation are largely the same thing: they are different expressions for the same reality in progress, i.e. the reproduction of capitalist social relations of production. In this sense the study of the accumulation process, with particular attention to its territorial features, is at the same time a study of social conflict. But this approach is not as simple as it looks.

Class struggles are fundamentally originated by capitalist exploitation relationships – mainly the direct extraction of surplus value from the immediately productive part of the working class. But, as we have already seen, exploitative capitalist social relations do not occur only in the strict production area but also and necessarily within the general social reproduction process which is formed to reproduce the very possibility of exploitation. In this sense exploitation not only strikes the productive workers in social relations other than the immediate production of surplus value, but it also involves various social groups, which cannot be considered productive workers, in different aspects of their everyday life.

This second kind of domination-exploitation relationship is determined by various different factors. In the first place the international market structure and the world organization of the economy originate various exploitative relations, through unequal exchange, to the advantage of the more advanced and concentrated economies and to the disadvantage of the weaker ones. These exploitative relations are also reinforced by political domination patterns; the dependent nations and areas are subordinated to strategies decided by the ruling classes of the more advanced countries. Various exploitative relations are originated by the patterns of the general reproduction process. The imposition of a mass consumption model, the marginalization of various strata of potential workers who cannot any longer be involved directly in capital accumulation activities, the development of an authoritarian control structure over the reproduction processes (ranging through bureaucracy, the education system, the public services, up to the repressive legal structure) are the most important areas where such exploitative relations are practised.

This approach interprets social conflict as generated by various exploitative relations which are suffered cumulatively in different terms and degrees by the large majority of the population as divided in various subgroups. Subsequent questions are: how does the objective exploitative situation determine the conflictual feeling; how do different anti-capitalist feelings interact and combine to create (or not) a general anti-capitalist movement?

Although exploitation is the ultimate cause of social conflict, the latter does not occur automatically, neither is it possible to determine an immediate relationship between the intensity and quality of exploitation and the quantitative and qualitative features of class struggles. Exploitative social relations raise a certain degree of consciousness in the exploited. This consciousness is at first (logically and not historically) an individual one, but through political class organizations it becomes collective and inspires conflictual collective behaviour. The relationship between collective class consciousness and political organization (not only parties or unions but also political groups and associations) is dialectical, in the sense that a political organization is the expression of a similar consciousness in a relatively large number of individuals but, at the same time, it transforms this common consciousness into something very different from the original individual feeling. Class confrontation and class balances of power are antecedent (in a logical sense) to the political trade-unionist organization of classes, but individual consciousness is an immediate aspect of a class divided society. This does not mean that every particular individual is conscious of his exploitation; on the contrary, some remain completely unconscious, but the common individual consciousness of the majority becomes collective class consciousness. At the very beginning, class consciousness is primitive and archaic, which is to say that it does not pursue any coherent political strategy (in early capitalism it takes the form of working class struggles against mechanization) but later it becomes increasingly subtle and political. The main point is that the chain of social relations of production, class strength and confrontation, and class consciousness, is wholly inside the social structure, although articulated in dialectical links.[14]

The problem of the unification of classes and movements is very complicated and controversial. Any single worker or capitalist can take part in more than one conflict at a time, apart from the fact that different strata of workers and capitalists are involved in different conflictual situations. Moreover, the objectives of the different social conflicts may appear incompatible, one with another. For example, some workers struggle simultaneously to get a higher wage in the factory and to force the state to make larger investments to provide better education or health services. If they get higher wages, the state is driven to spend more money to help the economic units to remain competitive in the world market, so that it is forced to cut the social investment programme, including the investments the same workers were interested in. The situation could also be reversed. But this apparent incompatibility gives a clear insight into the effectiveness of class struggles. The capitalist system is able to face partial struggles by sacrificing other sectors of the general context. In contrast it is absolutely unable to face attacks which come from any area where there is an exploitative relationship. A multi-exploitative system can reproduce itself if it cuts exploitation somewhere to increase it somewhere else. In this sense the competitiveness of interests between the various conflicts shows the limits of the reproduction of a capitalist society and the revolutionary potential of class struggles. Whilst capitalism is unable to face a generalized attack, social struggles cannot achieve a complete victory if they do not succeed in rejecting the social system.

Here we have two further problems: what is the class meaning of the short-term prevalence of some conflictual goals over others; and how is a unification strategy built up? The first point should be analysed within a specific situation, beginning with the condition of class hegemony. It is reasonable to say that capitalism, attacked from various fronts, will withdraw where the enemy is stronger and where the danger of loss of control of the general situation is minimal. This tactic also allows the reconstruction of the hegemonic social bloc through the provisional inclusion of some strata of the working class whose partial goals have been satisfied.

The unification tendency becomes explicit and strongest at the high point of class confrontation. On these occasions capitalists are forced to forget their internal divisions to defend their hegemony over society. At the same time the workers have to face two alternative outcomes: the possibility that a general defeat of the movement would impose enormous losses on every participant group or, by contrast, the possibility that a general victory realizes, although with different priorities, the interests of every subgroup. The unification process is usually led by a fraction of the class which expresses most successfully the hegemonic strategy needed for this massive confrontation. The very diffused assumption that the leading sections are always the most concentrated capitalists on one side and the trade-unionized workers on the opposite side is very probably outdated and incorrect. The problem should be examined carefully within different specific historical-geographical situations. In general it is true that these two fractions possess great contractual bargaining power, are well organized and, moreover, they are more easily represented within the democratic system of advanced capitalist countries. However, for these very reasons, these two fractions appear also to have the greatest interest in a reciprocal agreement at the expense of the interests of other components, when this is possible. In this sense, through much of the process of class unification, they are the least interested groups. By contrast, the most marginalized opposed groups, for example, petty bourgeois and unemployed workers, appear much more interested in unification strategies and more likely to assume the movement's leadership when the confrontation becomes generalized. But this remark is too vague to become an interpretative rule applicable to very different specific situations.

I shall now look at two important and closely linked theoretical questions. First, how do social classes become social forces, that is, for what reasons does consciousness ripen and express itself in class struggle? Second, how does the social behaviour of classes interact with the accumulation process? This involves asking how political institutions and organizations, mainly political parties and the state, are shaped by the accumulation process and how they interact with the accumulation process itself.

In the urban and regional field these problems have been mainly considered in the study of urban social movements and of state and local authority intervention in various territorial contexts. The complexity of studying such problems with a correct methodology has been largely underestimated; authors have usually avoided the theoretical problems or assumed a mechanical functional interaction between political institutions and the class-accumulation process.

I argue that a general theory is not applicable to the explanation of specific interactions between the accumulation process and the nature and activities of political institutions. Apart from the very general and vague methodological assumption that the nature of the state and of political organizations is fundamentally determined by the social relations of production, we should study such problems case by case. In fact it is impossible to establish a fixed typology of relations between class struggles and the accumulation process, on the one side, and the state and political actions and organizations, on the other.[15]

The reasons why, in a certain country at a certain point in history, the class confrontation assumes specific features and the state and local authorities have specific patterns of organization and intervention or pursue specific policies, are to be found in various complex factors; the international position of the economy, its specific history of capital accumulation, the origins of class hegemony and the cultural life of the country. These factors are by their nature unpredictable and cannot be embraced by a general abstract approach. Today, although the world economy is troubled by a generalized persistent crisis, the features of the crisis differ widely from country to country. So class balances of power, hegemonic strategies, patterns of state intervention in the economy and social and economic policies have different meanings. Such differences can be understood only through the analysis of the different features of capitalist, general reproduction processes in the various countries, the world market structure, labour and capital relationships, and the historical developments of class consciousness and movements in the specific areas. In this sense the Italian case, to which I will refer on various occasions, is to be taken only as a non-generalizable example. It is, however, important both for methodological reasons and for reasons of content. Through it, it will be possible to discover the origins of similar features in other cases and to put general capitalist trends in perspective. We can thus understand the reasons for specific phenomena and the particular features they assume in different situations. The Italian case seems particularly appropriate because it is very complex.

Having established these methodological points I now return to the discussion of class. As we have seen, the general object of the working class is to be free from exploitation, i.e. to establish a different mode of production where the workers themselves control the production process. This is a general and final goal, nearly impossible to identify in everyday class confrontation. The working class pursues the final goal through a complex and contradictory strategy built on intermediate partial goals. These should be evaluated by reference to the final goal (how much they contribute to its achievement), and have two complementary functions: to break the accumulation process, and recuperate, directly or indirectly, a part of the surplus value; to reinforce, increase and diffuse class consciousness and unity. Any tentative evaluation of class struggles should rest on these two standards, bearing in mind their relation to the achievement of the final goal. Such evaluation is a very difficult, politically involved, operation. Often short-term positive results may have negative effects in the long run, great victories of one sector of the working class on the real wages front (partial recuperation of surplus value) may determine a parallel disgregation of class unity and/or consciousness, and so on.

Urban social movements, so heterogeneous and politically disorganized, often only indirectly connected with official sectors of the working class, are even more difficult to evaluate. For these reasons, it is important to reach an understanding of the meaning of the different social movements in various situations. Squatters, rent strikers, ecological movements, local political committees and action groups may have very different meanings and interpretations within the general working class strategy. I shall now try to draw general lines of connection between capital accumulation and reproduction processes and social conflicts, with particular attention to the conflicts on territorially important issues. I shall then give some examples of recent developments which may clarify the general approach and evaluation. The specific connection between accumulation and conflict in the various ages of capitalism and in the Italian case in particular, will also be referred to in other parts of this work. Turning back to the situation of early capital accumulation described in Figure 1.1, certain points emerge.

(1) The early accumulation processes are characterized by a very high mobility of potential workers from the countryside into the new, developing industrial cities, with a consequent destruction of precapitalist productive capacities in the countryside, so as to continuously increase labour power at the very cheapest cost. Capital development has to face three main sources of conflict: the resistance of precapitalist groups to expropriation and capitalist diffusion; the existence and effects of ground rent in urbanization and rural crises; the necessity of paying high urbanization costs. The latter can be borne in three ways, either by the workers' wages, which in this case are higher than they theoretically should be; or directly by capital, which loses accumulation potentialities; or by a deterioration in the conditions of life of the workers, which results in their being less productive (because of the stress of bad living conditions) and more conflict-ridden.

(2) The resistance of precapitalist productive organizations, which is the main expression of the contradiction between the city and the countryside, cannot be interpreted as an aspect of the struggle between capital and labour. The precapitalist rural workers do not resist exploitation but rather the expropriation of traditional productive opportunities and the possibility of becoming a modern proletariat. This kind of conflict may also occur later, when capitalism tries to rationalize its economic structure by expropriating surviving traditional producers. The redevelopments of the European city centres are examples of such phenomena; craft units are expelled in favour of modern tertiary processes. In such cases, there may be a connection with the working class movement if there is a common struggle against the large corporations' interests in further capital concentration and centralization and an increasingly segregated and divided use of urban land.

(3) The interference of ground rent in the accumulation of capital is extremely complicated, both in early and contemporary capitalism.

(4) Capital needs to increase the urbanized, potential working class at low cost. But urbanization costs tend to increase and they have to be met either by capital or by labour (even when they are met by the state, they are finally repaid by one of the two). Moreover, these are always higher than other production costs because of the influence of rent and land speculations. Usually, urbanization processes give rise to a three-sided conflict: the rentiers and speculators want to impose higher costs to get an important share of the produced

surplus value; the capitalists theoretically oppose this tendency as they are obliged to pay for it through a direct subtraction of surplus value or through higher wages; the workers struggle for better housing and living conditions at decreasing costs because this is a means to higher real wages. From time to time the rentiers' interests coincide with the interests of some sectors of the bourgeoisie, if the latter owns land or utilizes rent revenue to promote financial concentration and industrial investment.

The temporary solution of this lasting conflict is historically determined by the specific strength of the three forces and by their reciprocal interconnections. To evaluate such phenomena it is important to understand the strength of the temporary complementarity of rentiers' interests with some capitalists, as compared to the temporary complementarity of the interests of the workers with other capitalists. Capital as a whole has always parallel and contradictory interests, here favouring financial concentration but at the expense of higher wages and a progressive division of perspectives between financial and industrial sectors; favouring cheaper reproduction of the working class but at the expense of land speculation and financial concentration and management. However, such opposed interests are differently distributed among the various capitalist sectors and at different periods of their development. The large concentrated corporations and financial groups gain from the connection with rent, whilst small developing capitalists desperately need to keep the cost of labour reproduction as low as possible. In times of expansion, this second issue is of most importance, while during recessions building speculation is usually welcome. This contradiction has created a complex cycle. In times of stagnation, capitalists have stimulated the expansion of rent speculation. Some of the reasons for this have been noted, others are low demand for new industrial land and the reduced bargaining power of the working class as a result of increasing unemployment. Alternatively, in times of expansion, capital is compelled to favour cheap urbanization against rent speculation, to meet the increasing industrial demand for labour power. At such times, the contractual strength of the working class is higher.

As I shall suggest later, the cycle may change in late capitalism, when even expansion does not lead to substantial increases in employment rates, and when concentrated corporate capital has become totally integrated with speculative financial units and has developed a clear strategy of under-accumulation and stagnation. In advanced capitalism (see Figure 1.2), the situation is even more

38   A Marxist Approach

complicated. The conflict between city and countryside is reduced to a minimum marginal level. But the overall class confrontation has enormously increased in its incidence, variety and intensity. Concentrated capital has become fully integrated with urban building speculation. The monopolistic financial-industrial corporations control a large share of land property and industrial capital. In this sense the conflict looks simplified – but this is misleading. The span of confrontation is much wider, among different capitalist interests, and between capital and labour. The working class is more segmented and divided. The trade-unionized and stable sectors of the working class have quite high contractual power in factory conflict because of the structure of the labour market in which workers in such sectors are not easily interchangeable, and have strong organization and mature consciousness. Moreover, within advanced capitalist societies the nationwide working class organizations become powerful enough to win social reforms at the expense of various forms of integration of large sectors of the working class. At this stage, different sectors of the working class become more interested in specific social issues outside the factories. The stable working class struggles for some kinds of social reform when it has obtained the maximum it can get in factory struggles. It attempts to further increase real wage levels through better housing, cheaper transport, a partial control over the consumption system and the ecological balance, etc. The different sectors of marginal or unemployed workers have no chance of gaining anything through factory struggles, so they fight for better social welfare from the capitalist state. In these various ways the contradictions which characterize various kinds of social formations in late capitalism are deep and numerous and are reflected in lasting and diffused social conflicts.

These conflicts express in different ways the general opposition between the degree of development of the productive forces and the organization of production and society in general. The latter has become too restrictive to allow further development of the productive forces. But conflict has become more diffused and at the same time more dispersed and divided. Many new fronts of social conflict are established on local or sectarian bases. With regard to the territorial structure; persistent regional underdevelopment, urban poverty and unemployment, the restructuration connected with new forms of suburbanization, ecological damage and waste, the fiscal crisis of large cities, the diseconomies of late capitalist concentration–decentralization processes, redevelopment of land and building speculation are among the most important sources of social conflicts. Class confrontations explode in a very diffused area but on a strictly local basis, so that it becomes more and more difficult to connect and organize them in general terms. In this sense, the process of disgregation of late capitalist societies is also reflected in these new features of social conflict. Local and limited conflicts, spreading everywhere for apparently different specific reasons, become very important in the generation of the general societal crisis. But they originate spontaneously, remain restricted, and cannot easily be connected with a general class strategy, which becomes lost, or at least more confused, both on the capitalist and on the working class front. In this situation class organizations meet greater and greater difficulties in controlling their rank and file. For this reason it is almost impossible to evaluate social conflicts from the point of view of the general class strategy. Every different conflict has some importance but cannot be situated in a class perspective which now appears extremely confused.

I want to conclude this section with some specific examples and cautiously evaluate their political significance. In general terms it is true that the capitalist organizations of contemporary societies have run into critical difficulties. Capitalism now faces the impossible task of increasing the level of exploitation of the working class and at the same time continuing to control a progressively disgregating social structure. Further, capitalist interests are very differentiated and difficult to combine and a large series of different localized sectorial conflicts promotes the disruption of the accumulation process.

On the other hand, the working class is so divided that partial victories are never translated into revolutionary general changes nor situated in an unidentified revolutionary strategy. In this sense I believe we have entered a long crisis-transition period, when capital is no longer in perfect control of the general situation but resists changes within a perspective of progressive social disgregation, while the socialist alternative is not yet clearly identified. I shall return briefly to this problem in the last chapter of this book.

More particularly, I want to mention some possible differences between urban conflicts in advanced capitalist countries. It is possible to distinguish three different situations. In the first, the local bourgeoisie, due to its capacity to accumulate surplus profit, is still able to integrate mass sectors of the working class, to pursue social democratic policies, to fragment, marginalize and minimize social conflict. Social conflicts are highly unconnected and peripheral. They have very weak links with working class organizations as part of the capitalist establishment. This includes the USA, West Germany, some Scandinavian countries, Switzerland, Japan (in part) and other minor but strongly industrialized economies. In the second situation, capital has been able to integrate large sectors of the working class in the past, through social democratic strategies, but in recent decades has lost this capacity. The most important example is Great Britain. Here working class organizations are recovering a conflictual class dimension, although with great difficulty. New social conflicts determined by the disgregative crisis of late capitalism are connected to some degree with working class organizations. They are not as isolated and marginalized as in the first case and they are not so much in opposition to the working class tradition. But class organization as a whole is weakened by the long integration experience it has suffered. An important aspect of factory and social conflict is the reconstruction of the working class as an opposition force.

In the third case, the local bourgeoisie has never been able or willing to integrate large sectors of the working class for relatively long periods. These examples are among the weakest industrialized economies for different reasons. This is the case in the southern European countries. Here the working class has a solid tradition of opposition strategy and organization. New social conflicts break out more violently because the economic and social situation is more critical. But the traditional working class organizations meet great difficulties in integrating conflicts which are quite out of character with their long experience. Later on I shall give examples of how the Italian Communist Party found it impossible to lead most of the recent urban struggles, regional uprisings, ecological protests and so on.

THE CAPITALIST STATE, THE FISCAL CRISIS AND TERRITORIAL POLICIES

Our ability to understand current societies is closely related to the question of whether we can explain the dialectical relations between the social relationships of production and their political expressions. I therefore turn now to how class consciousness and class movements become political institutions and organizations, parties and government policies.

While class consciousness and class struggles are inseparable aspects of socio-productive relationships (the structure), they never appear in reality at this abstract level because they are modified and transformed by political orgaizations and institutions (superstructure). It follows that any political question is a very complex bridge between structure and superstructure and we cannot clearly distinguish the former from the latter. Marx's historical class analysis of the 1848-49 events in France is a good methodological example of the complete merging of structural and superstructural factors in a class political analysis.[16]

Class struggles and events are influenced in the first place by the strength of each class in the social relationships of production, but they are also determined by several superstructural conditions, such as the specific culture and history of a class, the strength and qualities of its organizations, the loyalty and capacity of its leadership, the internal stratification and division into subgroups of each class, and so on. Gramsci tried to give a theoretically coherent answer to this problem, through his concept of 'hegemony',[17] which, however, was only vaguely shaped in his prison writings and could not be fully developed before his premature death. His followers have given confused and different interpretations of this concept so that its utilization remains difficult.

Gramsci argues that the fact that a particular social class is dominant in the social relations of production is not sufficient to make it the ruling class in a specific society. To control a very complex social structure any dominant class must form an articulated social alliance and must have instruments to integrate in its specific social organization the other classes characterizing that specific society. The need for a hegemonic strategy is even more evident when a very restricted minority dominates a large majority of the population. Moreover, any class domination context can theoretically express at least two or three different principles of hegemony, depending on the class fraction which leads it and on the structure of the social alliance. The antagonistic classes stay conflictual, but are forced to accept the hegemonic power of the dominant class, at least until they are able to destroy the conditions upon which the hegemony of the dominant class is based. Such conditions are to be found both in the specific social relations of production and in various historical superstructural elements, which might reflect and reinforce the structural relations or be totally different from them. Marx himself, in the case of the nineteenth-century French peasantry, gives a good example of superstructural conditions of hegemony which are unrelated to the productive relationships. French peasants were in favour of the Second Empire (a new hegemonic strategy established by the industrial bourgeoisie against the former financial establishment), because they remembered the advantages they had gained during the First Empire. But the economic and social situation had changed so much that they could not get from Napoleon III any reinforcement of their weak economic position. During the First Empire the small farmers' productive structure could be implemented by the expropriation of the large landlords, by war conquests and war economy. Fifty years later, the small farmers were being expropriated (proletarianized) and weakened by international competition in food production through imports from America and Asia, independently of any government policy. In this sense the Second Empire regime was established on a hegemonic project combining the interests of expanding industrial capital with only the purported interests, but active support, of the farmers, who, at that time, constituted the large majority of the French population. The hegemonic strategy of the ruling class is transitory within any one pattern of capitalist development, either because social productive relationships change and the various superstructural conditions worsen or because the class struggles of the dominated classes destroy the integration conditions. Newly determined class alliances are substituted for others, specific hegemonic fractions of the bourgeoisie lose their priority in the control of power in favour of other fractions.

Hegemony can be a very important concept with which to decode class relations into political organizations and institutions, and vice versa. For instance, Gramsci explains why the Italian national revolution (Risorgimento) was unsuccessful and gave rise to such a feeble and controversial capitalist development, and not to a different one. He argues that during the Risorgimento there were two different capitalist options for the formation of a hegemonic strategy: one more radical and progressive (republican and Jacobinian) and one more conservative (monarchist). The former was based on the possibility of completing the bourgeois revolution throughout the country, through the expropriation of pre-capitalist landlords, the formation of a large class of small farmers, and the accumulation of vast resources from agricultural rationalization to be utilized in rapid industrial growth. But this option could not succeed: the northern, more progressive, urban bourgeoisie was never able to forge a link with the large majority of the Italian peasantry, especially the southern peasantry, and finally gave in to the continuation of the precapitalist domination schema of the large landlords. The moderate sector of the bourgeoisie successfully created a hegemonic strategy, based on capital accumulation and industrial revolution in a small area of the north, and on the provisional and partial survival of precapitalist social relations in the rest of the country. As I hope to show in Chapter 2, this strategy had its advantages and disadvantages: the concentration of industrial growth in a limited area was achieved at the expense of a rather slow rate of growth, and of the freezing, for nearly a century, of important accumulation resources in a backward subsistence economy in the south.[18]

The study of the origins and structure of a specific class hegemony is certainly very complex. It must take into account class and productive relations and other cultural, historical and ideological conditions. Nevertheless, this analysis is essential to the study both of political struggles (and also specific class conflicts) and of government and state policies. As a methodological instrument, the concept of hegemony is very important because it avoids the utilization of functionalist methods. State or party policies must not be considered merely as mechanical consequences of specific class (or fractions of class) interests. They should rather be seen as parts of complex hegemonic strategies or counter-strategies, as the consequences of the need for the dominant class to keep its control over society and of the attempts by other classes to break such control. To use a different term, which requires considerable caution, I have proposed a theory of legitimation of class power.

The tentative schema in Figure 1.3 summarizes the conditions of formation and reproduction of the hegemonic strategy. Complex relations between structure and superstructure determine political relations. The specific relations of production, reflected in specific class structure and degrees of consciousness, condition class movements and struggles, which are related to the hegemonic strategy adopted by the ruling class and to the consequent organization of political relations in various parties, and in the state and public institutions. Hegemonic conditions cannot be considered only as structural, or superstructural, elements, since they result from the merging into a specific class project of both structural and superstructural conditions. Strictly, political relations are shaped by the hegemony of one class over the others. Hegemony retransfers both structural and superstructural preconditions into political relations. In this sense, political relations should finally be evaluated case by case and are not subject to 'iron' laws, and this reconfirms the view that no general theory of the state can be reliable, apart from very vague methodological assumptions. A class analysis of the state, its institutional character and its policies is not possible at the abstract theoretical level, because such an analysis requires an understanding of its specific class composition and history, the elements characterizing the class hegemony in a given situation.

A 'social base', as determined by specific socio-productive relations, develops a class consciousness, which expresses also the

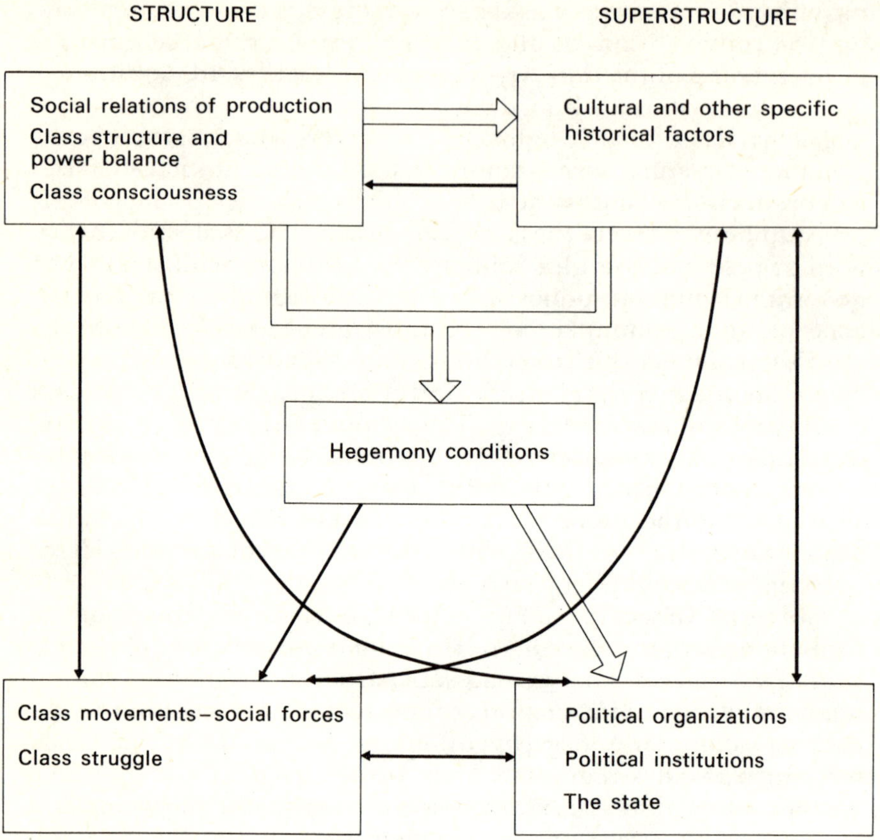

STRUCTURE   SUPERSTRUCTURE

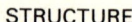

FIGURE 1.3   The conditions under which hegemony forms.

socio-cultural characters of such class. At this point the 'social base' is a potential 'social force'. Obviously a class, as a potential social force, is fragmented into different groups of interests, with different degrees of consciousness and different political potentialities. Every social class in a specific situation is reflected in various political expressions (parties or other organizations) which are connected with the specific interests of one or more subgroups of the class itself and which pursue different hegemonic strategies.

To understand both class conflicts and political institutions one must first consider the modes of formation and reproduction of class hegemony, as determined by its fundamental conditions and as modified by the specific circumstances of capitalist development. This explains why Marxist authors have *never* been able to conduct a plausible class analysis in an abstract and general way, but only in a specific context. Marx analysed France 1848–49, Engels, England at the beginning of the last century, Lenin, Russia at the beginning of this century, Gramsci, Italy during the Risorgimento period, and so on. This also explains the failure of recent general attempts to conduct a class analysis, among which the most ambitious but least impressive is Poulantzas.[19]

I turn now to recent literature on the state and state intervention in economic and social processes.[20] As a preliminary I shall try to answer an important question posed by these studies. Is it possible that the capital accumulation process has been radically modified by the new political dimension of advanced capitalism so that the whole approach to the study of current societies should be changed?

Both O'Connor and Offe seem to put forward an affirmative answer to this question. O'Connor is more explicit, he believes that advanced capitalism, among other important changes, develops a new process of production, appropriation and distribution of surplus value (indirect surplus value), through the intervention of the capitalist state in the economy. This point, added by O'Connor to the Marxist theory of labour value, is far from convincing, as O'Connor fails to explain how this new form of surplus value is actually produced. His writings in fact show that indirect surplus value, far from being new, is only a form of distribution of the surplus value produced in the traditional ways (absolute and relative surplus value). The state appropriates a part of the produced surplus value through the taxation system, and redistributes it through public expenditure and investments. But this does not necessarily change the general laws of capital accumulation. This interpretation is reinforced if we consider that the state reflects a capitalist hegemony in distributing its surplus value and, for this reason, is obliged to respect, by and large, the laws and contradictions of capital accumulation.

Other authors seem to believe that current societies, where capital is largely organized in monopolistic corporations, and governments frequently intervene directly or indirectly to implement and regularize the accumulation process, are no longer subject to market competition, and thus to various other accumulation laws indicated by Marx as typical of capitalist societies. In my opinion, the decadence of the capitalist market and of the traditional accumulation laws on a world scale is far from proved and documented.

The development of capitalism has created large and powerful corporations which, on a national scale, enjoy both a semi-monopolistic access to capital and good markets and a privileged relationship with the capitalist state. But market competition survives both on the international scale and the national levels, as far as the majority of economic sectors and exchanges is concerned. The late capitalist economy is a mixture of advanced concentrated units engaged in international competition and of less concentrated units which are active on a very differentiated and complex scale, local, national and international. The economic role of the state is not necessarily antagonistic to the accumulation laws; on the contrary, it is strongly complementary to them.

Firstly I should stress that state intervention in the economy is not at all a new event in the history of capitalism. In Chapter 2 I shall give evidence of the essential role that various states have had in fulfilling the conditions for capitalist take-off and fast growth in various countries of western Europe – through railway building, urban renewal, colonial conquests, re-armament and various other policies.

In the nineteenth century the intervention of the state in the capitalist economy was required mainly to break the resistance of precapitalist social structures, which were not easily won by market forces alone, or to accelerate the accumulation process, weakened by late take-off and menaced by the competition of more advanced countries. Subsequently state intervention has been increasingly associated with the growing complexities and contradictions of capitalist enterprises. On the one hand, the capital concentration process has never been generalized, so that a new form of dualism has progressively come into being, whilst, on the other, the increase of labour productivity has sharply attacked both levels of employment and the capacity of capital to realize the whole of the surplus value created. The great crisis of the thirties can be seen as the turning point of the restructuring of the capitalist accumulation process, although the final conditions for the new balance of late capitalism were created only later, through the massive destruction of productive forces during the Second World War. Not only was the new balance compatible with the main accumulation laws, but its results were essential to the reproduction of capitalism itself for the succeeding decades. This of course does not mean that capitalist contradictions were definitively overcome. The state intervenes in late-capitalist economies in two main ways. Through an artificial redistribution of surplus value it provides the means of survival of a now very complex capitalist productive structure, based on the co-existence of concentrated, advanced, expanding sectors with less concentrated, backward ones. Second, through an increasingly unproductive usage of surplus value, the state promotes the general reproduction of the social system, higher occupational levels (tertiarization) and a higher potentiality for realization of surplus value. In the long term both these kinds of intervention determine a serious compression of the accumulation rate and contribute to under-accumulation, waste, and the progressive fall of the general profit rate. The main internal contradiction of capital development, which in the twenties and thirties was expressed in the incapacity to realize the created surplus value, is now expressed in under-accumulation, stagnation and the fall of the profit rate.

Before considering urban and regional issues, we should raise two additional general points. The state operates in the capitalist economy within the limits of the accumulation laws and contradictions. This is reflected mainly in the difficulties the state and large corporations meet when they try to overcome capitalist anarchy through planning. The failure of capitalist planning, and, under many aspects, also of 'socialist' planning, is the main evidence that market anarchic forces and competition still survive and are strong enough to defeat any kind of policy intervention. The general contradictory logic of the market still directly conditions capitalist economies and (indirectly, through international exchanges) is strong enough to condition the economic development of the self-styled 'socialist' countries. Neither the state nor the large corporations have any powers to foresee the results of long term capitalist development. They cannot prevent overproduction, unemployment, distortions in the labour market, under-accumulation, and so on, chiefly because they cannot foresee the exact dimensions of a given trend. Moreover, they do not have the instruments nor the opportunity to implement radical changes in the trend of accumulation. Capitalist units and the different social classes are able to resist interventions made on long term objectives in favour of their immediate or short-term interests. In other words, even if it were possible to say that an investment would prove essential in twenty years' time, neither the state nor any capitalist unit would be prepared to give up twenty years' high profit for a possible gain such a long time hence.

The second general consideration is that state action can never be considered as mechanically functional to capital accumulation. Rather, it is connected to the complex contradictions and opposed forces which characterize the specific relations of production and the particular hegemonic equilibrium. State intervention is related to two sets of general social contradictions: the impossibility of optimally combining opposed socio-economic interests and the impossibility of further reproducing an outdated social consensus basis. The redistribution of surplus value, always operated by the state, is absolutely necessary to promote and reproduce capital accumulation but, in the long term, produces unmanageable contradictions on a world scale. There is no way to eliminate the critical contradictions determined by the exploitative and anarchic nature of the capitalist mode of production, such as the tendency to under-employ, to under-accumulate, to waste. Moreover, the continuous expansion of state expenditures produces new forms of expression of the general contradictions, such as an increasing inflation rate and the fiscal crisis of state and local authorities.

Such contradictions reflect in many ways on social-territorial relations: the failure of regional development policies, the fiscal crisis of the large cities, the worsening ecological situation, the unreliability of public services and housing policies. I shall now examine this range of problems.

Regional development policies aim to achieve two opposite goals: to enlarge and reproduce the basis for capital accumulation in less developed peripheral areas and to reproduce the social consensus (the hegemony conditions) in areas where traditional economic activities, occupations and social organization are progressively disintegrated by capital development itself. In late capitalism, these two goals are generally incompatible on a world scale. They may be compatible on a national scale only in the case of very wealthy, advanced societies, able to spend resources accumulated abroad to improve the economy and the social consensus of the less-developed, internal regions. But, even in these cases, regional policies become problematic when the rate of surplus accumulation decreases because of increased international competition and the rebellion of overexploited Third World areas. It may seem a paradox that, where regional policies could be relatively more successful in meeting both goals at the same time, they are operated not so much by the state but directly by concentrated private corporations. In their continuous re-organization, large corporations find it convenient to move productive activities to less developed areas in order to achieve a more profitable territorial division of labour. The traditional industrialized regions remain the seat of large financial groups and banks while industrial plants are decentralized in less developed, and consequently less expensive areas.

Take as an example the case of the USA. Gradually, the fastest industrial growth area moved from the east coast to the middle west, to the west coast and, finally, to the south. United States capitalist development left out various areas, mainly mountain or marginal ones, which remain poor and backward, but a great part of the national territory was suitable for use as industrial locations. Nevertheless, serious problems arose in the abandoned areas, and high costs of relocation and economic conversion had to be borne. The state had at various times to promote assistance programmes to subsidize excluded or abandoned areas and the unemployable part of the population (old people, females, young people, etc.). But no important regional development programme was implemented directly by the US state and local authorities for any length of time, although military and welfare development has certainly contributed to the expansion first of the western regions (1930–50) and then of the southern regions. Even recently, wage differentials and local authority incentives have contributed to push towards the south the development of some manufacturing industries (such as textiles, food processing, secondary chemicals, etc.). The greatest help the Federal State has given to the accumulation of capital has been to enter into several wars, to increase military expenditure, to expand the welfare budget, and to consolidate and support US imperialism abroad. But even in this case state intervention reached a critical point when the enormous state and local authority deficit became too heavy a burden for the accumulation process. No further expansion was possible without a more than proportional increase in state expenditure. At the same time, increasing state expenditure was reducing the accumulation rate too much. For the diminishing proportion of industrial jobs and the permanent productive restructuration imposed enormous costs in the form of maintenance of the social consensus, an acceptable rate of employment (mainly in the service industries) and a certain degree of assistance to the relatively impoverished strata of the population. In the seventies, the defeat in Vietnam, the Portuguese revolution, the loss of some important African markets, and more recently the Islamic revolution in Iran, menaced the surplus profits and benefits the USA had previously enjoyed. The increase of trade competition both with the Soviet Union and with other capitalist countries, mainly Japan and West Germany, has further worsened the situation. These factors are the background of the fiscal crisis of the US State and show how difficult it is for a capitalist state to provide a medium-term solid basis for capital accumulation.

It is likely that in the near future the regional issue will come to the forefront for US society and for the Federal State, when the tax revolt weakens the capacity of local authorities and of the state to intervene, and under-accumulation slows down development, with disastrously differentiated effects in the various areas. In the south, recent industrialization will be interrupted. In the old industrialized areas, the restructuration costs will be met with enormous difficulties. In the socially assisted areas, abandoned welfare programmes will give rise to new urban poverty and diffused conflict.

The Italian case is very different. Here the state is forced to intervene with vast regional development policies; the regional issue is one of the most important in Italian politics and economics. A large part of the country remains very poorly developed: unemployment and under-employment, the diffusion of irregular, low productivity economic units and the permanently critical state of agriculture are seriously endangering the possibility of renewing hegemony and reproducing capitalist assets. Italian governments have tried regional development policies in three different ways: through infrastructuration investments; through incentives favouring private settlements in less developed areas; and through a 'poles of growth' strategy, directly achieved by decentralization of large plants belonging to the state-owned industries and some large private corporations. As the next chapter clarifies, these policies have had some provisional results – both on the strictly accumulative ground and on social consensus level – but only in the short term, and without solving the problem of regional underdevelopment.

In the fifties, the state promoted massive investments to restructure agriculture and build modern infrastructures all over the country. These state investments had two main goals: to open the backward, self-sufficient rural market to the influences of rapidly growing industrial production and to build a new hegemonic bloc based on a new rural bourgeoisie, state bureaucracy and state-assisted strata in the less developed areas, in place of the outdated social order based on landed estates. This intervention promoted concentrated accumulation in the already industrialized areas but with increasing unproductive costs. In fact, investments in the south did not favour a productive reorganization of agriculture or an autonomous industrialization process, but only the increase of unproductive income spent in the south to buy goods produced elsewhere. Later, in the sixties and seventies, the state pursued the second and third strategies both together. The incentives to private industries to locate new plants in less developed areas did not work very well. Only a few large corporations chose to decentralize new plants in the southern regions, as the incentives were not enough to compensate for the more favourable situation of the market economies in the industrialized areas and the less expensive labour costs of the underdeveloped countries of the Third World.

Moreover in this same period the informal economy was developing in the only areas where favourable conditions for expansion were to be found, in some central and northern regions. In contrast to the large majority of the southern regions, these areas could offer the specific required background: a specialized surviving craft tradition (in textiles, tailoring, shoes, furniture, etc.) and a relatively good complementarity with agricultural production. In the south some financial groups speculated on state incentives and subventions and established uneconomic industries and ghost plants, using the grants available for financial speculations and not providing any form of permanent industrialization.

State industries decentralized the new capital intensive petrochemical and steel plants towards the south. In doing so they decongested the northern industrial area from a too-concentrated development, and saved some money, but they did not create an autonomous industrialization process or a permanent increase of industrial occupation in the southern regions. On the contrary, when the oil crisis led to excess capacity in these very plants, the south had to face a very severe decrease in the degree of industrial occupation and a high degree of waste in the productive capacity of these industries. Moreover, their settlement in the underdeveloped areas accelerated the crisis in local economic activities; as the modern industries competed with local small units in the purchase of resources and local qualified manpower, prices went up quickly and the small units had to close.

In this second period, state regional policies promoted short term accumulation. They could guarantee social consensus to a lesser extent, since during the building of the large plants industrial occupation was provisionally and locally increased; but in the long run they proved disastrous on both grounds. Agriculture has decayed into a persistent crisis which costs the state an increasing amount of money in assistance and the economy an increasing deficit in the food trade. The crisis of traditional manufacturers and the return of migrants has increased unemployment and underemployment, which could not be met by the very low increase of jobs in the modern, capital-intensive, industries or by the very expensive and parasitical expansion of the tertiary sector. The present deadlock is the most evident sign of such 'failure' of Italian regional policies in the long term.

The fiscal crisis of large cities must not be considered in isolation from the reorganization and crisis of the capital accumulation process and the fiscal crisis of the state in general. I shall very briefly try to explain how this phenomenon is connected with the features of the late-capitalist accumulation process. The fiscal crisis of large cities expresses the impossibility of raising the money necessary to manage the cities and provide the services traditionally required from local authorities. It is again a problem of 'who pays'. Urbanization costs have increased, and become more than proportional to the number of inhabitants who settle each year in a large metropolitan region. The re-organization of territorial facilities creates a very difficult situation from the financial point of view. The centre of the metropolitan area, the city, accommodates an enormous number of inhabitants during working hours and a decreasing number of residents. Very expensive urbanization costs have to be met both in the city centre and in the suburban areas. As the taxation system is based on residents, and any change discourages capital accumulation because it becomes – one way or another – a direct taxation on economic activities, the city centres become poorer and poorer and unable to meet the increasing urbanization costs. This phenomenon is aggravated by the fact that often a large proportion of the residual residents of city centres have a very low income. The state and local authorities cannot easily solve the problem by imposing double taxation on suburban residents who work in the centre; the result of this would be that labour costs and subsistence conditions would very rapidly worsen. This would immediately put the accumulation process in serious danger through an increase in labour costs, and would jeopardize the social consensus via social conflicts and tax revolts. The taxpayers' revolts in the United States constitute a good example of such phenomena. Thus, the deficits of both the central state and the local authorities increase to an intolerable level. This phenomenon is an important aspect of the late-capitalist accumulation crisis. The rate of accumulation is squeezed by resources that the state and the local authorities need to keep accumulation going and maintain social hegemony over the different social strata. Large metropolitan concentrations, functionally divided into a central service area and various kinds of economically specialized peripheries (mono-class housing, industrial settlements, trade, education, transport areas etc.) become more and more diseconomic to capital accumulation, since the organization, management and reproduction costs incurred increase much faster than average industrial productivity does. At the same time, this spatial organization, because of its various contradictions and incongruencies, becomes less and less tolerable to the large majority of the population. Yet metropolitan concentration remains essential to the extended reproduction of capitalism.

The crisis of public services follows the same contradictory logic.

I shall mention briefly some specific problems, which will be discussed at length in further chapters. State housing faces serious problems because it is increasingly conditioned by opposed forces. Capitalist development simultaneously increases the costs of housing and the necessity of providing new residents with cheap suburban houses. The persistent and increasing trend towards building speculation and property investment in the private sector contributes to an ever higher increase in building costs. At the same time, the workers employed in large factories or in the public sector, enjoying an increasing contractual and political power, demand better and less expensive houses. The marginal working class, oppressed by the distortions of the housing system – in terms of rent increases, worsening housing conditions and lack of rentable houses – becomes more and more conflictual.

The problems of public housing differ from country to country, depending on various factors, including: the traditional strength or weakness of the housing market; the degree and quality of state intervention; the specific features and timing of industrialization and urbanization. There are countries where the state and local authorities have intervened very little, leaving a free hand to private capital (USA), and others where there has been a long tradition of state housing (Great Britain). In most cases, state intervention in housing eventually becomes too expensive and fails to solve the increasing contradictions of the housing market. In general, but not necessarily in every country, the most important contradiction is due to a tendency to underproduce dwellings for low income groups and overproduce houses for the middle and high income groups. The point is that both rentiers and building corporations can make more money if they build new houses for sale or rent to the medium-high income population or for office use. At the same time the underproduction of houses for low income groups tends to increase prices and rents so that many families are forced to look for a flat which costs much more than they could normally afford (thirty to fifty per cent of their income) and which has been built for a much richer family. Moreover the overproduction of offices and high standard residential buildings constitutes a good method of freezing capital and speculating on inflation, which is also in part caused by the underproduction of low cost dwellings. Building corporations and rentiers continue to take advantage of the imperfect character of the market (which originates in monopolistic structure of land ownership) to the disadvantage of the long-term accumulation rate and, principally, of the living standards of the large majority of the population.

The housing problem is further complicated by other features of urbanized metropolitan areas; in particular by the tendency to segregate housing space. Specific social strata are pushed from the centres to the peripheries and forced to settle in mono-class segregated areas, either by the market mechanisms (prices of houses and levels of rents and/or by the state and local authority allocation policies.[21] In some cases, segregation is also selective and hierarchical; in the distribution of resources, the better off getting good houses in well serviced areas for a relatively low price, whilst low income groups get uncomfortable houses in poorly serviced areas for relatively high prices. This promotes social unrest and decreases the system's capacity for legitimation as it concentrates people with low living standards in segregated areas and worsens their subsistence standards.

The Italian case is among the most dramatic in the Western world, because housing speculation in the post-war period has created massive waste, a very backward and exploitative building industry and a persistent and dramatic housing shortage for low income groups in every large city.[22] Similar problems arise in the transport services. The capitalist state has long promoted transport policies based on the private car, at the behest of the powerful car industries lobby. These policies have meant enormous and increasing transportation costs, plus serious pollution and congestion problems and the increasing dependence of modern societies on oil production. This choice has also contributed to a rapid consumption of oil resources and to the very slow development of alternative transport and energy technologies which would conflict with the interests of the car lobby.

The early seventies marked a turning-point at which these transport policies began to impede rather than favour the accumulation rate and balanced social integration. Various governments have tried to reverse this policy by promoting collective transportation and less expensive energy technology. However, this late change of policy has meant tremendous social and economic costs. For example, the redevelopment of railways and transit systems on a national and city scale has turned out to be very expensive because technology had progressed very little in such decaying industrial sectors. At the same time it is impossible to abandon the private car suddenly as this would mean economic disaster in an industrial system largely activated by and dependent upon car production.

The situation remains critical, and no solution can be seen within the very complex articulation of world capitalism. Moreover, a new oil crisis is striking the capitalist economies more and more severely as a result of the Iranian Islamic revolution, and of the clash between Western powers and Arab countries over the separate Egyptian-Israeli peace.

State intervention does not solve the contradictions which characterize capitalist development, neither does it change the fundamentally capitalistic nature of contemporary societies. Market relations are modified by state intervention largely in the same manner as they were in the nineteenth century, although on different terms: the economy was not then as concentrated as it is now and competition among small producers was very severe. In this sense pure market capitalism has never existed.

Government policies redistribute surplus value in order to achieve two different and often opposed ends; to reproduce the best possible avenues for capital accumulation and to reproduce the legitimation of class power over a complex society under specific hegemonic terms. The present crisis represents the impossibility of simultaneously reproducing accumulation and hegemony in late capitalism. However, it does not offer the possibility of immediate solution through social conflicts, capital restructuration or new hegemonic strategies, as occurred in the cyclical crises of the past. Neither does the crisis indicate the very rapid and dramatic transition to a new socialist order which many Marxist scholars believe in and argue for. On the contrary, the crisis seems self-propagating as a long-term trend towards social disgregation, a slow rise in unemployment, the development of radical local and sectarian conflicts, the continuous provisional modification of the hegemonic order, and so on. The crisis of territorial balance and of state territorial policies is an important aspect of such general, long-lasting crises. They all reflect the impossibility of continuing to combine the further development of the productive forces with a conservative capitalist organization of society but, on the other hand, the productive forces are not yet developed to the extent that an alternative order could be created on a world scale.

THE NEW STRUCTURE OF THE LABOUR MARKET AND THE CRISIS OF URBANISM

The specific socio-territorial features of current societies will be dealt with in the last part of this book. However, to conclude this introductory chapter, I should like to mention some important aspects of the socio-economic structure of late capitalism, mainly connected with the labour market, and to analyse briefly its territorial consequences.

The last century of capital accumulation has deeply changed the structure of the labour market and the processes which it involves. Schematically, the most interesting changes are the following: rural overpopulation, which has fed the labour demand of developing industries throughout the age of capitalism, has been nearly exhausted; in the meantime, a large and fast-growing urban overpopulation has been established; as industrial occupation is not increasing overall at all the so called 'industrial reserve army' has disappeared as such and every form of unemployment has changed its role in the accumulation process; employment and economic activities in the service industries, both public and private, have grown rapidly. This has given rise to a vast process of tertiarization of current societies, although in different terms and with different rhythms in each country, depending upon their specific role in the international division of labour.

For the present case, three events and tendencies of late capitalism are particularly interesting: the territorial distribution, role and effects of various forms of persistent unemployment and underemployment; the tendency to social disgregation and to the 'local decentralization' of social conflicts and social problems; the features and consequences of the tertiarization process. Each of these topics could become the subject of a serious monographic study; here I shall only briefly mention some points I consider very important to a better understanding of current societies.

During the industrialization process, the reserve army of labour is mainly localized in the countryside, where it is active in agriculture at very low productivity rates. Two parallel processes progressively force it to urbanize: increasing demand for urban-industrial labour, and the rationalization of productive organization in the countryside. These conditions imply that increases in industrial employment do not bring about serious increases in the cost of the labour force because of temporary shortages of the workers required by expanding or new capitalist industries. Capitalist development progressively alters such a situation. Although manufacturing industries continue to develop their production capacities, this goal is now achieved mainly through increases in labour productivity rather than additional labour. At this stage, overpopulation – both the residual rural one, mainly located in the underdeveloped regions and countries, and the increasing urban one – no longer plays the role of an industrial reserve army. This is extremely important for two reasons: industrial wages tend to be decreasingly related to unemployment and under-employment rates and workers employed in different sectors tend to feel less and less *united* and become *competitive* among themselves and with unemployed and under-employed workers. In fact, capitalism moves from a relatively united labour market situation, with high mobility and competition, to a situation where workers are much less mobile. Many different and separate labour markets and working conditions emerge. The economists call this transformation the 'balkanization' of the labour market. Important, strong and stable internal markets co-exist with many local, highly competitive external markets.[23] The economic structure and the working class grow dualistic and highly disunited. Moreover, workers in the concentrated and advanced manufacturing industries enjoy a relatively good situation, with a safe job and a medium income, although that income is menaced by increases in tax outgoings and the costs of maintaining unemployed members of their families, even when salaries are automatically adjusted to the cost of living, and thus free from the effects of inflation (as is the case in Italy and a few other Western countries). Other potential workers, often selected minorities or foreign workers, suffer very long periods of unemployment, very unstable jobs and very low wages. This irregular working class group tends also to be heavily stratified in various ways, largely determined by local economic structure. The territorial features of social conflicts in late capitalism are largely different from the ones produced by traditional petty-competitive capitalism in the new character of the labour market which we have briefly sketched. The urbanization process is no longer determined by increases in industrial employment.

In some Third World countries and underdeveloped regions urbanization is still a massive phenomenon due to the persistent crisis of the countryside. It develops in the direction of an excessive expansion of the service sectors. (This will be discussed in Chapter 3.)

Peripheral cities and regions develop particular and dependent social conditions of production based on irregular occupation, on specific, backward, family structures and double employment, and on a very weak and sectarian process of capital-formation, which is totally controlled from abroad. In these areas, unemployment and employment in the services increase to intolerable levels and lead to waves of furious social conflict. But most of these conflicts are local and delimited. There is no overall solidarity in the national working class movement, so that their disruptive potential is rather low, even when the diffusion of the causes of conflict is in theory wide enough to subvert the capitalist order at any given moment (at least in the weak capitalist countries, like Italy, Great Britain, Spain, etc.).

Service expansion is pushed by two different factors. The increase in industrial productivity, with the parallel increase in the overall demand for services and capacity to produce them and the necessity to employ at least some of the surplus population. As we have already mentioned, this overpopulation is determined, on the world scale, by this same increase in labour productivity in the manufacturing industries, by the diffusion of labour-saving technologies, by the crisis in traditional economic activities and by the recent under-accumulation tendencies of world capitalism. Tertiarization has different meanings and consequences in the developed and underdeveloped regions. In the first case it is paid for by imperialistically accumulated surplus profits and becomes both a factor in and a condition of the continued imperialistic economic attack on underdeveloped regions. The exchange of values contained in highly sophisticated services and research activities, with values contained in raw materials and primary industrial goods becomes increasingly unequal, and imperialistic countries use their advantages to increase their privileges and reinforce their economies. By contrast, in less developed countries tertiarization is an overall economic deficit, and increases the dependence of the area upon the relatively more advanced societies. In both cases the two factors are present together and strictly interconnected, although economists would evaluate the first positively and the second negatively. This strict interconnection means that we cannot clearly distinguish a positive development of tertiarization from a negative one. Further, in the most advanced capitalist countries tertiarization has some markedly parasitic features, connected with the necessity of rapidly increasing the employment of the surplus population and the maintenance of highly differentiated levels of income, in order to disunite the working class and impose advantageous consumption models.

The tertiarization process is paralleled by a huge increase in white collar jobs within manufacturing industries themselves. The latter is again determined by the same process of tertiarization, plus the necessity to win new markets by any means (publicity, market research, political pressures, etc.) and a parallel decay of strict control of production costs within a much more concentrated economic structure. These two phenomena have a strong influence on the social structure of contemporary urban settlement. Most large cities become the concentrated workplace of a large number of white collar workers employed in industrial management, in banks, and public and private service industries. But these people only work in the urban centre; they live in outlying suburban settlements. The tertiarization process, both in advanced developed countries and in underdeveloped regions, leads to a huge increase in general production costs, and forces capitalism to reshape its territorial structure completely, through a general tendency to over-urbanize in proportion to the direct production capacities and revenues of the metropolitan area. The late-capitalist city becomes economically non-viable, not primarily because of the increase of the direct costs of industrial production – the ones borne immediately by the economic units – but because of the enormous increase of indirect production costs – the ones paid by the local authorities, the state, the local communities. Thus we have an increasing opposition between industrial units, mainly the most concentrated ones, which push for a continuous process of territorial concentration, division and reshaping (suburbanization, advanced division of functions across space), and other social forces, which run into difficulties because of the increasing costs of such developments. Again the problem is connected with the fundamental anarchy of capitalist societies, where economic units act to realize selfish, shortsighted goals, which lead in the long run and on a general level to explosive contradictions.

The tertiarization process also contributes to the breakdown of current societies into a complex hierarchical organization (whose results are outside centralized control), increasingly conflictual and highly disgregated. Service workers, not being immediately involved in the necessity to keep production costs as low as possible, are differentiated from other workers – more stratified, less professionalized, often less efficient. This phenomenon is most widespread where increasing unemployment forces indiscriminate and parasitic increases in service occupations in order to maintain social stability (class hegemony). In these cases, the income and role of white collar workers in service industries depend more upon political protection and the capacity to serve specific class interests than upon professional qualifications.

Territorial social stratification is greatly affected by such processes. The differences between developed and underdeveloped regions tend to increase and the social structure of a metropolitan area reflects the various hierarchical differences of an increasingly white collar population. Urban conditions of life deteriorate generally, due to the difficulties the social system meets in covering higher and higher urbanization and urban management costs. The very consensus of the mass, urban, middle classes, mainly tertiary white collar workers, is endangered by these contradictory developments. Ecological movements, some of the community protest organizations, and some of the large city commuters' movements, show how much the late-capitalist use of land is perceived as repressive by a large part of the middle classes. Since in every country the middle classes remain the strongest source of mass support for bourgeois hegemony, middle class conflictuality is an important sign of the economic and legitimation crisis of late capitalism.

The late-capitalist working class (in a wide sense, including all dependent workers without managerial or directive responsibilities) is stratified into three different mass sectors: the stable workers employed in oligopolistic manufacturing industries; marginal workers employed or employable in competitive industrial and service units; white collar workers or non-manual workers employed or employable in private or public service industries. The third category should be further divided into two components. First, a strong one (from the workers' point of view), which includes workers employed by the state, local authorities and banks and insurance under stable and protected contracts and including highly qualified professionals still in short supply in the labour market. Second, a weak component,[24] including executive non-manual workers employed in both private and public sectors in a temporary and unstable manner, and professionals over-supplied to the labour market by the mass education process. Whilst the first component remains privileged and enjoys higher incomes and better living and working conditions than the stable industrial worker, the second component suffers the same troubles as the marginal worker, although under different terms. In fact the over-population created by capitalist development is most menacing to the conditions of life and work of marginal workers and the second component of white collar workers. Although this pattern of stratification does not change the contradictory nature of late-capitalist societies, it does affect the main contradictions of the capital accumulation process. Social conflicts are generated by a crisis which is characterized by the simultaneous occurrence of explicit or implicit unemployment, a strong under-accumulative tendency, the increase of waste and unproductive expenses and overproduction in some industrial sectors. These conflicts reflect the new stratification of the working class, as does the territorial structure, which is also affected by the different social interests generated within the working class by capitalist development. The central, advanced industrial areas, the capitalist metropolitan cities, suffer an inevitable continuous increase in the costs of production and life, to the point of unavoidable diseconomies. On the other hand, various kinds of capitalist peripheries suffer growing economic and social marginality, increasing unemployment and deprivation of local resources. The process cannot be stopped and reversed, being a natural part of the accumulation process. On the contrary, any form of economic decentralization increases territorial dependence and long term social contradictions. I shall deal with this question more fully in Chapter 3.

One of the most important theoretical problems is that no clear alternative to the crises of capitalist development in general and urbanization in particular can be outlined. Reference to existing 'socialist' experience has proved unsafe. As I explain in Chapter 4, these experiences resemble capitalist development too much. At the same time the working class movement in the West is being disgregated by the very features of the capitalist crisis. Although some Western working classes have perhaps been more conflictual over the last two decades as compared to the previous twenty years, they appear, at the same time, to be more confused and divided. However, I shall attempt nevertheless to deal with two problems. What alternative currents and prospects are expressed in the conflicts concerning the use of land in present day societies? What theoretical evaluation of existing socialist experience within a capitalist world can be offered? The answers are closely connected. Socialism is the process through which capitalist societies are overthrown on a world scale and an alternative social organization established. The social force which implements this revolutionary change is intended to be the working class, the exploited part of the population inclusive of various different social strata, forming a wide class coalition under an alternative social-hegemonic strategy. In this sense socialism is not a state but rather a process, already going on under different terms and to different extents in every current society.

It may be useful for a better understanding of accumulation-territorial problems to offer a few further theoretical remarks on socialism, which will be developed in the last chapter. Individual, historical experiences of socialism are unreliable as a guide to the general features of socialism because the name describes a protracted world-wide process. In addition, it should be remembered that the self-styled socialist countries are societies where the productive forces remain less developed than in advanced capitalist ones and where the world capitalist market plays an influential role. Hence their experience can tell us very little about the possible socialist character of future societies. These countries have to be at least partially competitive with capitalist economies in world trade and this affects their whole socio-economic organization. They are forced to develop a specific, exploitative technology, and in this area they suffer from a dramatic deficit. They must increase the productivity of labour, abusing manpower in the process. They must try to produce the same goods and impose the same consumption models instead of alternative ones. To control production in this exploitative way they are forced to employ a very authoritarian and centralized bureaucratic organization.

When production is organized in this way, social organization cannot be wholly under the control of the majority of the population nor can it be democratically planned.[25] This kind of society does not escape the major contradictions of late capitalism, although they are manifested in very different ways. Integration into the international capitalist market on terms restricted by bargaining with capital, introduces into national economies important features of capital accumulation. On the other hand, it is practically impossible to keep a national economy and society isolated from international trade for very long periods, whether it be a large country or a very small, unimportant, partially self-sufficient one.

Similarly the use of land is also affected by exposure to the international market and to capitalist contradictions. Concentrated urbanization cannot be stopped and the spatial division of labour and uneven regional growth are developed in parallel with the process of industrialization. Centralization and decentralization processes take place in a very similar way to capitalist societies.

The degree to which alternative socialist possibilities can be realized in a limited area of the world depends on two major conditions: how far a country can stay partially independent of market impositions and the strength and effectiveness of the decentralization of power to the masses. When a centralized political elite and bureaucracy exerts power through a hegemonic strategy based on rapid industrialization and its absolute centralized rule over society, socialist characteristics are totally lost. In theory, socialism should be a completely alternative process to that of capital accumulation. It should be based on two fundamental conditions: direct immediate control over the organization of production by workers and the development of very sophisticated and advanced production capacities, able to satisfy larger and larger collective and individual needs. A hypothetical society based on these conditions will also be able to produce an alternative use of land and to progressively overcome the contradictions developed by capitalism in its territorial structure; ecological imbalance, regional inequalities, waste of land, diseconomies, heavy concentrations, urban and rural poverty, the continuous increase of the division of labour, segregated and hierarchical housing and living standards, and so on.

We know very little about the specific features this socialist process might have. Some indications can be deduced from the experiences of two large countries which for some time and for different reasons, enjoyed an almost complete isolation from the capitalist world market: the USSR from 1917 to 1922 during the war communism period and the People's Republic of China from the late fifties to the early seventies. But these indications cannot be interpreted as a model of socialist development, because of the specificities of both experiences, and of the very backward development of productive forces which characterized their social situation. With these qualifications I refer the reader to the study of the Chinese experience in the last chapter of this book.

Indulging in some fantasy, I believe that socialist territorial structure should be based on undivided, partially autonomous productive and population units, where, through advanced technological capacities, the collective is able to satisfy most of its needs directly without any form of strong or permanent division of labour. These local communities will not resemble pre-capitalist ones. They will exchange goods and services with other units, but such exchange, at the beginning unequal and partially exploitative, will have to become less and less exploitative and equal with the progress of socialism. But this process will only be completely successful when socialism becomes dominant and hegemonic on a world scale.

RECENT URBAN AND REGIONAL STUDIES

I have so far assumed as an important methodological point the refutation of urban or regional sociology as an independent scientific discipline. This refutation, however, cannot be argued solely on the grounds that urban reality exists only as an ideological device invented by bourgeois scholars. Uneven territorial distribution of population and resources is a fundamental aspect of the general reproduction process of capitalist societies. Capitalist use of land reflects various contradictions originating in the exploitative character of its social organization. There are no urban or regional questions as such: urban as opposed to rural or to regional is not a fundamental characteristic of social problems. It is only a feature of the general reproduction of current societies. So, although it is possible and reasonable to call a social problem urban or regional or rural, as the academic description of division of labour teaches us to do, this definition has no precise scientific meaning, apart from its obvious descriptive content. I shall briefly survey here the most important neo-Marxist studies on this subject, and discuss the question of how far these studies can go in bypassing the limits of traditional studies and in contributing a new methodology capable of understanding current social development.

Urban sociology became an important independent branch of social studies in the first half of this century, as a consequence of the research activities of a group of American scholars mainly based in Chicago (the Chicago School).[26] Some work on urban and urbanization problems was done in various earlier social studies,[27] but only the Chicago School focused attention on urban reality so precisely as to create a methodological separation, which is now considered totally artificial, between urban social problems and other social problems.

Traditional urban sociology was mainly based on the straightforward observation of a peculiar social reality, particularly that of large US cities, without any attempt to explain the origins and causes of such reality.[28] Any connection between urban social structure and the general class structure of society, and between the urbanization process and the capital accumulation process was carefully avoided. At the very beginning, this was due more to the lack of a general methodology than to a specific policy. In fact the results of the Chicago School studies were also utilized by radical politicians to denounce US society in the thirties as repressive, segregative, unjust. But when functionalism became the predominant social science methodology and the justificatory principle of sociology itself, under Parsons' programme,[29] urban sociology found a place in a scientific system and became part of an overall functionalist theory of modern societies. 'Urban' became a branch of a very segmented, divided, artificial scientific system, a device meant to break down social knowledge into various independent sectors, where the general dialectical interconnections were denied and concealed, to protect the interests of capitalist reproduction. Under this methodology, the social 'status quo' was totally justified by its functional inevitability and by its strictly artificial segmented structure. It is only at this stage that 'urban' became an ideological device, meant to isolate from the complex social process a supposedly separate part of reality. Moreover, the creation of an official, academic urban sociology is only an aspect of the vast process of progressive division of scientific knowledge: geographers and economists accept the same division into various artificial subdisciplines.

The scientific research activities on increasingly urban societies have been largely monopolized by functionalist methodology, successfully exported to Europe and other parts of the world in the fifties and sixties. Wright Mills' powerful early refutation of functionalist methodology[30] and of the division and dispersion of intellectual knowledge was either fiercely opposed or almost ignored until the late sixties. Then a new wave of social conflict and the crisis of late capitalism created the conditions for a new discussion of the methodological approach of the social sciences. Beginning in the late sixties, a large number of critical and materialist studies were developed in various countries. This was a by-product of the contradictions slowly maturing in the post-war period, ranging from the decolonization process to the creation of an extended mass consumption structure with its enormous overproduction difficulties and its rapid exhaustion of raw materials and energy reserves. More immediately, it can be seen as the consequence of three important recent events: renewed class conflicts, begun by the students in 1966-68 and taken over by the Western working class in 1968-70; a new dimension in international class confrontation, with the Vietnamese resistance to US intervention and the diffusion of the contents of the Chinese cultural revolution; the economic crisis of capitalism and the clear failure of the welfare myth.

These studies have important objective and subjective limits. Their content is very rich on the critical side – a radical rejection of previous functionalist and historicist methodologies – but rather poor from the positive point of view – the achievement of an alternative materialist-dialectical methodology for a comprehensive understanding of social realities. These neo-Marxist intellectuals are unlikely to achieve great successes in this field chiefly for the following reasons. First, they are integrated into the traditional academic division of scientific labour so that, for example, sociologists have a very poor training in economics and vice versa. Second, the Marxist background utilized is the traditional one, as elaborated by dogmatic academicians divided into branches of different philosophical schools and deeply separated from the praxis of the various sectors of the national working classes. Third, social scientists have a very limited autocritical sense and a low consciousness of their limitations. They are confined in an artificial academic world, as separate as possible from class praxis. Further, when they are connected with organized sectors of the working class (mainly the Italian, French and Spanish Communist parties), they are obliged to accept a traditional division of labour and to depend upon a bureaucratic authoritarian organization. As a consequence of these limitations, they end up reproducing many methodological elements which characterized the traditional functionalist or historicist analysis.

The French works on 'collective consumption' and 'urban social structure' are perhaps the most important of such new radical studies on urban and regional problems produced after 1968. I shall try to explain the reasons which led such scholars to identify urban problems with collective consumption processes. The idea of isolating the area of consumption from production is typical of a Marxist structuralist approach, which tries to argue for at least the partial autonomy of various groups of social facts (political relations, consumption, cultural relations, etc.) from the structural social relations of production.

Specifically urban problems are seen by these authors as a set of collective consumption, social relationships, by contrast with general economic or industrial problems which are defined by collective production processes. Thus urban conflicts are interpreted as a class confrontation in terms of collective consumption. Capital attempts to maximize profits, although with various contradictions between different capital sectors, and as a result confines the reproduction of the working class to the minimum possible standards of collective consumption, that is: poor housing, segregated areas, high taxation of wages for inefficient public services, expensive transport and so on. On the other hand the working class struggles to gain a better share of and control over collective consumption processes, better and less expensive housing and public services, fast and free transport, democratic decision-making on urban renewal, and so on. This view of urban problems is reductive and misleading for particular reasons.

(1) The consumption process is only a partial aspect of the general production process. Production (in a strictly technical sense), distribution and consumption relations are highly interdependent and together form the social relations of production, i.e. the social structure. One cannot consider consumption processes separately from the other two aspects of the capitalist reproduction process.

(2) If we add the adjective 'collective' to the word 'consumption'

we raise a number of questions which French, neo-Marxist, urban sociology scholars have not answered. What can be called collective consumption and what individual consumption? Is it possible to establish scientifically what can be consumed individually and what has to be consumed collectively? Are there other phenomena, apart from the urban, which can be classified as a collective form of consumption? Can urban problems really be defined by a category as vague and confused as collective consumption? There are many other questions, listed by Pahl in a recent essay.[31]

(3) French neo-Marxist scholars have defined collective consumption in a number of different ways, thereby generating great confusion.

I would argue that the 'collective consumption' theory is the result of two opposed intentions; to see urban social processes in terms of class needs and to redefine the urban sector as an autonomous object of social studies. I strongly sympathize with the first intention but disagree with the second for the reasons already expressed.

In a class analysis, it is very important to determine what are the general and specific class needs on basic social issues such as housing, transport, the use of land, regional development and so on. This operation may permit the association of specific class conflicts and contradictions with general social processes. But the problem of social needs is extremely complicated. What appears to be an immediate need of the working class may be a misleading long-term goal for the workers' political movement. On the other hand, some important goals do not appear as immediate, essential class needs. Furthermore, we should assume that it is impossible to isolate 'urban' needs from 'non-urban' ones. The consumption process itself is not definable in a purely territorial context, it does not correspond to any 'urban question' but is rather an important part of the general social question. In fact, class needs, the consumption model and process, the different styles of life of various social strata, the environmental balance, are only parts of the general capital reproduction process. This must be conceived as including the enlarged reproduction of fixed capital and the labour force, the consumption in a peculiarly selective way (and waste if necessary) of a large part of the produced goods and services, the selection of needs to be satisfied and needs to be repressed. Finally, it includes the social reaction, permanent conflict, created by the impossibility of satisfying all social needs in a society organized on the opposition between two different classes.

Some additional criticisms can be levelled at specific works in the

French school, and particularly against Castells' *La question urbaine*, which was the first and most important essay from this scientific standpoint.[32] Here, the strong structuralist emphasis isolates the nexus of urban problems from its historical origins and its dialectical complexities. The author succeeds in giving a good account of what he calls 'urban structure', which is also expressed in complex diagrams, but he disregards essential social connections and relations and, worse, he reduces some important social relations to mechanical roles and functional links. The dominating interests of the monopolistic sector of the bourgeoisie appear to determine every social event.[33] Moreover, in Castells' work the economic aspects of the urban question are examined in such a weak and confused way that they disappear under a set of vague sociological concepts. It is impossible to understand how the capital accumulation process determines the features of urbanization and why the urban social structure takes the form it does under specific productive strategies. Contemporary societies appear to be determined by the prevailing social interests of a class fraction, monopoly capital, rather than by a complex and comprehensive class confrontation, which we usually call the class struggle or the capital accumulation process. Thus the ghost of functionalism, which Castells explicitly throws out of the window, comes back through the door.

This theoretical confusion originates mainly in the fact that Castells and others pre-select a range of problems and codify them into a semi-autonomous structure which they call 'urban'. The correct scientific process should be rather the opposite. By studying the accumulation process in its complexities first, both at the abstract theoretical level and at more specific levels, we can decodify the problems we are more interested in and explain them fully in relation to that process itself.

Other methodological criticisms could be made against the contribution of the Marxist geographer David Harvey.[34] Harvey's work is not as vast or documented as that of the French neo-Marxist group but he raises interesting points in analysing the reproduction cycles of the built environment. Again, however, the built environment question, as an identifying feature of urban problems, is a mistake, though the analysis of the role of urban infrastructure and building is often useful in understanding capitalist development. Any mode of production, and in particular any social formation, involves a process of reproduction of a specific built environment, which is essential to the reproduction of society in general. In capitalist societies this is very complicated because it involves financial reproduction, the shaping of essential production means and long term consumers' goods (for example, housing and urban services) and the employment of a relatively large, unskilled sector of the working class. Harvey is, in my opinion, interested too much in the function of the built environment as a part of dead capital and too little concerned with the complex relation between the renewal of the built environment and the accumulation of capital, intended in a broad sense.

The main limits of Harvey's analysis are:

(a) the built environment is not exclusively 'urban' but includes other kinds of lasting social infrastructures located outside cities;
(b) the analysis of built environment reproduction is by no means exhaustive of the various territorially important social problems raised by capital accumulation;
(c) the social conflicts and contradictions raised by capitalist built environment reproduction are oversimplified, and often reduced to a mechanical opposition.

The built environment can be a specific part of fixed capital or a long term, lasting consumption good or infrastructure. As such it has a particular position within the reproduction of capitalism as a dominant social formation, in that the specific form, cost and lifetime the built environment assumes in the history of capitalism, is important in understanding the terms of capital accumulation and class confrontation. But, although Harvey is sometimes tempted to claim this, the reproduction of the built environment does not follow any specific 'iron law' because it occurs within specific accumulation terms, as determined, historically and dialectically, by the social class confrontation, the organization and relative strength of the classes.

For a better understanding of this point, a short example may be useful. During the Second Empire, French capitalism achieved a successful acceleration of accumulation through the renewal of an important part of the built environment, the restructuring of central Paris. Through this manoeuvre financial speculation was promoted, and employment and the demand for industrial goods grew very rapidly, so that new capitalists could realize high profits and achieve high levels of investment. But this example does not mean that any urban renewal process need have the same motivations and results. In different historical class conditions, the rebuilding of an important part of the built environment can easily reflect or be an attempt to manage economic stagnation, or even be a form of deceleration of the accumulation process. On the other hand it is worth adding that it is not inconceivable that French capitalism would have achieved the same accumulation goals through quite different trends, policies, or interventions.

Finally I want to suggest also that Harvey's diagrams describing the reproduction of built environment and the connections between built environment, class structure and productive structure, are not very convincing.

I would again suggest that the built environment be approached by a different path, that is to say, starting from the study of the accumulation process and not, as Harvey too often does, starting from a prejudicial selection of problems concerned in the development of urban settlements.

The refutation of the traditional functionalist methodology of urban studies is not enough to establish an alternative radical Marxist approach. The definitions of the urban context by the two authors mentioned are too narrow and cannot include the complex social relations which determine urban and regional development. In my opinion, trying to define non-autonomous social relations, such as urban and regional ones, is always a mistake, leading to the re-introduction of functionalist methodology. Any delimitation of the object of study actually compels the scholar to assume a set of independent variables, whose influence on the object is finally explained as a mechanical and functional link. Facts, however, tell us that the object of our studies is not in any way distinct from reality in all its aspects; its dialectical relation with social reproduction problems is bilateral and complex, since its effects are not easily predictable. This is the chief reason why I do not attempt to define the urban question, but rather try and relate urban phenomena to the dialectical process of capital accumulation in its whole, real complexity.

The re-utilization of functionalist or historicist methodological approaches is dangerous, but at the same time extremely fascinating, because it offers the possibility of a much easier and simpler explanation of complicated social questions than the materialistic approach. Functionalism allows a straightforward explanation of the relations of causality, which, although false, is easier and apparently more convincing than a complex dialectical explanation. Moreover, using a functionalist methodology it is possible to visualize the whole social situation in terms of wide schemata which appear (but are not) useful to a comprehensive understanding of complicated social situations.

Historicism, on the other hand, expresses its interest in urban questions mainly through the elaboration of social typologies of urban situations. Max Weber's typology of cities is the best known sociological example.[35] Typologies may also seem convenient for a better understanding of social realities but they do not take into account the complex connections between different processes and situations and miss their causal relations. As I have argued elsewhere,[36] the main problem raised by an historicist methodology is the difficulty of arriving at a comprehensive scientific understanding of the social processes. Historicist typologies, no matter how articulated and precise they are, cannot explain the causal origins of social phenomena. In urban studies this becomes very dangerous since urban realities can be understood only through comprehensive reference to the social phenomena of which they are very partial aspects. The failure to do this empties urban studies of any scientific content and leaves only more or less accurate descriptions of specific historical cases.

Finally, neo-Marxist urban studies often contain another danger. Many scholars are prepared to abandon the historical dimension of urban processes in order to achieve a more comprehensive understanding of current realities and a general theory of the urban question. This is because they do not sufficiently investigate the connection between accumulation of capital, as an historical process, and specific urbanization trends and characteristics. Most traditional urban studies, however, have made the opposite mistake, emphasizing the pragmatic analysis of specific historical features and missing the general theoretical dimension. Considered from this aspect, most recent urban studies express an over-reaction to the superficiality of traditional pragmatism and so they lose completely the historic dimension of our social problems.

CHAPTER TWO
Territorial Division of Labour and Capitalist Development

MODE OF PRODUCTION AND TRANSITION

I shall begin by discussing Marx's concept of the mode of production remembering that for Marxists all social phenomena are ultimately determined by the specific historical and social forms of organized production.[1] Marxist research in urban sociology has been criticized for its *a priori* assumption that territorial organization in modern Western society always depends on the capitalist relations of production. This, it is suggested, precludes the possible contribution of other variables such as the development of productive forces and of productivity in general.[2]

I shall try to clarify the problem, bearing in mind that for Marx the history of humanity is a succession of different social-formations each characterized by different relations of production – that is to say different relations between social classes. In every socio-economic context the forces of production – seen as a network of social relations which determine the capacity of mankind to produce and consume at a given historic stage – develop towards a point of inevitable conflict with the very socio-economic context which generated them. At this point the prevailing mode of production becomes an obstacle and is overthrown so that a new mode of production can be established. The new order will have taken shape within the old social order and, more precisely, within the development of its productive forces.[3] One must add that the new social-formation will embody many characteristics of the old and this will be more marked where the forces of production are less developed. Unless these surviving elements become essential to the new order they will eventually disappear when the productive forces on which the new social-formation is based reach a stage of full development.[4]

In a general way one may therefore claim that for Marxists the socio-territorial division of labour, the structure and use of land, depend ultimately on the dominant relations of production, bearing in mind the dialectic development of forces of production within the dominant mode. What this entails for the origin and the subsequent development of capitalism will be discussed later. The picture is further complicated theoretically by the debate on the process of transition and transitional society.[5] The change from one social-formation to another is slow and complex and even if in its final stage it often assumes a revolutionary character, it involves long term processes which constitute transitional phenomena. During the course of their dialectical development the forces of production, and in particular the revolutionary social class, develop patterns of social organization which are typical of the future society and which thereby undermine the old.

PATTERNS OF CAPITAL ACCUMULATION AND URBAN DEVELOPMENT

The capitalist mode of production established itself in Europe first in England then in the other countries of the Continent between the seventeenth century and the end of the nineteenth century. But the process of transition from a feudal to a capitalist society had begun long before. Historical phenomena connected with this process can be traced to the end of the eleventh century, i.e. to the period of Carolingian decline. The process of transition can be seen as the dialectic interplay of two different phenomena: the crisis of the feudal mode of production and the primary accumulation of capital.

The division of territory represented by the great mercantile cities in the late Middle Ages and the complex problems surrounding the break-up of feudal agriculture from the eleventh century onwards[6] are beyond the scope of this study. We shall limit ourselves to the immediate prehistory of capitalism – i.e. the formation of industrial cities, the widespread commercialization of agriculture, the growing division of labour between industry and agriculture and the formation of the capitalist market. This we will refer to as 'the original accumulation of capital' since we are obliged to ignore the lengthy period of gestation of the phenomenon for practical reasons. This original accumulation of capital brought dramatic changes to socio-territorial structures, for it replaced a widespread socio-territorial organization, based on production for immediate consumption and characterized by little division of labour, with a highly specialized and concentrated socio-territorial division of labour, typical of the capitalist mode of production.

Once established the new mode of production was far from static (neither were those preceding it, though capitalism is immensely more dynamic than its forerunners). It reproduced itself on an increasing scale, reinforcing the division of labour and aggravating socio-territorial contradictions. I shall examine the process by which capital is accumulated in terms of its concrete influence on territory, looking beyond the mere economic mechanism to the dialectic of the social process played out between the classes and especially the capitalists and proletariat. Neither urbanization nor urban concentration necessarily derives from the general progress of industrialization, except inasmuch as progress and industrialization are factors in the accumulation of capital. Recent experience in China has demonstrated how industrialization and the modernization of an economy may take forms other than those peculiar to capitalism and so lead to very different socio-territorial structures.

But more complex problems have to be confronted when analysing the imperialist aspects of the accumulation of capital and of present day socio-territorial structures as well as when dealing with the symptoms of transition from capitalist society to socialism and its socio-territorial implications. On this point I shall limit my attention to certain hypotheses.

The prefiguration of a socialist alternative by the working class in present capitalist society invariably raises the question of the socio-territorial structure of any future, socialist society. To solve such a complex problem it is not enough to make comparative studies of existing socialist societies. Problems would still remain even if these studies were less scant and more reliable.[7] Socialism is not a dominant mode of production on a world scale: no one country can therefore claim to have fully undergone the process of transition into a truly socialist society. Given this, it follows that within such transitional societies there must exist a whole series of socio-economic processes which are still fundamentally capitalistic in nature.

A socialist society can be distinguished from one where the capitalist mode of production is still dominant by the presence of an explicit attempt to overcome the residues of capitalism. It is to such efforts – which manifest themselves in the socio-economic strategy of the new hegemonic class – that one turns when searching for the specific characteristics of a society in transition, i.e. a society with a socialist perspective. In it the capitalist mode of production is no longer dominant although the sparse development of productive forces still obliges it – locally and even more on a world scale – to retain some typically capitalistic features. But I shall discuss this problem more fully in the last chapter.

PRIMARY ACCUMULATION AND INDUSTRIAL 'TAKE-OFF'

What does the primary accumulation of capital amount to at the start? In so far as it is not the direct transformation of slaves and serfs into wage earners (a mere change of form), it signifies nothing other than the expropriation of the immediate producers, this is the end of private property based upon the labour of its owner.

Later on Marx clarifies his conception of the transition from a pre-capitalist society to a capitalist one.

At a certain level of development, this method of production brings into the world material means which will effect its own destruction. Thenceforward there stirs within the womb of society forces and passions which feel this method of production to be a fetter. It must be destroyed, it is destroyed. Its destruction, the transformation of the individual and scattered means of production into socially concentrated means of production, the transformation of the pigmy property of the many into the titan property of the few, the expropriation of the great masses of the people from the land, from the means of subsistence, and from the instruments of labour – this terrible and grievous expropriation of the populace – comprises the prelude to the history of capital.[8]

Thus for Marx primary accumulation is a total socio-economic process taking place outside 'the economic laws of capital' which will later regulate its reproduction. In view of this one ought not to reduce the process to a mere economic mechanism or even a generic historical evolution.[9]

Although Marx focused only on the specific forms in which primary accumulation presented itself in England, he did not exclude the possibility of several variants occurring in other countries. The English example remains an interesting one, for accumulation took place there before any other country. For this very reason, however, it cannot typify the general process of primary accumulation throughout history.

Marx's analysis of the English case can be summarized as follows: land expropriation and expulsion of the rural population; concentration of land ownership together with an increase in agricultural production due to more intensive exploitation and a net increase of arable land, matched by an even greater expansion in the agricultural sector producing raw materials for industry (sheep farming for wool, cultivation of cotton and silk); accumulation in the colonies, via slavery and commercial monopoly; birth of a modern banking system with international ramifications (international credit system) and the start of the National Debt.

These factors, so typical of English primary accumulation, are not all found in subsequent developments in the other European countries; notably the agricultural revolution and the relations between agriculture and growing industry underwent different developments in different countries. Each case does, however, reveal certain fundamental aspects of primary accumulation which entailed a radical change in existing social relations. A case in point is the introduction of the capitalist market in industry and agriculture, on both the national and international level. On the one hand this brought with it the seeds of destruction of any productive activity directed towards self-consumption, on the other hand it aided the growth of an evermore differentiated division of labour.

Flight from the land and creation of industrial towns are the first territorial by-products of intensified division of labour between industry and agriculture and also within their various respective branches. By and large it is the countryside that finances this process by supplying it with the necessary raw materials for industrialization, i.e. surplus population, new materials, food for the growing urban proletariat.

The new industrial centres can exploit the countryside by rapidly increasing its yield or by inducing an agricultural crisis. Although it may seem to be a paradox, such a crisis can be advantageous to industrialization provided that the division of labour now operates on a world scale and that capital can be accumulated through other means than the hoarding of surplus agricultural produce. Given these conditions, industry develops by using displaced peasants for its labour-force and by recycling depreciated agricultural capital, since it has also access to other sources of capital and of cheap food and raw materials.

Rapid and continuous urbanization is but the most obvious socio-territorial by-product of primary accumulation. The commercialization of agriculture – which requires crop specialization – revolutionizes social relationships in the countryside; likewise industrial take-off reshapes the size and functions of both small and large towns.

ROLE OF RURAL CLASSES: PRIMARY ACCUMULATION AND URBANIZATION

The growth of a deep contradiction between town and country – which is characterized by a drainage of resources from agriculture and their rechannelling to newly born industry – is an essential element in societies which are developing towards capitalism. Problems arise as soon as one attempts to give this contradictory relationship between town and country a concrete and systematic meaning in the process of primary accumulation.

Basically one is faced with testing whether the conflict between town and country is general or whether Kemp was correct in suggesting that 'only in England agriculture was "sacrificed" to industry and the establishment of a world-based division of labour'.[10]

In order to answer this question, and also to throw some light on the implicitly exploitative nature of the town-country dichotomy, we shall start by considering the economic roles of the towns, beginning with the development of large towns in the late Middle Ages based on commerce and handicrafts.

... the growth of trade carried in its wake the trader and the trading community, which nourished itself like an alien body within the pores of feudal society; ... with exchange came an increasing percolation of money into the selfsufficiency of manorial economy; ... the presence of merchant encouraged a growing inclination to barter surplus products and produce for the market ... .[11]

Dobb is right to point out that

So far as the growth of the market exercised a disintegrating influence on the structure of Feudalism, and prepared the soil for the growth of forces which were to weaken and supplant it, the story of this influence can largely be identified with the rise of towns as corporate bodies, as these came to possess economic and political independence in varying degrees.[12]

However, it took a few centuries before the development of the market and urban commercial and financial accumulation could assert itself more generally, thus overcoming the marginal role assigned to them by the still dominant agricultural and feudal order; by the time this occurred those towns which had prospered at various times between the fourteenth and the seventeenth centuries were no longer centres of primary accumulation and of capitalist development.

Urban development coincided completely with industrial development only where primary accumulation had become so dominant as to dismantle the whole pre-capitalist society. By and large this took place after the bourgeoisie had conquered state power following a revolutionary struggle against the feudal hegemonic class. In fact an ambiguous relationship prevailed at first between town and country. Towns – city states in particular – exploited the surrounding countryside. Peasants were made to work for the town, but they were not allowed to compete with the guilds which controlled the manufacture of goods, and as soon as more workers were needed they were forcibly recruited in rural areas and brought to the cities. The prosperity of these, however, was still limited by the enduring supremacy of the mode of production which centred round the agricultural hamlet. However, town and country played different roles in the intense stage of primary accumulation, which involved the complete breakdown of pre-capitalist relations of production and of the limitations that these had placed on the advance of productive forces. At the high point of primary accumulation, exploitation of the countryside by the town – once an increasing but marginal phenomenon – became the rule. This resulted in rapid urbanization and produced mass migration on a scale which in turn led to disruptions of the territorial equilibrium such as had never been experienced before.

Commercial and industrial cities underwent a massive and continuous growth which ultimately led to the complete depopulation of certain regions. Every society undergoing a transition to capitalism has experienced these symptoms, although different conditions have resulted in variations in the speed of these processes, and the role played by the existing feudal classes – i.e. mainly by the feudal lords and the peasants. In England the modernization of agriculture and the exploitation of mines, which both directly and indirectly stimulated capitalist development, were mainly brought about by large landowners – mostly noblemen but also merchants who had acquired large holdings. Landowners completely did away with the rights of agricultural communities (through enclosures, expropriation of land and resale to merchants, etc., etc.) thus transforming subsistence agriculture into extensive production or more often using the land for modern sheep farming. In the meantime many merchant-entrepreneurs set about exploiting the surplus rural population thus created, by establishing the cottage-based textile industry until later technological advance (steam power and mechanization) made its concentration in factories an even more profitable business. Landowners were instrumental to the exploitation of the countryside and because of this not only did they survive as a social group, by merging into the new dominant class, but they also enriched themselves considerably in the process. It was not until the repeal of the Corn Laws when English agriculture was made to compete on the open market with colonial and American products, in order to augment industrial profitability by a reduction in the cost of living, that wealthy landowners who had not previously invested their large agricultural profits in industry found themselves in difficulties. But the fact still remains that the leading role played by landed aristocracy during the period of primary accumulation allowed it to become part and parcel of the bourgeoisie in England. Evidence of this can be found even today since former land-owning and mining families are among the wealthiest in the country and hold key positions in banking and industry. Yet another peculiarity of the English case consists in the sudden and rapid decline of agricultural employment hand in hand with the specialization of agriculture and early dependence on foreign agricultural produce. One can now give a concrete meaning to Kemp's remark quoted above. The inherent tendency of capitalism to create territorial disparities was pushed to its extreme limits in England by the near annihilation of its least productive sector – namely agriculture.[13]

The role of Germany's landed property follows the English pattern in Prussia but it becomes more complex in the remaining regions. Large Prussian landowners carried out successive plans for rationalizing agriculture which involved disposing of peasants and smallholders who thus paid the price for expansion and modernization of agriculture, a process that had its beginnings in the reforms carried out from above in the early part of the nineteenth century. Unlike their English counterparts, the Junkers always operated under protective market conditions (partly because modernization took place in a different environment at a different time) and they never did give up their land even though by putting their capital in circulation they contributed to the extremely fast economic growth witnessed by Germany at the end of the last century (and of course largely benefited from it). The aforegoing should not lead one to assume that Germany was free of the town–country contradiction or of its exploitative nature which worked to the detriment of the countryside. Peasants and craftsmen were driven into the factories and down the mines in their thousands, the massive involvement of population in the booming industry and its resultant effect on the regional equilibrium was all the more noticeable because of its extent and rapidity. However, Germany, even more than England remained a dual economy, with enormous industrial concentrations on the one hand, and on the other a surviving, small and quasi-artisan industry and a widespread traditional agriculture.[14]

The French experience – resembling later developments in parts of Italy, some northern European countries and West Germany – is of interest because it allows us to consider further the process of primary accumulation and the expropriation of independent producers such as peasants and craftsmen. The French gentry resisted the development of the productive forces through the use of absolutist power, following the pattern already set by the English aristocracy in the previous century. In spite of this, the transition to capitalism got under way with the slow erosion of feudal agricultural supremacy and the development of urbanization, international trade and a sizeable manufacturing sector concerned with luxury goods. The revolution smashed the gentry's opposition and established socio-juridical structures suited to the development of a capitalist mode of production at the same time as it created a sizeable stratum of smallholders who had benefited from land redistribution.[15] It is the presence of these peasant-owners which has given rise to controversy. Some commentators[16] have argued that the existence of small landowners caused delays and anomalies in French industrial development, postponing the expropriation and exploitation of the countryside, which is a fundamental aspect of primary accumulation.

In my opinion, however, the survival of small landed property in France should not be viewed as an absolute hindrance to capitalist development. Kemp himself, in the context of the dispute surrounding the possibility of agrarian reform in Italy following unification, underlines the contribution made by modern small land ownership to capitalist expansion.[17] Firstly, it promotes the full development of a consumer oriented market which in turn engenders growth in some crucial industrial sectors and in the long term counteracts the tendency towards an exclusive and artificial expansion of heavy industry. Secondly, smallholders as a group are more likely to modernize agriculture than large landowners, who may remain insensitive to change. Thirdly, small property sets free market forces in the countryside, on the one hand delaying the expulsion of the labour force from the agricultural sector, and on the other hand progressively strengthening the medium-sized family agricultural enterprises, which are most profitable in the long run. Some characteristics of French primary accumulation matured over a long period so that at times one cannot distinguish these phenomena from those more appropriately relating to capitalist accumulation. Expropriation of the peasants and their subsequent urbanization, for example, occurred very slowly, starting from the mid-nineteenth century. The expropriation of agricultural resources also took place over a long period of time, during which it took such forms as predatory taxation and usury on agricultural credit. Throughout the process small farmers were left at the mercy of the laws of the market, which forced them to tighten their belts and to continuously reduce the price of their products (it should be remembered that at this time the whole of Europe, except England, operated protective customs policies towards agriculture). In any case France (and countries that followed the same pattern of development) initially had enough reserves during the period of primary accumulation to guarantee capitalist take-off. Indeed the demographic revolution and the feudal upheavals of the two previous centuries had already provided a reservoir of industrial labour power in all big cities and especially in Paris. Accumulation based on commerce and handicraft was a good starting point for French capitalism provided that it concentrated on productive sectors not directly in competition with the more advanced English manufacturing industry. (From the sixteenth century France had been producing a large quantity of luxury textile goods – following the collapse of Italian production and the displacement of European commerce to the north.)

PRIMARY ACCUMULATION AND URBANIZATION IN ITALY

Italy became a national entity in 1860. Unification was arrived at through the annexation of 'liberated' Italian regions to Piedmont under the Savoy dynasty, witnessing the continuation of an existing kingdom rather than to the birth of a new state. Analogy to Germany's unification pattern is all too obvious, but one difference is worth noting for it helps clarify the diversity in the balance of social classes present in the two processes. The Monarchy and the hegemonic section of Prussian landed property, which had sponsored German unification, represented the least progressive section of that country from the point of view of capital. The opposite holds true for Italy where the Savoy and the northern bourgeois and landowning classes were by and large the capitalist vanguard within the ruling class as a whole. Therefore one finds that in Germany the agrarian class had actually led the national as well as capitalist revolution by playing a crucial role in the process of primary accumulation, introducing reforms and rationalizing Prussian agriculture. In Italy on the contrary the northern bourgeoisie which headed unification found itself confronted by agrarian strata which, in the southern regions, from Tuscany downwards, were still enjoying enormous privileges thanks to the survival of numerous feudal vestiges and aided by the economic stagnation of the last century. There were two options open to the Italian bourgeoisie. On the one hand it could have rid itself of the agrarian strata starting a process of revolutionary reforms such as the expropriation of latifundia and redistribution to peasants; on the other hand the bourgeoisie could have created a power bloc in partnership with the agrarian strata with whom it would share economic and political power. A third alternative such as the implementation of moderate reforms from above, as had happened in Germany, was not possible because southern landed property would have opposed it. This last option also had to be ruled out from the start because of class considerations; one cannot imagine that once reforms had begun they would have been enough for the peasant movements which it would have brought into being. The moderate social strata that had played the leading role in the 'national revolution' could easily solve the dilemma presented by the above alternatives. In fact the first was automatically ruled out since the south lacked a strong peasant movement which might have forced the option upon the bourgeois ruling class. Indeed once the strength of the masses had been unleashed it might even have uprooted the very social structures upon which stood the power of aristocracy and bourgeoisie which had brought unification about.[18] Hence an alliance between the northern bourgeoisie and the large landowners of the whole kingdom was a foregone conclusion. Garibaldi's expedition was in line with this political option, suppressing as it did the Sicilian peasant uprisings in 1860. The Italian national revolution, even more than that of Germany, brought together deeply divergent regions in terms of economic, political and social structure. In some cases the capitalist unification was the means of homogenizing the many regional inequalities which had resulted from a totally different historical tradition, in other cases the differences were drastically sharpened.

First of all one must point out that some northern regions had undergone an early development of capitalist mercantilism. Between the thirteenth and fifteenth centuries, for example, Florence and Milan as well as the surrounding countryside constituted very advanced socio-economic structures with a high level of urbanization and a very productive agricultural sector which were matched by a very clear division of labour between agriculture and handicraft, the latter being highly specialized and concentrated.[19] The socio-economic crisis which affected these regions in the seventeenth century did not completely destroy past achievements.

The relative overpopulation of cities did not result in a return to agriculture and handicraft based on the small village. Agriculture was in the hands of wealthy city dwellers and of a large group of medium-sized landowners who were more liable to invest in agriculture than big landowners. Irrigation and modernization of agriculture were still carried on and large numbers of skilled craftsmen kept up their tradition in the textile sectors of wool and silk and in the production of iron.

In its early stages territorial duality is mainly an agricultural phenomenon but it is also rooted in class antagonism. In the north the landed gentry and the bourgeoisie were stimulated by the Napoleonic occupation and somehow managed to continue developing during the ensuing restoration. In the south the repression following the events of 1799 and the return to Bourbon rule hit the bourgeoisie very hard, while it propped up the conservative bloc represented by the absolutist Monarchy and the owners of latifundia.

The most striking differences relate to social relations in the countryside. In central and southern Italy one finds the entrenchment of conservative large landowners. In Sicily the end of feudalism was relatively recent dating back only to 1832, and then it left the old property relations practically untouched. The only change was the addition of a few thousand excise-men (who contracted land on behalf of gentry) to the few dozens of wealthy landowning families. For the rest, Sicily's hundreds of thousands of peasant families were left with their poverty at the margins of society. The same story could be repeated for continental south and central Italy, where the largest landowners, an untitled group which had replaced the bankrupt gentry, ended up being as resistant to change and modernization as their predecessors. The only exceptions to the rule are to be found in Apulia and Campania in the second half of the century. In the north social relations are more varied and from the end of the eighteenth century some landowners began a process of considerable modernization of agriculture; the same applies to many medium landowners and to bourgeois entrepreneurs who rented the land. In the last decades of the century, for example, Emilia Romagna saw reclamation of land and intensive investment in agriculture which increased productivity and gave it a capitalist outlook.[20]

A statistical analysis of some crucial indicators will show how badly the southern economy fared compared to northern performance: output per unit of labour is 30% lower in the south, here one finds only 19% of the total number of cattle, compared to 47% in the north, and only 16% of silk production (at this time an essential resource for Italy) compared to a staggering 78% in the north.[21]

Urban organization also shows remarkable differences, with the north having developed a network of cities which for centuries had specialized in skilled handicraft production, as well as large markets well connected to the countryside and centres for productive and cultural activities. In the south one finds an economically weak Naples, a place for the gentry to consume their agricultural surplus and the refuge of a numerous lumpen proletariat which had inflated its population to half a million, making it the largest Italian metropolis and third in Europe after London and Paris. Excepting Messina and Palermo which nevertheless are witnessing a centuries old decay, the other southern cities are no more than enormous agricultural dwelling centres for the peasant masses who are brutally exploited by the owners of latifundia.[22]

Table 2.1 provides a basis for a discussion of regional territorial differences. First of all the high rate of urbanization (taking the number of communities over 20,000 strong as an index) experienced by Italy at the time of unification is not to be put down to industrial development so much as to peculiar agricultural structures in some of its regions. So central Italy, where one finds share-cropping methods of agriculture foremost, and some southern regions, where peasants live in large centres and commute to work land which is sometimes very distant, are also the areas with the highest percentage of urban growth – Liguria in this respect must be viewed as a case apart since it is the peculiar geography of the region that imposes urban concentration along the coastline. The more developed regions, such as Lombardy and Piedmont, have a relatively lower rate of urbanization. The pattern so far outlined is confirmed by looking at figures relating to communities with over six thousand inhabitants and to the incidence of people living away from the main centres, isolated in the countryside. Sicily and Apulia, in which the commuting phenomenon is most marked, have also the largest numbers of compact communities. The socio-territorial structure of regions where share-cropping prevails also presents a high incidence of large municipalities, but here a section of the population does not live in its main urban centre but scattered in isolated dwellings or small agricultural hamlets. So for these regions the proportion of people living within a municipality but actually located outside its main centre is rather high. To this one should add that in the south the peculiar commuting arrangement on which agriculture is based bars the rise of small hamlets and isolated dwellings that were said to be typical of central Italy but are also to be found in the north. Figures relating to 1871 show that the population spread outside the main centres accounted

TABLE 2.1 The socio-territorial situation in the regions in 1861 (using the boundaries of the day): (I) Percentage of the population living in towns of over 6,000 inhabitants; (II) Percentage of the population living in municipalities containing a town of over 6,000 inhabitants; (III) Percentage of the population living in municipalities of over 20,000 inhabitants.

Regions	I towns %	II urban municipalities	III municipalities with over 20,000 inhabitants	IV difference in % between II and I
Piedmont	14.7	20.6	13.0	+5.9
Liguria	24.3	26.4	31.7	+2.1
Lombardy	14.1	17.3	16.7	+3.2
Emilia Romagna	18.0	31.3	30.2	+13.3
Tuscany	16.9	25.6	29.5	+8.7
Umbria	12.1	29.2	29.1	+17.1
Marches	12.1	22.8	13.3	+10.7
Abruzzi and Molise	9.9	13.1	12.8	+3.2
Campania	33.6	39.2	25.1	+5.6
Apulia	58.5	63.7	20.8	+5.2
Basilicata	29.0	31.8	0.0	+2.8
Calabria	15.0	17.9	6.7	+2.9
Sicily	59.7	66.8	27.0	+7.1
Sardinia	14.5	15.4	10.8	+0.9
Italy	25.2	31.5	19.3	+6.3

Sources: I and II from ISTAT, Statistical Yearbook, development of the Italian population from 1861 to 1961, pp. 181, 182; III extrapolation from ISTAT data, *Municipalities and their populations at the censuses from 1861 to 1961*, Rome 1964.

for 23.5% of the total in Piedmont, Lombardy and Liguria; 42.5% in Venetia and Tuscany; 46% in Emilia Romagna, Marches and Umbria; 14% in Latium, Abruzzi, Campania and Calabria; 6% in Apulia and Lucania and 6.5% in Sicily and Sardinia.[23]

This seems to demonstrate convincingly that, for Italy at least, one should not blindly assume that patterns of urbanization are indicated merely by computations concerning the incidence of urban centres with over twenty thousand inhabitants; but I shall return to this point later on when comparing urbanization trends in various European countries.

The reasons for the slow and contradictory nature of Italian industrial development were many. The lack of raw materials and of a modern finance and banking system plus the absence of agricultural revolution on a national scale subordinated Italian industrial growth to foreign economic centres; first to England and France, later to Germany.[24] Northern agriculture could only partly finance the industrial take-off with the surplus it produced and the slow introduction of an internal market. There was a great gap between the productivity of Italian agriculture and that of other European countries, therefore lack of competitiveness prevented it becoming a solid base for capital accumulation. The average revenue per hectare was £it. 79 in Italy, £it. 170 in France, £it. 213 in England; at the same time average wheat production per hectare was 9 quintals for Italy, 15 for France and 32 for England.

On top of all attempts at agricultural rationalization its capitalist transformation had to contend with the enduring latifundia and other feudal vestiges in southern and central Italy. As Sereni has shown,[25] capitalist transformation of agriculture took place mostly as a result of redistribution of church and state land. In some southern areas even this redistribution was not followed by agricultural development because the plots of land merged into stagnating structures. The growth of agricultural production was very limited and always lower than 3% per annum. Without a doubt the low magnitude of capital accumulation based on agriculture is one of the causes of the slow pace of industrialization. Gerschenkron[26] has calculated the average annual rate of industrial growth to have been 4.6% in the 1880s; 0.3% in the 1890s; 6.7% in the twelve years of the take-off (1896-1908); and down again to 0.3% in the following five years. Over the whole period under consideration the average annual rate was below 4%; meanwhile at the turn of the century it was 7% for Germany which was itself witnessing a decline. For other countries which saw a delayed development and were then at a point of take-off we have a noticeably greater rate of growth: 12% in Sweden, 8.5% in Japan, 8% in Russia.

This does not mean that in Italy there was no primary accumulation. This did take place along with phenomena typical to it such as sharp division of labour, geographical concentration of development, decay of local markets and regional division of labour. Nevertheless capitalist take-off was slow and contradictory since it was restricted by the backwardness in which the vast agricultural areas of the country remained.

Emigration is one of the socio-territorial by-products symptomatic of the weakness of Italian development. The strong wave of migrations of Italians towards the Americas and other European countries was the result both of the rationalization and crisis that hit agriculture. Most of these came from the northern countryside but many came from the south too. The migratory process increased over the years and the annual rate went up from an average of 180,000 units between 1880 and 1890 to reach 300,000 in the following decade, eventually topping the half million mark in the first fifteen years of this century, at a time when Italy was already considered a major contemporary industrial power.

Italian industrialization certainly increased the north–south gap but one could neither claim that the south was drained of its resources by the industrial accumulation in the north, nor that the process established a colonial-type relationship between the two areas. (Lest one should forget, the south had scanty mineral and agricultural raw materials and its agricultural surplus was not even enough to stimulate a local market let alone one involving the large masses; the industrial revolution in the north did not change this: in fact when southern agriculture entered a critical phase after 1888, its labour-force did not drift north but migrated to America.) Uneven development did however take place. While the north, drawing upon its economic and social advantages managed to take off industrially, the south lagged behind because of its antiquated pre-capitalist economic and social structures.

The weakness of the southern market and the small proportion of agricultural surplus related to it meant that the north did, nevertheless, marginally benefit by the backwardness of the south. In particular Italian industry enjoyed territorial monopoly since there was no competition from the south; taxation also weighed proportionally more heavily here than in the north; moreover state demand for the products of northern enterprises in preference to southern ones, in the former's competitiveness, also worked towards widening the gap between north and south. Because of this the very few industries that had originated under the stimulus of the Bourbon state, especially in Naples, were at best being overshadowed if not completely destroyed, with the single exception perhaps of the steel plant in Bagnoli (Naples).

Little can be said about the difference between the north and south in relation to their respective rates of manpower engaged in industry since these figures are based on the first census data, which are hardly reliable if not positively misleading. So, for instance, it would appear that the percentage employed by industry over the whole active population is greater for the south than for the north. Variations over time are of more interest to us; whereas for Liguria and Lombardy the population employed by industry increases by

TABLE 2.2 Percentages of the active population among the resident population, and of the population employed in agriculture or in industry as opposed to the professional classes – taken from certain Italian regions according to the censuses of 1861, 1911, 1951, 1971 (in respect of present boundaries).

Regions	Active population %				Employed in agriculture %				Employed in industry %			
	1861	1911	1951	1971	1861	1911	1951	1971	1861	1911	1951	1971
Piedmont	69.5	55.8	50.5	40.5	81.1	57.9	32.6	12.2	11.5	26.6	43.4	55.7
Lombardy	63.7	50.9	47.9	40.1	69.3	46.3	20.1	5.5	19.8	36.9	53.0	59.8
Venetia	54.8	45.2	44.2	37.2	72.5	62.3	43.1	14.0	13.7	21.1	32.8	48.7
Emilia Romagna	56.9	49.2	48.7	41.4	67.8	64.0	51.9	20.0	18.8	19.2	25.2	42.5
Tuscany	57.0	49.8	44.4	37.9	67.8	54.7	39.6	11.5	18.5	26.9	34.0	48.3
Latium	58.8	46.5	41.3	35.7	71.0	50.4	33.1	9.8	11.5	21.1	25.6	31.9
Campania	57.3	46.5	39.2	32.4	62.3	58.0	46.6	23.9	23.2	21.9	27.1	38.0
Apulia	57.8	45.0	41.3	34.9	65.9	63.4	58.2	36.9	23.0	21.0	22.0	32.0
Calabria	70.6	50.6	40.0	32.9	62.0	65.7	63.3	32.6	28.8	21.9	20.1	36.3
Sicily	49.9	48.8	41.2	30.7	53.9	53.9	51.1	28.7	23.1	20.0	22.2	33.6
Italy	59.5	48.2	43.5		69.7	58.4	42.2		18.1	23.7	32.1	
Number ('000)	15,535	17,497	19,577									

Sources: For census data from 1861, 1911, 1951 cf. ISTAT, Statistical Yearbook, Development of the Italian population from 1861 to 1961, pp. 223, 224 and 225. The 1971 data are based on the provisional results of census XI of the population.

more than 10% – i.e. from 19% in 1861 to 30% in 1901; for Campania, Apulia and Sicily, the most significant and populated regions in the south, over the same period we see an actual decrease from 23% to just over 20%. The relative size of the active population in agriculture is even more telling; during the four decades under consideration there is a decrease of about 15% in the north, whereas in the south the rate goes up by a few units (Sicily and Calabria) or falls only slightly as in Campania and Apulia. The relevant figures are given in Table 2.2.

To summarize, Italian regional inequalities deepened during the period of primary accumulation before the industrial take-off which is placed at the beginning of the present century by Gerschenkron; the unevenness of the process can be simply put down to the fact that while accumulation did take place in the north the same cannot be said for the south.

Naturally this difference is mirrored in the socio-territorial structure of the two zones. The northern urban network was considerably strengthened; some large cities – like Milan, Turin, and Genoa – became industrial centres and the receiving end of the agricultural exodus from the surrounding valleys; the same applies for some secondary but specialized industrial centres such as Sesto St. Giovanni, Novara, Biella and Brescia. Meanwhile to the south, cities were undergoing a radical crisis; in particular, Naples, having lost the advantage of being the capital town of the largest Italian state and the centre of industrial concentration (it does not matter here that Bourbon steel and engineering industries were very backward) soon showed the weakness of its economic structure. A demographic analysis tells the same tale; Milan, Turin and Rome doubled in size in the last four decades of the century, Naples only increased its population by 29% and its annual average fell below the natural growth rate for the south as a whole, as can be seen in Figure 2.1. Later I shall discuss how the regional differences discussed in this section went on to deepen in the first decade of the century at the time of industrial take-off.

FINAL THOUGHTS ON THE COMPARATIVE ANALYSIS OF PRIMARY ACCUMULATION AND URBANIZATION

The study of specific cases of primary accumulation and the rise of capitalism, with its influence on the town-country relationship, allows us to draw some conclusions. We agree with Kemp when he says that England is the only case where the countryside is com-

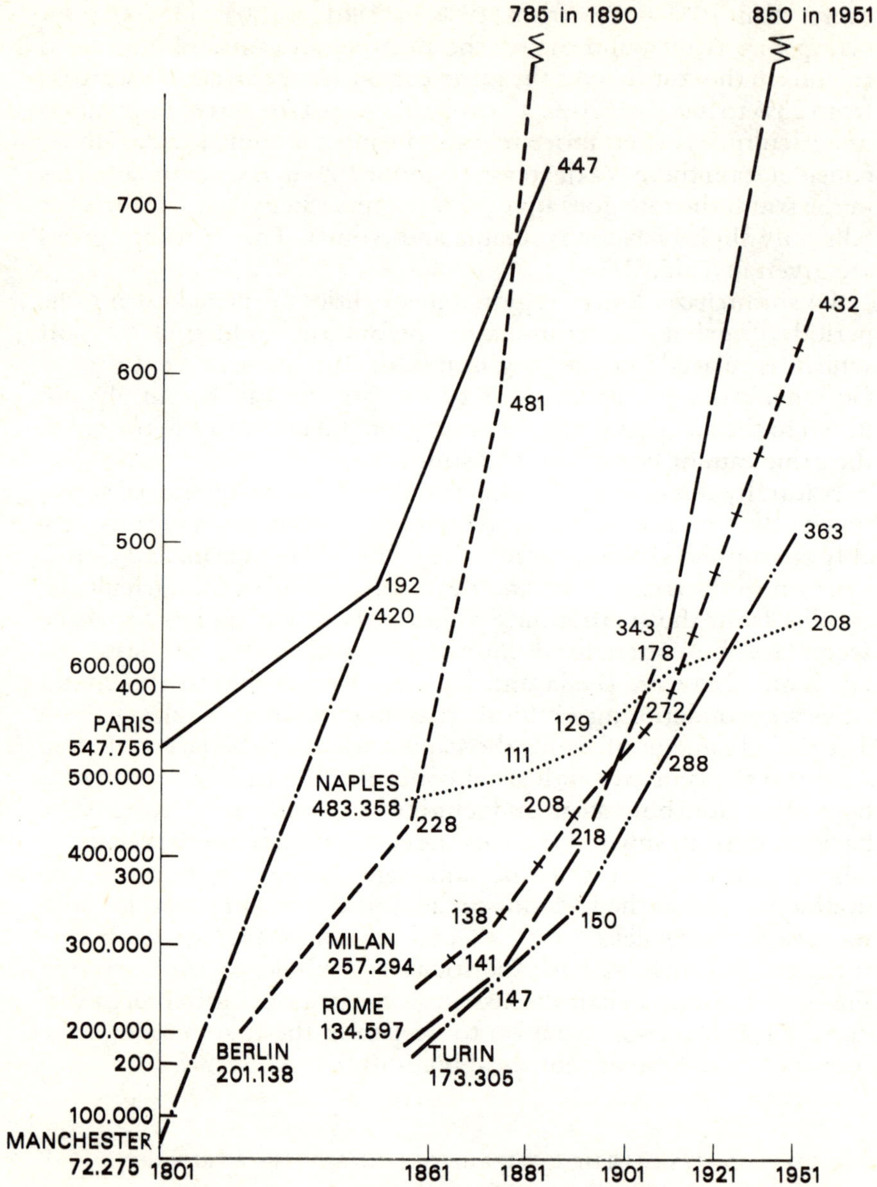

90 *Territorial Division of Labour*

FIGURE 2.1 Urban growth in various European cities. (Index numbers: starting date=100.)
Sources: Berlin and Paris, A. Weber, *The Growth of Cities in the Nineteenth Century*, New York, 1899; Manchester, L. Mumford, *The City in History*, Penguin Books, Harmondsworth 1966; Italian cities, ISTAT population census.

pletely sacrificed to capitalist accumulation as well as being the only example with a clear cut tendency to expropriate independent producers – a characteristic which for Marx was the very essence of capitalist accumulation. England also shows a definite connection between urbanization and the rise and development of capitalism. Except for London the country was hardly urbanized before the industrial revolution.[27] But within a few decades it suddenly witnessed regional and demographic shifts leading to a concentration of population in a few large industrial centres. We shall later see how urban concentration, especially in England, is closely related to the characteristics of capitalist accumulation. The smooth linear pattern typical to England is in my view largely due to the fact that the country's industrial revolution antedated the continental one by a few decades. This meant that England could not rely on some alternative means of primary accumulation like foreign financial help, cheap agricultural imports from the Third World, or the development of very specialized sectors of manufacture. This is also the reason why other experiences of primary accumulation were much more controversial than the English. Everywhere, sooner or later (but this is a fundamental difference), there was a remarkable drainage of resources from the countryside and these went towards financing urban development and industrial growth; never again was this process as drastic in the first period of primary accumulation as it had been in England. Indeed one might say that in most other cases capitalist take-off left enough resources in the countryside so that it could exploit them at a later date rather than exhaust them completely in the pre-industrial stage. This made the beginning of capitalism slower and more complex in countries like France and Italy, or it introduced lasting contradictions, even though initially there were viable substitutes to the complete exploitation of the countryside (as in the German case).

Sources of primary accumulation other than the exploitation of the European countryside were indeed available only because industrial take-off was not so much a European phenomenon as a global one. European capitalism thrived despite the fact that it had not fully utilized its rural areas because the gap was filled by the exploitation of the Third World countryside. In addition, underutilization was furthered by the fall in price of agricultural commodities thanks to the forceful entry of North American farmers into the market, the selectivity of European agriculture (cereal production was abandoned because no longer profitable), intense circulation of finance capital, international borrowing and the development of National Debt. In the long run the expropriation of

92 Territorial Division of Labour

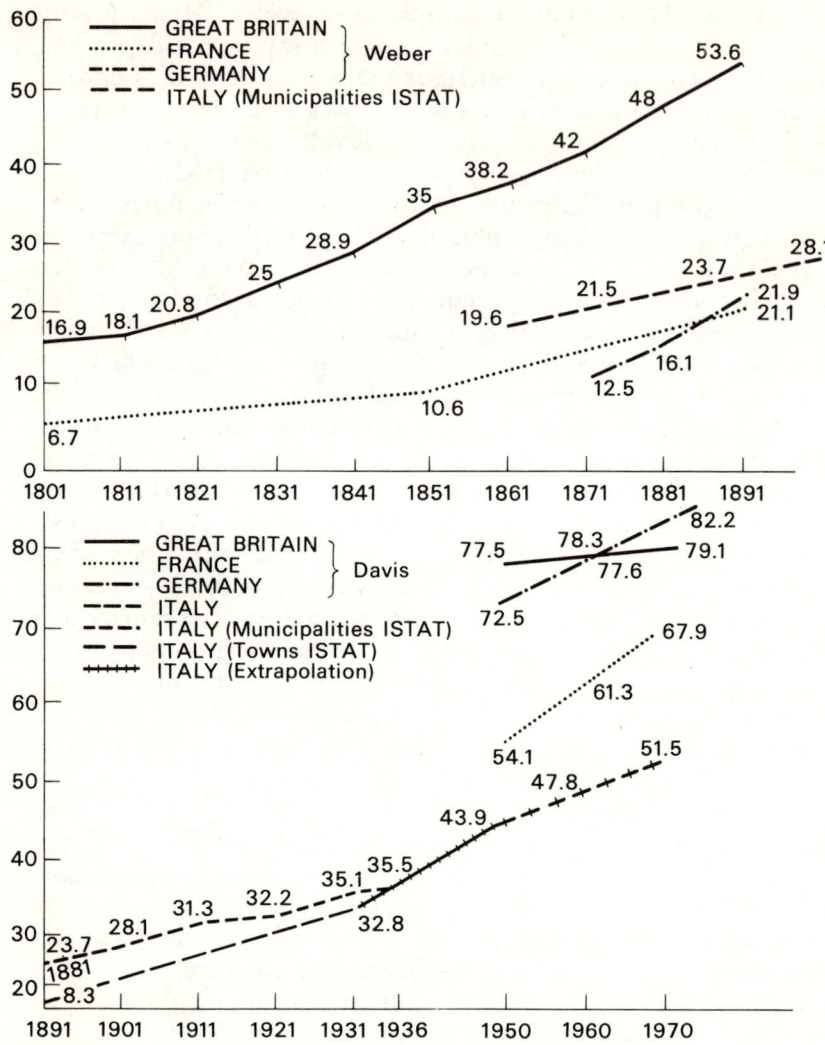

FIGURE 2.2 Urbanization in the nineteenth and twentieth centuries.
Sources: A. Weber, *The Growth of Cities*; K. Davis, *World Urbanization 1950–1970*, 2 vols, Population Monograph Series, University of California, 1969–72; ISTAT population census.

independent producers, peasants and craftsmen, did take place in every capitalist country and it resulted therefore in the total subordination of the countryside to urban development: but it happened in different ways and at different times.

In some countries, what had not been achieved by primary accumulation was accomplished through the capitalist laws of competition – whose tendency to diminish costs of production led to the expropriation of small farmers and craftsmen so that their labour power as well as their tools might be used for capitalist expansion.

Patterns of urbanization (Figure 2.1) and of the formation of large cities (Figure 2.2) are a reflection of the different types of capitalist growth and conditions under which primary accumulation took place.[28] Before we deduce anything at all from such figures serious doubts must be expressed concerning their comparative value; for one thing different countries use different statistical methods, so some census data, the Italian in particular, are rather suspect; moreover levels of urbanization and size of towns mean different things according to the country and the date.

The diagram representing the process of urbanization points to some interesting considerations. For England the process is marked and continuous over the whole ninety years between 1801 and 1891 (but we have to keep in mind that in this case data relate almost exclusively to the period after completion of primary accumulation). Therefore the English urbanization curve starts fairly high and proceeds to increase markedly without any sudden jump. One might infer that the process of urbanization was rather slow before industrial take-off and quickened only after it had taken place (especially for towns exceeding 20,000 inhabitants). This hypothesis can be deduced from French and German patterns both of which show a sudden increase at the time of industrial take-off. The diagram also shows the survival of a large agricultural sector in France and the rapidity of the German process of urbanization.

The Italian graph is particularly interesting in that it shows a very high starting point; this is largely due to the fact that the data are not homogeneous with those of other countries since for Italy they refer not to the population of the town itself but to all those living within the boundaries of the municipality. In fact, as can be seen from the graph, the curve relating to the towns only is six percentage points lower than the curve relating to the population of municipalities at the start of the period, but the former does eventually overtake the latter. Data relative to the northern regions in 1951 are presented in Table 2.3. There are plausible explanations for the high level of

TABLE 2.3 Percentage of the population living in towns of over 20,000 inhabitants in 1931 and 1951 (columns I and II); percentage of the population living in municipalities of over 20,000 inhabitants (column III) in 1951.

	Towns % present population		Municipalities % resident population
	I 1931	II 1951	III 1951
Valle d'Aosta	0.0	34.2	25.7
Piedmont	31.9	36.9	35.5
Liguria	55.1	64.1	61.2
Lombardy	34.3	38.9	36.0
Trent + Alto Adige	17.1	23.9	25.2
Venetia (and Friuli – 1931)	22.8	31.5	32.0
Venezia Giulia (and Friuli – 1951 and Istria 1931)	45.2	39.5	35.7
Emilia Romagna	37.6	45.8	42.5
Marches	17.1	24.4	34.0
Tuscany	36.0	43.2	42.4
Umbria	19.8	23.7	53.2
Latium	52.9	59.5	59.1
Abruzzi + Molise	4.1	12.3	20.6
Campania	36.9	43.8	46.7
Apulia	37.8	49.5	53.4
Basilicata	0.0	10.0	10.0
Calabria	8.3	13.4	19.8
Sicily	39.4	46.4	52.6
Sardinia	12.9	18.4	23.6
Total	32.8	39.9	40.8

Source: For columns I and II cf. ISTAT, *Statistical Yearbook, Development of Italian population from 1861 to 1961*, pp. 176–178. Column III, derived from ISTAT, *Municipalities and their population at the censuses from 1861 to 1961*, Rome 1964.

urbanization in pre-capitalist Italy. In the north, commerce and handicrafts had developed at the end of the Middle Ages; there were ten or more capitals of independent states, and Naples and other southern towns had grown disproportionately to their actual economic power. But without a doubt the peculiar concentrated structure of some agricultural southern regions (Sicily, Campania, Apulia) is the single most important reason for the high level of urbanization. Urbanization was by and large a slower process in

Italy than in other countries once industrialization got underway (this is so whether one looks at the curve relating to municipalities or whether one looks at the one representing the towns only – the latter grows faster because it starts from a lower level).

This same phenomenon can be found by looking at the diagram for urban growth: no Italian city had a high growth at the end of last century (Rome is an exception but its rapid increase of population during the present century is not due to economic development but to other bureaucratic and political factors). During the five decades between 1861-1911 Milan and Turin doubled in size while becoming centres for industry; such a rate of growth is not very remarkable when compared to other foreign cities also in the process of industrialization. Paris, for example, trebled in size between 1840 and 1890; Manchester increased four-fold in the first half of last century; Berlin grew three-and-a-half times in less than thirty years (1861-1890). Northern Italy's urban population increased at an annual average of less than 1.5% up to 1901; only later did this rate reach 2% and not until after the Second World War did it reach a high level (2.64%). (Unfortunately Italian data again refer to municipalities.)[29]

MECHANISMS OF CAPITAL ACCUMULATION AND THEIR COMPLEX EFFECT ON TERRITORY

Once capitalism becomes the dominant social form it reproduces and expands itself amidst continuous and fundamental changes in the socio-territorial structure. We shall briefly discuss the characteristics presented by capitalist accumulation in its various historical stages so as to better understand their territorial implications.

These characteristics can be summarized in the following schematic form.

(1) Capital exploits workers by extracting surplus value which provides it with the means for continuous and ever greater expansion. With every productive cycle there is a relative growth of fixed capital (investment in machinery and infra-structure) compared to variable capital (the workers) since production has to be increased in order to retain competitiveness; therefore capital concentration grows continuously, at least in the sectors which offer high profits, and is re-invested rather than being consumed.

(2) In general the progressive concentration of capital leads to the exclusion of a section of producers from the market, since they

cannot keep up with competition because their limited basic capital does not allow them to produce at ever lower costs. The bankrupt small and medium concerns are absorbed by big capital which thus receives a push to concentrate even further.

(3) At the same time capital's discrimination between more profitable (where concentration is taking place fastest) and less profitable sectors (where concentration is slow or doesn't take place) reproduces constantly, at world level, a deep economic dualism. Highly concentrated capital increasingly exploits and discriminates against those capitalist sectors which are least able to practise capital concentration, like agriculture and some sectors of industry and commerce.

(4) As big capital goes on concentrating so it can afford to control capitalist sectors with least concentration and in this way to rob them of profits and resources: monopoly industry reaps great profit at the expense of non-capitalist and less capital intensive sectors. Such exploitation can take place in several ways: through the difference in price between commodities produced by concentrated monopolistic capital and those produced by less concentrated branches of industry, through monopolistic decentralization towards social or geographical zones which permit a more intense exploitation of labour, or through low prices, imposed on producers of raw materials and semi-manufactured goods for which monopoly (monopsonic) is the sole purchaser.

Stages of capitalist development are characterized by the extent of capital concentration and thus by a different configuration of the phenomena listed above. Besides, as we already saw for primary accumulation, concrete historical and sociological analyses of different countries show that there is no single pattern followed by the stages of capital accumulation because for each case one must take into consideration a variety of internal and external economic and other factors.

As a first approximation I shall take three stages of capitalist accumulation, each characterized as follows:

(1) The first stage is characterized by low concentration of capital and by widespread competition among capitalists. More and more productive sectors are industrialized. Capitalist production is diversified and gradually spreads to all branches of production thus continuing the expropriation of small independent producers not yet accomplished by primary accumulation. The reinvestment of high profits, made possible, amongst other factors, by the super-

exploitation of an overcrowded labour market, provides the financial backing of most capitalist advance.

The middle classes increasingly make up the market outlet for expansion in production while the working class is kept at subsistence level and unable to react against its complete submission to capital for the very reason of its extreme weakness on the labour market. The phenomenon is also accentuated by the development of transport, which breaks down geographical barriers, and engenders long distance migrations and the creation of an international labour market, a factor which will be taken up later when dealing with territorial displacements.

(2) The second stage is characterized by further concentration and by the primacy of banking and financial institutions as a means of gathering and recycling capital. Productivity increases and the market expands towards all social groups and regions of the earth. The concentration of production in large factories now means that only one section of the labour market is utilized; children are no longer needed and the super exploitation of women ceases. The exploitation of labour is intensified and the working day shortened. These developments also result from the rise of parties and trade unions at a time when the working class – which has by now absorbed the surplus manpower coming from agriculture – has managed to emancipate itself from internal competition. As working class living standards rise they provide capital with more market outlets and yet further opportunity for concentration.

International duality is sharpened; large finance and industrial conglomerates which head and control industrial development, face less concentrated and profitable sectors. In expanding throughout the world capital gives this duality a clear territorial dimension, which also coincides with the more noticeable 'specialization' of capital and with the division between developed and under-developed countries or regions.

(3) In the third stage there is an extreme concentration of capital along with its specialization (large stock holding companies controlled by a minority of shareholders and the growth of State industry). Large monopolies are more closely intertwined with the structure of the capitalist state, which can co-ordinate the survival of capitalism much better than the banks. Further capitalist expansion is drastically reduced; to open new industries one must shut some of the old ones down; wastage and parasitic growth are rife. The bourgeoisie uses political power to lengthen its life span.

The level of employment stabilizes itself in the most advanced countries because of the gradual disappearance of relative surplus population. The main cause of such developments is the shrinking size of the active population; less and less of the labour force is at work, while the majority is not active (housewives, students, pensioners, etc.). Moreover, growth in the tertiary sector concentrates a large number of workers in unproductive occupations. In these countries the working class wins for itself a relatively high standard of living; meanwhile capital seeks to recuperate the costs partly through inflation and mainly through a very tight control of consumption and life styles. The exploitation of underdeveloped countries reaches higher levels by means of unequal exchange and foreign investments, which allow the accumulation of enormous profits.

The exploitation of the working class and the process of accumulation of capital require a continuous process of urbanization, that is to say the amassing of population in large industrial cities. The capitalist thirst for ever lower costs of production and higher productivity favours geographic regions which allow savings in production. This applies to existing large urban agglomerates, which have a concentration of labour power and infrastructures, to ports and mining centres where raw materials either cost less or are closer at hand, as well as providing marketing points, and to financial and administrative centres, which are close to the largest markets and to the decision-making centres as well.

The revolution in transport makes this territorial division of work less relevant, but capitalism's urban concentration in fact dramatically increases (actually, it can easily be shown that usually faster transport has been used in the interests of further concentration), whilst the depressed areas become even poorer and do not benefit from the technological advance. Under capitalism and under capitalism alone – i.e. a system whose sole driving force is the maximization of profit – the provision of socio-economic infrastructures necessary for industrialization becomes selective and hierarchic: i.e. it is too costly to provide a widespread infrastructure to give long term benefits for the collectivity rather than for capital. In fact the growing economic duality between large conglomerates on one side and small firms, agriculture and production of raw materials on the other, constantly increases territorial disparities; on the one hand we have an enormous concentration of the control on profits and superprofits, on the other the constant theft of resources engenders more relative poverty in the economically underdeveloped areas. These may be areas whose industrial production is not concentrated and which have been relegated to the secondary sector, in countries which produce agricultural and mineral raw materials, as well as underdeveloped countries with massive reserves of labour which are exploited by foreign monopolies inside factories which are labour intensive and pay low wages. The spreading crisis of capitalist society further accentuates the contradictions between large and small towns, between overpopulated areas and those agricultural zones that have been abandoned, between capitalist concentration and the deserts of underdevelopment. Evidently capitalism – that is the hegemonic social formation – is responsible for the clash between economic development and socio-territorial structures. Indeed socio-territorial contradictions, uneven geographic distribution, hyper-urbanization and urban hierarchy as well as chronic economic depression of immense areas of the world are all fundamentally the result of capitalist division and exploitation of labour. We shall attempt a verification of these contentions through a brief but concrete discussion of urban development in some countries in Europe and Italy in particular.

FROM THE CITY AS A FACTORY TO THE IMPERIALIST METROPOLIS

Nineteenth- and twentieth-century urban history shows how capitalist society developed and how the contradictions, implied by division of labour and exploitation, came to a head. I shall not dwell too long on the different characteristics of capitalism's socio-territorial structure, which vary from country to country; instead I shall try to depict a synthesis, by means of some examples. During the first period, which I shall call the 'period of the factory-city', there is fast urbanization on a national scale, and steady growth of some large production centres, in which the great factories are concentrated (because of the economic and geographical advantages already mentioned).

The population shifts occur mainly on a regional scale and correspond to the abandonment of the countryside, brought about by two opposite factors: in some cases by the rationalization of agriculture and thus by its expansion (England offers the clearest example of this), but more often by a crisis in agriculture, promoted by the development of the international agricultural market, the fall in prices and the constant deterioration in the living standards of the peasantry. In every case the growth of the big industrial cities is mainly due to the movement of people from the vastly overpopulated agricultural sector, people whom capitalism inherits from pre-capitalist society. It is important to note that every expansion of a city population, during this period of urban history is paralleled by an increase in the quota of workers employed in industry; industrialization and urbanization proceed *pari passu*.

The earliest case is the English example of a structure and of socio-territorial processes typical of the factory-city phase of development, for it is not contaminated by the phenomena characteristic of later phases such as financial concentration or state intervention in the economy or long range emigration.

In the nineteenth century workers employed in agriculture declined from about 40% to about 10% of the working population, while the population resident in the cities rose from just over 20% to little less than 80% of the total.[30] This change was all the more radical in view of the fact that the population increase remained higher in the country than in the towns, at least in the first three-quarters of the century, due to the high mortality rate in the industrial towns. Meanwhile the production of certain industrial sectors was increasing several fold.

At least in the first half of the nineteenth century the growth of wholly industrial towns, Birmingham, Manchester, Liverpool, etc., was distinctly faster than the rate of growth of London which, though the greatest consumer market and the administrative and financial centre of nation and empire, was not the main industrial centre.[31]

The connections between the labour market, the cost of labour, the productivity of labour, and the conditions of urban life and migration to the cities are interesting. Given the relatively low productivity of labour (relatively because despite the big jumps in productivity within manufacturing industry and the great factories, the productivity of the individual worker grows little until it becomes possible to intervene in the rate and organization of work) and the great amount of work available, the working class wage-earners barely subsist and the living conditions of the working masses are atrocious. Working class families are crowded in unhealthy dwelling places, they lack clothes and fuel for the winter and they lack medical assistance. Food is periodically in short supply.[32]

Again for basic economic reasons one can say that during this period the price of houses and the building industry obey market rules (that is, the price rises because demand for housing rapidly outstrips supply). For the moment two contrary tendencies due to appear later are not observed. These are speculation on housing areas (which will raise rents and labour costs) and subsidized construction (which will bring a measure of official control to the housing market).

The second phase of the urban development of capitalism is characterized by an interplay of complex socio-economic factors and by the effects on territory of a revolution in transport systems which permits a new utilization of land. The heavy concentration of capital makes the fortune of the great cities, seat of the banks, industrial management and centres of governmental power: thus the financial capital, which draws to itself all the activities of economic management, takes over the lead from the factory-city, and a new territorial distribution of labour is effected. The example of London cannot be overlooked. While the capital city had taken a secondary role throughout the first phase of the industrial revolution it came back to the fore in the second half of the nineteenth century, both in terms of political and economic power and in terms of its urban growth and size.[33]

Exploiting the revolution in transport, the great cities are able to grow beyond their previous limits and divide their territory into residential areas, productive areas, areas for offices and for the tertiary sector. Speculation in different areas and urban repression, together with the first attempts at planning and the birth of public housing schemes and of a modern local administration reflect deep changes in the labour market on an international scale, as well as the birth of the workers' movement.

In the developed countries a progressive reduction of the over-population typical of rural areas takes place: the process of urbanization completes itself and the increase in work opportunities is now principally based on rationalization and on the movement from depressed areas all over the world to the most advanced areas. This new quality of the labour market offers an undeniable advantage to the working class. Since capitalist management in large factories has an interest in preserving the stability of the highly productive workforce it employs and cannot cheaply replace, the workers can begin to organize themselves and fight for improvements, higher salaries and greater job security.

Land speculation in urban areas thus becomes a system for control or repression of the working class in the city, thus recouping whatever is lost to capital within the factory. The construction sector of a market economy, incidentally, is of great importance during this phase of urban restructuration and rapid growth of the larger cities, for while the demand for housing and offices increases rapidly, the supply, by reason of limitations on urban space increases very slowly. The laws of the market cause a constant rise in the price of urban accommodation and property and thus ever heavier deductions from workers' salaries.

The other side of the contradiction is that where the working class is strongest and developing industrial capital disposes of substantial resources drawn from outside (e.g. imperialistic and colonial profits), ways of adjusting the property market (like the building of council houses) develop with the following double effect. They limit the amounts drawn on salaries from home purchase thus keeping the cost of labour low and they limit the cost of housing new workers in the city, thus opening new occupational areas to capitalism.

London was able to achieve, by the end of the last century, a vast concentration of five million inhabitants, mostly employed in the tertiary sector or in industrial management, inasmuch as it was the capital of the biggest colonial empire that has ever existed. A large part of Asia and of Africa were directly ruled by London while almost all the countries of Latin America existed in virtual economic subordination to England. Almost all the import-export business of the most advanced country in the world – that is to say a very large slice of world commerce itself – was governed by London companies.

London was the most important financial centre, home of the great banks and of the central markets in industrial and agricultural raw materials. All this goes to explain the precocious expansion of the great metropolis at the heart of the British Empire but it also explains its subsequent weakness in relation to other cities such as Paris, New York or Tokyo, which are overtaking its economic primacy during the twentieth century. Ultimately London's dominion owes too much to its colonial empire and too little to the monopolistic concentration of British enterprises. Capital attained its greatest degree of concentration and power in other cities, especially in the United States to begin with, then, after the Second World War in Germany and Japan, where industrial specialization yielded great increases in the productive capacity of the two countries, bringing them to a position of great economic strength.

In the underdeveloped or colonial areas the arrival of capitalism, not now in the shape of an economic revolution affected by local forces but as a form of hyper-exploitation conducted from outside, leads to a revolutionizing of socio-territorial structures very different (despite certain superficial similarities) from the patterns of urbanization in capitalist countries.

Even when the rural areas of underdeveloped countries manage to produce a surplus by rationalizing their productive processes, this agricultural surplus does nothing to subsidize local industrial development but is absorbed by imperialist countries stepping up the export of industrial commodities to the underdeveloped country in question. Any increase in per capita income goes to boost imports and consolidate the economic dependence of the underdeveloped countries rather than going into investment and industrial development. Colonial or underdeveloped cities ultimately grow into great areas where labour is unutilized for productive work. The growth of cities in underdeveloped areas does not promote large industry but rather the growth of the tertiary sector, as a structure devoted to administration and consumption, and of light industry and crafts, as a structure which, while being productive, offers no immediate competition to the imperialist monopoly.[34] Taking into account the high birthrate of underdeveloped countries and in many cases the rapid destitution of the countryside (more a feature of Latin-American than of Asian or African economies) the aggravation of relative overpopulation in the big cities takes on a dramatic quality. Shanghai before the revolution, Singapore, Bangkok, Calcutta, Bombay, Cairo, Buenos Aires, Rio de Janeiro, Mexico City are all, in different ways, vast concentrations of poverty and at the same time instruments with which monopoly capital continues to penetrate and exploit the rural areas: they are seats of commercial companies, of branches of the great industries of the West, of corrupt public administration lacking real authority, of import and export companies. Whereas during primary accumulation rural deprivation was paralleled by the enrichment of the cities (at least in terms of work and productivity), under imperialism the impoverishment of the countryside (which in many cases does not even mean an increase in agricultural production and productivity) is only echoed in a rapid worsening of urban poverty. The surplus enriches the imperialist metropolis and the crumbs that remain or return to the underdeveloped area (even in the form of so-called economic aid) are cornered by those restricted social strata in order to subdue the masses, thus favouring the reproduction of underdevelopment and imperialist exploitation.

The present phase of capitalist socio-territorial structuring develops the contradictions of preceding phases to their limits. The highest degree of concentration and the most destructive imbalance, supported by an economy and a society which on the whole is stagnant and which suffocates human progress or promotes it in abnormal forms, are the most important features of our territorial division of work.

Alternatives in social, economic and territorial terms are cultivated behind the deepening social conflicts, through the self-organization of the exploited classes, whether the Western working class or the urban semi-proletariat of the Americas, Africa and Asia.

I want now to suggest what goes to make up the socio-territorial structure of the most recent phase of capitalism. The great metropolises, after years of congestion and the rises in cost due to millions of people living together in a limited space, move their centres of production out towards the periphery – but they continue to centralize management and decision-making, which, in the long run, obstructs any form of territorial decongestion.

The great city in the West, and the great city of an underdeveloped country, both end up, at a far different extent, by promoting a new radical division of labour, becoming the centre of tertiary rather than productive activity. Management, scientific research, high finance, import and export centres, power in public affairs, the centres of distribution all increase their influence in the multi-million city. All this manifests itself in the rapid specialization of space, on the one hand the office blocks of the centre, on the other the residential suburbs. Productive activities are decentralized and placed according to their importance in different peripheral zones. High technology, capital-intensive industry, if it does not contaminate the environment, remains in the hinterland of the great cities and completes the picture of the metropolis. Those sectors of mass industry only moderately capital intensive, such as the great mechanical engineering industry, continue to be localized in the big industrial cities but their productive cycle tends to be split into two sub-cycles in order to allow decentralization of the simpler work processes which are less satisfying and dirtier, towards underdeveloped areas where local manpower can be utilized at low cost. The less densely concentrated sectors tend to remain in the specialized areas as ever and become progressively more subservient to the enormous interests of capital lodged in the metropolis – either because of state takeover, or the orders placed by heavy industry, or debts contracted with the great banks or the central finance houses. Finally, the production of semi-manufactured goods in squalid conditions, the petrochemical industry and the initial processing of raw materials are moved out along with other low productivity processes to underdeveloped areas. Here they further shackle the local economy to the interests of the metropolis without favouring any degree of autonomous development. This territorial division of work represents a social and productive order full of contradictions and extremely unjust, as its high cost in social terms and the tensions and conflicts which it engenders make clear.

In the great metropolis the problem of disaffection among workers is worsened by the time wasted in commuting. Despite the rigid and repressive structuring of space, the housing market continues to function in contradictory fashion. Supply cannot swiftly meet demand, which swells out of proportion to the increase in urban population, on account of the restructuring and specialization of areas. The poorer classes, numbered in hundreds of thousands, continue to live in ghettos. Substantial groups of new immigrants remain unhoused for long periods and camp out in whatever shacks they find. The high cost of housing is a constant worry to the poor and the intermediate strata of society in almost all the developed countries. All this comes about while the economic crisis is eroding workers' living standards, building up the numbers of unemployed and reducing the proportion of city dwellers actively employed.

Meanwhile, in underdeveloped areas urbanization or the demographic build-up or movements of refugees and immigrants following work, continually boost the population of the great cities, while job opportunities remain few, especially in the advanced sector of the economy. Thus an economic dualism spreads, with most of the population in the big cities of underdeveloped countries making a living out of the building industry, local handicrafts, street vending, domestic service, odd jobs and, in the last resort, illegal activities. The narrow base on which this economic sector operates, a sector by the way constantly threatened by the possible expansion of concentrated capital, always produces poverty. Where the dominant class of an underdeveloped country is unable because of economic crisis, or its own voracity, to keep the impoverished city masses quiet by bestowing upon them a part of the surplus created in the countryside, social tensions periodically explode in the form of revolts.

The highest price for this division of labour, however, is paid by the rural areas of the Third World, which cannot even rebel against the situation because of their scattered forces and the political and social disorganization which is typical of them. Economic and social stagnation, catastrophic periods of famine, the lack of even partial re-investment in the land, the total dependence of the producers of raw materials on imperialistic monopolies make up the ugly face of a plundering economic organization by which the division of work is effected.[35]

URBANIZATION AND ECONOMIC DEVELOPMENT IN ITALY

I shall now test my general theory of the relations between the territorial division of labour, territorial imbalance and capitalist development against the concrete realities of the Italian situation. The Italian situation is certainly not an ideal paradigm of capitalist development. On the contrary, its uneven economic growth and the successive exercise of three different types of economic policy (liberal, fascist and liberal-planning), its dearth of industrial raw materials, the profound inequality of the different regions and a marked economic dualism make Italy anything but a typical case.

There are, however, two answers that can be offered should objections to the example chosen arise. Firstly, no single long-term development process can be considered typical and exemplary. Secondly, by its very complexity Italy presents an extensive range of territorial disparities brought about by capitalist development.

It has recently been pointed out that economic development in Italy presents aspects typical both of developed and underdeveloped countries.[36] Furthermore the fact that Italy cannot simply be explained as the geographic sum of a developed region and an underdeveloped region adds interest to the case.

In this brief analysis, I will dwell principally on the two periods of rapid industrial development in Italy: that at the beginning of the century and that which followed the Second World War. I will be particularly brief in dealing with the fascist period, limiting myself to a few remarks on modifications made to the socio-territorial structure. I have shown how the original accumulation of capital in Italy was a limited process which was restricted geographically. Up to the beginning of our own century and in particular between 1896 and 1908 there was a period of intense industrial growth and transformation. After this initial industrial boom Italian economics followed a slow and controversial course until the Second World War.

During this period the value of Italian agriculture rose by an average annual rate of 2%, a distinctly unimpressive rate which indicates that agriculture was not important in financing industrial development. But during this same period, as the cost of merchant shipping diminished, the force of international competition meant that the price of agricultural products dropped steeply, which certainly favoured industrial growth. Between 1880 and 1895 corn dropped 40%, rice 25%, hemp 20%, edible oil 18%, pork 28%, butter 22%, silk cocoons 22% – this last figure becoming 40% by 1897.

Only wine noticeably increased in price during these fifteen years, going from around 30 to around 40 lire per hectolitre.

Though it was the textile industry which in many ways conditioned this first industrial boom, metals, chemicals and machinery are the industries which accelerate their development with average annual increases of respectively 12.4%, 13.7%, and 12.2% as against the 3.5% of textiles and the 5.5% of foodstuffs.[37]

The development achieved by these specific sectors of industry was dependent upon the prior fulfilment of three important conditions: state orders for the rearmament of Italy, the development of a new finance and credit system based on banks of the German type (the most important being the *Banca Commerciale Italiana di Milano*) and the exploitation of electric energy. It is of importance to emphasize these facts because one way or another each of these three factors intensifies industrial concentration, and bestows further privileges on the areas already more highly developed, especially in the case of the financing and banking system, which, being situated almost exclusively in Milan, offers enormous advantages to the development of Lombard industry.

Another essential factor in the industrial boom is the availability of almost unlimited cheap labour. Emigration statistics indicate how much was available in every region of Italy. The critical state of rural Italy and the rationalization of agriculture in this period made available an enormous surplus population: in the first decade of this century there was an annual emigration of Italians numbering an average 597,246, of which 211,000 came from the north, 108,000 from the central regions and 278,000 from the south. In the decade therefore, something like six million Italians left the country. That is to say almost a fifth of the population figure for 1911.[38] In 1913 emigration reached its highest peak with a figure of 873,000, that is to say almost a fifth of the active population in that year.

Such unlimited supplies of manpower naturally allow Italian industrial development to make high profits on the difference between salary increments (which were made, though the levels were always low) and the increase in productivity. In turn this allows a high rate of re-investment, which is certainly a factor in industrial intensification, for re-investment is to the advantage of the bigger, more efficient industries, those more favoured by the local economy, and those most closely linked to political power.

One must further consider that the rate of industrial production in the first ten years of the century rose by 5.2% in Lombardy, 4% in Piedmont, 3% in Liguria, while it fell 0.3% in Campania, 1% in the Abruzzi, 0.7% in Apulia and 4% in Calabria. Thus the overall rise of

108 *Territorial Division of Labour*

1.4% in the rate of industrial output in Italy during the decade is an algebraic sum composed of the higher rises recorded in the industrial areas together with the almost constant decline (Sicily must be excepted) registered in the southern and agricultural areas.

This first period of rapid industrial development is not exceptional when compared to what happened in other European countries (we have already quoted the rates of development in Germany, Japan and Russia at the time of industrial take-off: all of these being, as Gerscherkron emphasizes, superior to that 6.7% a year which the same author attributes to Italian development).

Various reasons prevented industrial development from being complete, among which were the modest scale of capital accumulation, the lack of raw materials, and a lack of mobility in the home market, which was largely locked up in a pre-capitalist agricultural system. In 1910, that is to say in full industrial take-off[39] Italy's per capita consumption of raw materials[40] is far behind that of England, Germany and France, and Italy also lags behind France and Germany in the numbers of her population employed in agriculture, the figures being 59.8% for Italy, 33% for France, 23.8% for Germany.

If one could to some degree counter these data concerning the consumption of industrial raw materials with the objection that Italian development was less dependent on heavy industry and was turning more to hydroelectric energy than coal one would still not be able to deny that of the four countries Italy was the only one overwhelmingly agricultural in nature.

Now let us look in greater detail at the territorial processes which followed the industrial take-off and the new territorial division of labour. Emigration hit different rural regions equally hard and affected in like manner, both the north and the south, where the agricultural crisis was at its worst. Venetia and Campania provided almost half the numbers of those who emigrated between 1870 and 1900 and Venetia alone provided two-fifths of the total. By the first ten years of the century 56.3% of emigration in general and a much higher percentage of permanent emigration in the direction of the Americas all came from five regions, of which four were situated in the south. These were Venetia with 16.5%, Sicily with 12.6%, Campania with 11.8%, the Abruzzi with 8.2% amd Calabria with 7.2%. Lombardy and Piedmont also had a high rate of emigration, 9.2% and 8.4% respectively, although in this case it tended to be temporary emigration to other European countries. Emigration thus begins to upset the balance of population in different territories even if one cannot as yet talk of inter-regional population shifts.

The great cities like Milan, Turin and Genoa grew rapidly in this period because of the numbers who abandoned rural life in the mountain valleys to dwell in towns. In the case of Milan, it was the neighbouring municipalities which grew rapidly, rather than the city itself, following the spread of industrial development and according to the price of land.[41] One thus witnesses a process of intense urban growth and colonization of territory around the four Italian cities which saw the greatest development in this period, that is to say Rome, Milan, Genoa and Turin. When the process was complete the cities were changed beyond recognition, their population mainly consisting of people from the neighbouring, crisis-ridden agricultural areas.

At this time the so-called industrial triangle took shape (the Milan-Turin-Genoa area) which consolidated its primacy during the fascist era and also became the basis for more recent industrial development. In Milan, which, after Naples, is the most heavily populated city in Italy and the only great industrial centre, were concentrated the metallurgical workshops of Breda and Falk, the rising giant of the chemical industry, Montecatini, and some great engineering concerns such as Marelli. But above all, it was here that the great finance and banking groups of the time had their headquarters.

In Turin Fiat was founded and became, within a few years, one of the most colossal engineering concerns in Italy and all Europe. In Genoa, along with a port serving the major Italian industries, naval shipyards grew where the military and mercantile fleet were constructed; the great steelworks of Sampierdarena also developed at this time.

'Indeed,' to quote Castronovo,[42] 'the northern regions had the majority of factories, with the larger industrial capacity, 71% of industrial enterprises employing over 500 workers (and 68% of those employing over 1,000), and with more mechanization (58% of the total). It was in the provinces of north-west Italy, in fact, that more than half the firms employing over ten men and almost half of those which used mechanized energy were situated.' The strength of the industrial triangle – Castronovo rightly remarks – resides in the 'capacity for expansion of the mechanical engineering sector' and in the links already established by this sector with the banking and finance organizations and with state protectionism. On the other hand there was a grave reduction in industrial employment in the south (686,000 men in the thirty years between 1881 and 1911, that is to say a loss of 30% of industrial employment).[43]

All this is not immediately reflected in the statistics for people

TABLE 2.4 Population of municipalities of over 20,000 inhabitants per region in 1911 and the percent increase since 1861 and 1871 (for Venetia and Latium).

	N.	% of the resident population	Difference in % since 1861 (or 1871)	
Piedmont	773,144	22.6	9.6	
Liguria	643,258	53.3	21.6	
Lombardy	1,330,267	27.9	11.2	
Venetia+Udine	693,439	18.6	—	1.4
Emilia Romagna	948,834	33.7	3.5	
Tuscany	998,140	37.4	7.9	
Umbria	223,544	36.4	7.3	
Marches	205,869	18.0	4.7	
Latium	592,204	33.4	—	11.2
Abruzzi+Molise	160,799	10.6	7.8	
Campania	1,200,378	38.7	13.6	
Calabria	134,228	8.8	2.1	
Apulia	913,838	41.6	20.8	
Sicily	1,786,404	46.9	19.9	
Sardinia	137,734	15.9	5.1	
Italy	10,742,080	30.0	10.7	

N.B. Valle d'Aosta and Basilicata are not included as they do not have municipalities of over 20,000 inhabitants.

Source: Based on data from ISTAT, *Municipalities and their populations at the censuses from 1861 to 1961*, Rome, 1964.

living in the municipalities with over 20,000 inhabitants, as Table 2.4 shows. The most advanced regions in the 1861 statistics, that is Liguria, Sicily, Apulia and Campania, notably increased their level of urbanization (in this connection the regions of central Italy were exceptionally slow). In the southern regions this phenomenon reflected a progressive impoverishment of the countryside and the depopulation of the smaller centres in favour of the larger ones which offered better chances of survival. In the north, on the other hand, urban concentration was not remarkable and the progress of industrialization is mirrored above all in the frenetic growth of the big cities and of a few large centres of specialized industry.

Thus the critical state of the countryside led only in part to urbanization because of the slow and contradictory nature of urban development. In the sixty years between 1861 and 1921, as our first graph illustrates, the urban population rises from 19.6% to 34.1% of the total population with an average annual rise of 2.5%, a slow rate of urban development when compared to that of England or for that matter France and Germany. Moreover, this urbanization is largely due to the pressures exerted upon life in the countryside, and consists mostly in migrations to cities which are not industrial centres.

Only because Rome was the capital of the realm, did its inhabitants multiply from 194,500 in 1861, to 667,500 in 1921. This was the greatest urban expansion of the period, but Naples and Palermo also, which were oversized in terms of the scant industrial activity they provided, increased their populations remarkably despite the stagnation of industrial activities in the south.

The twenty years of fascism saw only the most feeble urban development and that mostly due to general population growth. Both emigration and urban growth ceased almost completely. The halting of urbanization is partly explained by the economic policies of fascism and partly by laws which forbade change of domicile. With regard to the first point, fascism, by a basic economic choice and out of political concern to avoid any repetition of the socialist alliance between poor rural and urban workers seen in 1919 and 1920, committed itself to agricultural reclamation and investment in the countryside, without, however, modifying the status of landed property and the conditions of exploitation. This commitment, though it brought no substantial results either in the way of increased agricultural production or revaluation and modernization of Italian agriculture, managed, however, to freeze the crisis and to delay its outburst until after the Second World War.[44]

Indeed the urban concentration which did take place during fascism increased the importance of industrial cities and of Rome; between 1921 and 1936 Naples and Palermo grew at a minimal rate and were affected by a measure of emigration, Genoa, Florence and Venice and many other cities of small size grew only at the general rate of population growth, but Rome passed from 670,000 inhabitants to 1,150,000, Milan from 699,800 to 1,111,500, Turin from 499,100 to 629,100.

The process of urban concentration reflects the economic policy of Fascism, which favours industrial restructuring so as to benefit the big concentrated industries[45] and the consolidation of heavy industry. At the same time it favours the agricultural class and preserves overpopulation of the rural areas.

MONOPOLISTIC DEVELOPMENT IN ITALY, AND URBAN STRUCTURES

The geography of the post-war economic situation in Italy is highly unusual. An outmoded agriculture and a productive organization which were pre-capitalist and inefficient, still employed over forty percent of the working population. That is to say it tied up a relatively large population, which various politico-economic interventions in agriculture would in time have liberated. There was still great concentration both of heavy industry and of certain sectors of technologically advanced industry, in particular chemicals and mechanical engineering, all of which had been seriously damaged by the war. Light industry, especially textiles, was relatively outdated and not densely concentrated but, more importantly, had maintained its plant in working order and could call upon large reserves of manpower, since the unemployed numbered almost two million. The infrastructures of the great industrial cities, Milan and Turin, had suffered badly in the war.

These conditions, along with the drive provided initially by the textile industry, organized in many small centres throughout central and northern Italy,[46] and the abundant manpower available in the centre and south, could have given the country more balanced economic development. But the demand for a great concentration in terms of capital and territory was a condition of the recovery of a capitalist economy. Rapid industrial development was therefore accompanied by the growth of a considerable territorial imbalance between the few big cities and the little ones, between city and country, between industrial areas and underdeveloped areas. Reconstruction was brought about by the great mechanical-engineering and chemical industries and the powerful financial groups of the industrial triangle.

Payments for war damages, building speculation and US aid under the Marshall Plan allowed further consolidation of large-scale industry in the north. The degree of concentration of capital, which also has territorial implications, was primarily dictated by Italy's effort to win a place in the Western capitalist market and her need to compete against more advanced foreign industries. At the beginning of the 1950s the strategy of the utility motor car was launched. The small car, which does not have US rivals, soon transformed Turin and Milan into two automobile capitals and at the same time accelerated the development of a great number of connected industries; paint, windscreens, tyres, plastics, steel, electrics, petro-chemicals and so on.

The south and agriculture were the real victims of the rapid post-war industrial development. Agriculture was destined to remain a marginal or reserve sector in economic development, constantly devalued, never modernized and never competitive in foreign markets since it had yielded much of its work-force to industry. The south began by producing cheap labour and a consumer market for the industrial products of the north and then became the theatre for industrial decentralization of a devastating and exploitative nature, frustrating its chances of progress and prosperity.

The partial agricultural reform of 1951, rather than initiating rationalization of Italian agriculture for the sake of efficiency and productivity simply prepared for the long term rundown of the agricultural work-force caused by the excessively small scale of post-reform agricultural enterprises, and the neglect of agriculture in economic politics.[47] The average annual rate of increase in post-war Italy's gross agricultural product equals, or almost equals, that of countries with a highly developed agriculture like Holland, Great Britain and Denmark (2.4% by comparison with 2.3% or 2.4%) but is distinctly inferior to that of other countries, like Germany (2.9%), France (3.5%), Austria (4%), Greece (4.8%) and Yugoslavia (5.1%).[48]

Capitalism exerts contradictory influences on Italian agriculture. The medium-sized family-run capitalist enterprise finds it hard to establish itself in rural areas as it lacks the tradition and generally finds economic conditions unsuitable. Agricultural structures in Italy continue to experience extreme polarization between the great capitalist enterprises and enormous numbers of small, inefficient and run-down businesses which depend upon part-time labour or industrial work taken in and done at home by members of the peasant family, or remittances sent by emigrants.[49] Thus the most interesting phenomenon in the agricultural areas, as far as capitalist development and socio-territorial structure are concerned, is the rising rate of emigration which, in the last twenty-five years, has totally revolutionized the human geography of Italy.

All who write on the subject[50] agree that post-war economic development in Italy was based on two factors: the almost unlimited availability of cheap labour provided by Southern agriculture and the position won by Italy in the capitalist manufacturing market. This permitted constant expansion of exports both in the traditional sectors; shoes, hides and leather, clothing and textiles, and then more especially in the field of mechanical engineering which produced consumer durables (automobiles and electrical appliances) and eventually the chemicals monopoly.

It is not easy to define in a few lines the territorial manifestations of this phase of industrial development but we can attempt a quick outline. The great centres of the mechanical-engineering industry, the undisputed backbone of the industrial boom, had from the beginning of the century been almost exclusively concentrated in the industrial triangle. The manufacture of automobiles, electrical household appliances and the factories making electric motors and machine tools were all concentrated around Milan or Turin. Metallurgical industries were more widely dispersed but prevalent in central or northern Italy, with the exception of the old centre of Bagnoli near Naples. The economic policy of the I.R.I. was of fundamental influence here for it aimed to construct huge capital-intensive steel mills, following the Japanese example so that steel might be produced as cheaply as possible: The great private centres of the steel industry in Milan suffered as a result of this, but, on the other hand, enormous advantages accrued to the mechanical-engineering industry, which acquired cheap raw materials, and to the small privately owned metallurgical industries which prospered as their more powerful rivals suffered, due to the fact that the State steel industry could not produce what small metallurgical industries produced (rods for reinforced concrete in particular). The private sector of the metallurgical industry was situated predominantly in the province of Brescia and it was this area, once again in the north, which reaped the benefits of capitalist development, for, as we shall see, the decentralizing of steel-manufacturing complexes was detrimental to the areas which received them.

Principally for reasons of 'market economy' the small and medium export industries grew up largely in the centre and north, if not wholly within the triangle. For this reason industrial employment developed in sectors not particularly concentrated (footwear, clothing, paper-making and printing, textiles, leather and building materials) even in central northern areas outside the triangle. All this came about without interfering with the process of monopolistic and territorial concentration of capital, indeed it reinforced it. The dominant sectors of industry, along with high finance and public administration, remained exclusively attached to the great cities of the triangle, and to Rome. Thus, though employment in the manufacturing industries, which were concentrated in Lombardy and Piedmont, had fallen from 48% to 45% of the active population by 1971, its redistribution was of no benefit to the south which, if its seven regions are taken together, dropped from 17.2% to 13.5% employed in manufacturing. The benefit accrued to certain regions of central northern Italy (Emilia Romagna, the Marches, Venetia,

Latium and Tuscany, in order of increased employment) which ranged from 26.1% to 33.3%. But the monopolistic and concentrated structure of capitalist development is not disproved by this spread of employment precisely because the fundamental sectors of industry remain concentrated in the triangle and especially because the apparatus of control is ever more securely in the hands of the financiers and industrialists of Milan and Turin and of the politicians of Rome. In a word, post-war Italian development shows, even in the brief outline we have traced, a strong tendency to increase regional imbalance, and the socio-territorial division of labour.[51] I return to the present Italian crisis in the next chapter.

The economic and demographic data, though they furnish irrefutable proof of the process of territorial concentration in Italian development, only shed light on certain large-scale features of the grave imbalance and of the territorial and economic dualism which was planted deep in Italian society by developing capitalism. Clarification of other features is only achieved by research on specific areas or situations.[52]

Between 1951 and 1971 the five cities of Milan, Turin, Genoa, Rome and Bologna absorbed 35.6% of the total national increase in population. Milan and Turin alone, in 1971, absorbed 21.6% of industrial employment in Italy. It can be said, however, that Milan, Turin and Rome by themselves have almost complete control of the economy, for the great industries and banks of Italy all have their seat in these cities.[53] But, and here we have the most interesting feature of the phenomenon, territorial imbalance is worsened by the decentralization of productive processes and by the recent economic crisis. For example, Mondadori, which is the biggest Italian publishing complex, a quasi-monopoly, has its headquarters in Milan, whereas its factories are in the province of Verona. A part of the work done is carried out in Mondadori's factories but the major part is decentralized and given to small industries which live off work farmed out by Mondadori. They are underpaid and this perpetuates an exploitation of workers whose salary levels range from forty percent of those usual in the great industries. The excess profit is absorbed almost completely by Mondadori and recycled as capital in the Milan stock exchange.[54]

A different type of decentralization, creating a different kind of territorial imbalance occurs in the petro-chemical and steel industries. Both industries are capital intensive, productive of noxious waste, and have high congestion costs because they depend upon enormous structures for the transport and processing of their raw materials, a network of pipelines, large ports, etc. I shall analyse the

116 *Territorial Division of Labour*

effects of this decentralization in Chapter 3, after which I shall try also to analyse the development of peripheral industrialization in various regions of the north-east and centre.

Post-war industrial development has considerably accelerated the pace of urbanization. Whereas it was forty years for the percentage of those living in municipalities of over 20,000 inhabitants to rise from 31% in 1911 to 41% in 1951, in the twenty years between 1951 and 1971 the rate increased by over eleven percentage points. Meanwhile, the population of cities and towns became larger than that of municipalities as the city expanded outside the municipal areas and outlying suburbs were absorbed in the development of the cities.

This is particularly notable in the most recent period: Rome (increase of the population from 1951 to 1971, 68%), Turin (62%), Bologna (45%), Milan (36%). These rates of increase clearly outpace the growth of other cities, medium and small in size, or situated in the south. Incidentally, the narrow municipal boundaries of Milan conceal the expansion of a city of impressive dimensions. Urban expansion in every direction is a recognized fact and large cities like Monza or Sesto San Giovanni are districts of Milan, even if they preserve administrative autonomy. Between 1951 and 1971, the province of Milan grew at a greater rate (56%) than that of its chief town: a unique occurrence in Italian history. But if one takes the thirteen municipalities within the Milanese conurbation[55] which between 1951 and 1971 passed the 20,000 inhabitants mark, one notes that the sum of their growth was 271% with an average annual increase of 13.7% and a total population which rose from 125,167 to almost half a million.

The congestion and the gross overcrowding in the big northern cities are too well known to need further description here. The pattern of regional urbanization illustrated in Tables 2.3 and 2.5 reflects both the traditional territorial structure of regions and the industrial capitalist development together with the increase of territorial imbalances. The urbanization curve for the northern regions, especially Piedmont, is certainly more pronounced than that for other regions and all the more so in recent years. In the central regions of Italy, however, and in Emilia Romagna pre-eminently, a more dynamic process of urbanization is demonstrated, especially by those cities with over 100,000 inhabitants. The statistics of levels of urbanization, it has to be said, have become more and more meaningless. The great northern cities, Genoa and Milan especially, pursue their expansion through neighbouring municipalities. The city extends its influence and commuters come

TABLE 2.5 Percentage of the population living in municipalities with more than 20,000 inhabitants and in municipalities with more than 100,000 inhabitants in 1961 and 1971.

	1961 +20,000 inhabitants	+100,000 inhabitants	1971 +20,000 inhabitants	+100,000 inhabitants	Difference between the % population with over 20,000 inhabitants between 1971 and 1951
Piedmont	44.2	26.2	51.0	31.1	15.5
Valle d'Aosta	30.3	—	33.8	—	8.1
Liguria	65.5	52.2	66.2	50.7	5.0
Lombardy	41.9	25.2	46.7	25.5	10.7
Venetia	36.0	19.9	41.0	23.7	9.0
Trent	28.0		30.7	12.3	5.5
Friuli	38.4	22.6	40.5 −	30.6	4.8
Emilia Romagna	50.4	30.3	56.7	41.1	14.2
Tuscany	52.0	21.5	58.6	25.4	16.2
Umbria	54.7	14.2	58.9+	30.5	5.7
Marches	37.4	7.5	44.3 −	8.1	10.3
Latium	67.6	55.3	75.2	59.5	16.1
Rome	55.3		59.5		
Abruzzi+Molise	24.8	—	30.3+	8.2	9.7
Campania	53.6	27.3	58.6	27.4	11.9
Apulia	55.5	18.3	58.0	20.4	4.6
Basilicata	12.7	—	16.8+	—	6.8
Calabria	23.3	7.5	28.6+	13.5	8.8
Sicily	57.3	25.6	60.6+	30.3	8.0
Sardinia	30.4	12.9	36.4	22.6	12.8
Total	47.0	24.7	52.4	29.2	11.6

+ = regions where the total population has decreased between 1961 and 1971
− = regions where the total population has increased less than 1% during the decade
Source: extrapolations from ISTAT data for population censuses X and XI.

from ever farther afield. Some years ago it was calculated[56] that the gravitational pull of Milan on commuters embraced hundreds of thousands of workers and easily extended beyond the regional boundaries themselves into Piedmont, northern Liguria and Emilia.

On the other hand the urban structure of the south is only apparently reinforced by selective migration from the more critical rural areas; and the demographic importance of the cities increases only relatively. Indeed, with very few exceptions their rate of growth is very low. Between 1951 and 1971 Palermo and Syracuse in Sicily, along with certain cities in Sardinia and Apulia, may be considered exceptions. Urbanization in the south does not mean industrial development or modernization. It does not even denote that imbalance between urban and rural territory usually aggravated by developing capitalism. The southern city tends to become a fixed world in itself while the more intractable parts of the countryside are simply abandoned along with their villages. The big cities survive by speculation in building and a parasitic tertiary sector. The great factories of the southern cities are the administrative offices of municipality, province, region and state, the hospitals, the schools and universities which in the last resort provide work whether real or fictitious for a majority of the active population.

In the last twenty years in Italy regional disparity has grown not only between north and south but also within single areas. In the north, Milan is a city so congested that the new waves of workers migrating to it are not able to find accommodation even in the vast provincial hinterland which surrounds it. At the same time the hilly and mountainous areas of Lombardy itself are gradually turning to deserts. The little provincial cities which thrived during the economic 'boom' now live off loans or the orders from monopolistic enterprises or from the state.

The development of industrial dualism and the process of selection of the work-force are the most important factors to modify the territorial division of labour. Alongside the great monopolistic industries, numerous small businesses survive, and in given periods develop, utilizing the abundant work-force rejected by the big industries, the young and old, women, the illiterate or semi-illiterate. This type of industry generally has little autonomy, either because it works to order for big industries or because it is directly controlled by monopolistic finance groups or because it depends on them for its raw materials, or for other reasons. Naturally this organization of industry is quite different from the traditional

TABLE 2.6 Population of the nine largest Italian municipalities according to the census figures from 1861 to 1971, index figures for 1861 and 1951.

	1861 N.	1921 N.	Index figures (1861 = 100)	1951 N.	1951 Index figures (1861 = 100)	1971 N.	1971 Index figures (1861 = 100)	Index figures (1951 = 100)
Rome	194,597	667,468	343	1,654,074	850	2,781,993	1,429	168
Milan	257,294	699,840	272	1,276,178	496	1,732,000	673	136
Naples	483,358	860,378	178	1,005,384	208	1,226,594	253	122
Turin	173,305	499,118	288	719,216	415	1,167,968	674	162
Genoa	242,944	541,765	223	685,102	282	816,872	336	119
Palermo	199,986	397,793	199	491,744	246	642,814	322	131
Florence	151,799	280,828	185	374,943	247	457,803	302	122
Bologna	116,871	210,368	180	338,926	290	490,528	420	145
Venice	128,000	222,720	174	316,160	247	363,062	283	115
Province of Milan				2,505,153	—	3,903,658	—	156
Province of Turin				1,433,001	—	2,287,016	—	160
13 municipalities in the conurbation of Milan				125,167	—	464,805	—	371

Sources: derived from ISTAT data for population censuses.

competitive network. Industrialized provinces and regions depend entirely on external monopolies and accumulate capital for them. Mondadori provides a good example of this.

The peripheral areas of Lombardy and Piedmont, Venetia, Emilia Romagna, the Marches and Umbria, where work done at home and part-time work is very common and where hundreds of small or medium-sized industries grossly exploit an abundant work-force which might be described as marginal, function as branches of the economic and decision-making centres in Milan and Turin, and show an unprecedented degree of dependence.

Within the south also, examples of great territorial inequality develop. Where industry has been decentralized those areas which receive it develop in dependence upon northern or state or foreign capital. They are transformed into modern industrial centres but riddled with contradictions. The Naples area including Caserta and Cassino with the mechanical engineering industries of FIAT and IRI (Aeritalia and Alfasud) has in a few years been turned into an industrial centre. The creation of new jobs has not however resolved the local problems of this ancient urban area, where a chronic surplus of manpower had already resulted in chronic underemployment in the urban proletariat and the formation of a vast sub-proletariat.

Therefore, the inability of an advanced capitalist economy to substantially increase employment is particularly high in areas which have the lowest rates of industrial employment, and high unemployment, underemployment, or occasional work. From 1961 to 1971, while the rate of unemployment was diminishing a little in general in Italy, it was increasing considerably all over the south, reaching a peak in Calabria, where it provided the fundamental cause of the fascist revolt in Reggio.[57] The employment crisis is aggravated in the southern cities when, for national or international reasons, the escape valve of emigration is closed, as has happened in recent years. Swelling in size as the surrounding countryside is abandoned, the southern cities, and in particular Naples and Palermo, do not, however, offer sufficient job opportunities. This problem is compounded by the fact that these cities are not touched by the mainstream of economic development. They are poor in resources and live by speculation, which means that adequate infrastructures and urban services cannot be provided and that the price of a house remains very high, while living conditions do not come up to the national average.

The rural south, especially those of its regions which are hardest to farm, retains the exclusive function of providing manpower, until that day – which cannot be far off – when the residual population becomes too old. They will then lose even this function and survive in a condition of extreme decadence. Agricultural productivity remains unchanged. The only growing source of income is provided by the remittances of the emigrants, which are used to balance subsistence family budgets. As the countryside is deserted the agricultural heritage of centuries is lost. The extremely precarious equilibrium which embodies more and more profound contradictions in the organization of production and its territorial structure, finds its breaking point in economic crisis. When the economy can no longer expand and thus can no longer guarantee rises, however differentiated, in income, or jobs, even on a provisional basis, to the unemployed or under-employed, the social tensions concealed behind economic inequality will explode.

In this context the present condition of Italy is interesting because behind its deep inequalities different causes of potential and imminent conflict are at work. In Naples the unemployed are organized in action groups. The weaker regional economies in central Italy and Venetia have reached a critical situation which has made thousands of workers redundant. The Alfa Romeo factory in Milan was occupied by workers when some thousands of them were put on unemployment benefit for five days. Italsider in Taranto was occupied for some months by workers taken on for the construction of new plant, then left without a function in the cycle of concentrated production. In Calabria the current flood of criminal activity is one of the signs which suggest how economic stagnation in the region, where construction of the fifth National Steelworks is unlikely even to begin, may generate explosive social conflicts. Finally, in Turin the FIAT employment policies have made it necessary to fire or put on unemployment benefit over 25,000 workers, causing a general strike, a local strike lasting over a month, and an unsettled national climate.

These are only a few examples of the circumstances in which social contradictions develop. In any case capitalism in Italy demonstrates the economic, political and social fragility of the different capitalist strategies of development used for many years and it demonstrates the irresistible tendency towards the imbalance and the contradictions typical of the mode of production. The free enterprise project of Vera Lutz[58] which favoured spontaneous growth of economic activities in the regions already best provided with infrastructures, and use of the depressed areas as reserves of manpower and for tertiary agricultural activities, was rejected as being too reactionary, but nevertheless largely applied during the

1960s in Italy. The migration of over 3 million southerners (twenty percent of the southern population) towards the industrial areas is sure proof of this. The limitations of this strategy are also revealed by the resulting congestion of the northern cities and the decline of those activities in the south which ought, in theory, to have gained by the thinning out of the relative overpopulation. The strategy of decentralization has proved to be even less workable in practice. The decentralization of high-intensity capital ultimately breaks down local economic structures which are too flimsy to compete with the gigantic factories, and it does nothing to help alternative economic initiatives.[59]

Furthermore, the way in which the big industries operate is made worse by class conditions in the south. The frantic competition for jobs reinforces the patron-client relationship. The degree of power wielded by the local bosses makes it advisable for the northern managers to come to terms rather than clash with them. Often the union itself is involved in patronage and ends up enjoying a special relationship with the management. All this naturally contributes to social and political immobility, even when the economic development of the area, in terms of production, is outstanding.

The decentralization of highly work-intensive activities has also failed to correct regional imbalance, for only the most flourishing industries can decentralize in this way; Italian and foreign multinationals in particular being, along with certain large Italian monopolies, the only economic activities able to expand. To begin with they decentralize the practice of exploitation, not only of workers but also of consumers, of small local industries, and of agriculture. As a result, local resources are depleted out of all relation to the new jobs created in the underdeveloped area and the poor suffer from inflation, agricultural crisis, concentration of business and the closure of certain sectors of local activity.

The inability of Italian capitalism to manage a situation of unequal development is a sign of the specific weakness of the Italian economy within the international framework. Other Western countries have managed to survive so far, even while economic and social contradictions were aggravated in their territory by the progressive territorial division of labour. But this has been due to the enormous advantages of excess profits obtained by exploitation of the Third World.

Both blue and white collar workers, paid relatively high salaries, accept the inconveniences of life in the great metropolis; commuter travel, territorial segregation, alienation. Those who emigrate make social sacrifices because they have some guarantee of social promotion. The countryside can be left half abandoned because agricultural specialization in developed countries reaps benefits at the expense of peasant producers in the Third World. In the long term, when the resources of outlying areas are exhausted and/or the chronically exploited areas rebel and emancipate themselves, the inequalities within capitalist development will generate social conflicts throughout the spectrum of territorial organization.

CHAPTER THREE

Uneven Territorial Development and the Crisis of Advanced Capitalism

INTRODUCTION

Economists have mainly studied the problems of regional imbalance through methodologies which are both sectorial and self-limiting, and therefore overlooked social relationships as a whole. Basically, regional economists – be they classical and neo-classical or Keynesian and neo-Keynesian – have always created models which forecast a development of the capitalist economy capable of gradually recovering regional imbalances within the general development schema. The former think that the market mechanisms can impose a diffusion of the conditions for economic development; the latter underline the need for well-defined development policies, provided obviously that these policies can solve the problems of regional underdevelopment and, on a more general level, territorial contradictions as a whole. Both these lines are based on a false assumption: i.e. the available technology of advanced capitalism will concretely drive towards an equalization of the conditions of economic development. In other words, they refuse to consider some essential and very complex relationships between social classes; the ones, namely, which determine the ways technological progress is used. The result is that technological progress is considered as an independent and abstract variable, as far as its operating conditions and shaping interests are concerned.

Theoretically, today's technology would easily balance some geographical and social disadvantages (for instance, the lack of energy sources or of geographically near markets); but, as things are, technical-scientific knowledge is an instrument of a process of capital accumulation based on monopolistic concentration, on an articulate hierarchy of firms whose aim is profit conservation and maximization, and on as much exploitation of both resources and the work-force as possible. In other words, the actual lines of development strengthen the imbalance, and are contradictory even in purely territorial terms – neither can they be modified through political and economical interventions by the state or other public agencies. In this sense, we are still facing the old problem: it is impossible to plan a balanced development, even in territorial terms, because it happens to be impossible to rationalize the class contradictions which generally characterize capitalist societies. Territorial resources cannot be used at their best when the social structure is based on exploitation of labour and profit accumulation: and this applies both within a simple capitalist demand-and-supply logic and a modified one, whose 'corrective' factors are large scale state interventions in the economy. Therefore, territorial imbalances are purely aspects of the general class dialectic which is a characteristic of advanced capitalism.[1] The fact that regional imbalances remain and worsen confirms our hypothesis; however, this is not enough to overcome a rather dogmatic theoretical circularity. Here we can only rely on examples which are often non-generalizable, whilst to build a general 'law' would require the full documentation and articulation of all its elements and mechanisms.

It is important to try and explain concretely the relationships between, on the one hand, the dialectical process of contemporary capital accumulation and, on the other, the territorial contradictions which keep coming up – both on world and local level. Moreover, today, it is extremely important to explain both the factors and the territorial effects of the crisis of advanced capitalism – i.e. the long recession and economic stagnation, the serious political and social conflicts, which began in the sixties and give no sign of abatement. Of course, all this is far from easy, and can be done only by trial and error, within a wide, general, discussion. For a start, analyses on a national basis do not allow the development of a general theory, whereas sweeping remarks can very easily be too vague and unsupported by facts. One typical pitfall is shown, as far as generalization of specifically national experiences is concerned, by the neo-classical and neo-Keynesian economists' work in this field. Williamson's Law for example – about the gradual re-absorption of regional imbalances in advanced capitalism – is totally based on the economical development of the USA and Canada.[2] The main fault is basically that the two countries are, in an international context, quite exceptional. They do not have internal work-force reserves; they have always obtained these through international migrations; this gradually made the mother-countries of the work-force pay the social costs of US and Canadian development – in terms of new regional imbalances. At a later stage – when the USA and Canada had become ruling imperialist countries – it was even easier to partially balance their internal imbalances, thanks to the underdevelopment of large chunks of the Third World. Even a cursory look at countries where capitalistic development has been marked by important internal migrations shows that regional imbalances persist and tend to get worse.

THE INDUSTRIALIZATION PROCESS AND ITS TERRITORIAL LOGIC

The beginning of modern industrial production undoubtedly deeply upset precapitalist territorial balances. Industrialization means territorial concentration, i.e. a rapid urbanization process increased even more by a remarkable demographic growth. At this stage, industrial settlement is conditioned by three factors (which are unevenly distributed over the whole of the territory): the existence of energy sources, the presence of industrially useful raw materials, and the existence of a local market which can absorb at least a significant portion of the industrial product. Obviously, the latter factor has a strong multiplicative role. A high growth of urban concentration created by a developing industry means that the industry itself will find it advantageous to settle in large cities, because of the relevant market economies implied. Some large cities with a complete and unspecialized industrial structure have progressively acquired giant metropolitan dimensions. The work-force is a productive resource which can be moved about the territory at reasonable cost, especially since a large part of the economic and human-social costs of labour mobility is directly paid for by the workers themselves. Therefore, in the course of a long industrialization process, migrations are the main factors of change in territorial patterns. Strong socio-territorial imbalances are caused by several kinds of migrations: from the rural areas surrounding the first industrial cities, from the over-populated, less developed regions and countries to the developing areas, from the internal mountain regions to the plain and coastal regions, etc.

Emigration areas undergo several different social shocks, which sometimes mean a constant slowing down of the local industrialization process or, more often, a national or regional underdevelopment process. This is because, in both cases, the pre-capitalist productive unit in the countryside is steadily destroyed. Peasants and village artisans are forced to specialize in agricultural production, and increasingly depend upon the urban production of industrial goods. Agricultural production is at a disadvantage in that industrial capital accumulation is quicker, and the city/countryside imbalance steadily increases. On the other hand, the different socio-economic relationships which substitute for the original pre-capitalist community in the countryside tend to create different situations. In areas of early capitalistic penetration, the growing dependence of countryside on town and the unfavourable exchange ratios are partially compensated by large increases in agricultural productivity and by an actual revolution in agricultural production. Even if the accumulation of agricultural capital is slower – both because the goods produced are subsistence ones and because the landowners keep compressing the potential profits – some rural areas do undergo development, thereby granting the peasants a lifestyle which is not very different from the urban workers'. However, in most agricultural areas – both extensive dependent agricultural plantations and intensive agricultural smallholdings (very important because they reproduce most of the latent relative overpopulation) – industrialization creates a marked underdevelopment.

Capitalism penetrates different world areas with different chronologies and modalities – both in terms of the industrialization process and of market integration. It is important to remember that even in the fifties, many Third World areas and even a part of the European countryside were still characterized by forms of autarchy and self-sufficiency.

Improvements in transport technology and exploitation of energy sources do not change the trend towards further territorial imbalances – which are always determined by the modalities of capital accumulation. Indeed it is capital concentration and centralization, rather than the new production technology, which tend to multiply territorial imbalances. Our industrial societies' technology allows, on one hand, a better diffusion of some advantages of industrialization, and, on the other, a more centralized control of the semi-developed or underdeveloped peripheral areas. Obviously, capitalism particularly uses technology in this second way. Suburbanization, the development of large urban areas whose organization is hierarchical and segregated, the total abandonment of hill and mountain areas, the steady trend towards territorial concentration: these are the main ways in which capitalism uses transport, communications, and new energy technology. Of course, the size and modalities of the present territorial concentration process differ from last century's. The concentration area is much larger – region-city or conurbation are current terms – and space is more and more organized according to a complex value-and-function hierarchy. However, contradictions and territorial imbalances tend to increase: the present economic and social crisis makes them essential factors within the unavoidable dialectic between the needs of further development of the productive forces on one side, and capitalistic production relationships on the other.

MONOPOLISTIC ACCUMULATION AND TERRITORIAL TYPOLOGIES: THE INDUSTRIAL AREAS

In advanced capitalism, the accumulation process is dominated by the big industrial concentrations, which – more or less directly – control a large share of the market, and of society, on an international scale. Multinational oligopolies condition and determine the whole accumulation process precisely because competitive capital circulation is blocked by a growing stratification of a firm's financial and development possibilities.

At a certain stage of the development of capitalism it becomes almost impossible for small independent capital to enter the key sectors of the economy, where large, very concentrated capital makes considerable super-profits. This stratification is made even more rigid by the considerable integration between banking and financial systems and industrial enterprises. The multinational oligopolies are simultaneously powerful concentrations of industrial capital and financial holding companies with interests in large banks and in almost all the profitable industrial sectors.

At the same time, one can observe the increasing importance of the direct and indirect intervention of the state in the management of the capitalist economy, whether as a substitute for certain market mechanisms which no longer function (the safeguarding of low-profit sectors and the re-balancing of profit levels), or because its support has become essential for the expansion of accumulation at home (expansion of services) and abroad (the acquisition and maintenance of markets).

Moreover, state intervention in contemporary capitalist economies is largely a concentration factor. Firstly because the great corporations, having tremendous national or multinational economic power, have a much better chance of getting privileges and aid from the state (also working in their favour is pressure from the trade unions to gain better conditions for workers employed in the large corporations, from state welfare or economic intervention). Secondly, national or regional capital cities, as the concentrated headquarters of state bureaucracies and power elites, are further valorized by state intervention in the economy (concentration of private agencies and offices in connection with economic activities).[3]

Finally the productive structure and the occupational structure of late capitalism is very widely articulated and differentiated as a consequence of technological disparity, of different capital intensity, and of the rigid non-communicative organization of both capital and labour markets. While some large corporations are able to re-organize at least part of their production under a very modern and labour-saving technology, other corporations are obliged to slow down technological progress to avoid the danger of increasing unemployment too much, and the risk of social riots. At the same time there is a generalized and new re-development of the informal economy. Dependent or independent industrial units, sometimes offshoots of decentralization of concentrated corporate manufacturing production and at other times more spontaneous re-organization of traditional economic sectors, spread across the industrial peripheries. They make use of black market, irregular, underpaid labour, easily recruited when the unemployed population grows, due to the decrease of industrial jobs because of the new labour-saving technologies. This neo-dualism, also a product of the tertiarization process and the growth of the unemployed or under-employed urban population, strongly modifies the class structure of advanced capitalist countries by markedly differentiating the composition of the working class on one side and of the capitalist class on the other.[4] The working class is more and more disunited because the working and living conditions of its various strata are more and more differentiated: from the trade-unionized, highly paid blue-collar worker, employed permanently in a large corporation, or the white-collar worker, regularly employed by the state, the large banks and insurance companies, down to the unskilled day-labourer irregularly employed in small building industries, the female home-workers, semi-employed by small textile units, the retired person, working part-time and irregularly to supplement a very low pension, and so on.

A second very important characteristic of the accumulation of capital in the monopolistic phase is the difficulty of maintaining a high and increasing rate of profit, due to the progressive exhaustion of reserve areas for the penetration of capitalism. Rapid development, chiefly in the twenty years after the war, has brought about progressive integration into the capitalist markets of partially involved areas and, as a parallel, the indiscriminate increase of exploitation of available resources with ever greater intensity. The consequence has necessarily been the diminution of the development rate, the rebellion of a number of Third World countries subjected to unrestrained exploitation, and the continuous increase of competition between the various advanced capitalist economies. Moreover, in the monopolistic phase, competition between industrial powers no longer gives rise to increases in the productivity of labour and the diminution of production costs, but, rather, to a continuous battle to obtain the greatest possible measure of control of markets by means of instruments independent of the price and production costs of the goods (e.g. the granting of political protection by the world powers to authoritarian regimes, the supply of arms for wars against their neighbours, the destructive effects of such wars serving to open up new productive areas for the oligopolies, the cornering of certain agricultural products, the sale of which on the market is more remunerative but risky and exposed to price fluctuations, etc.).

The characteristics of accumulation in the monopolistic phases which have been briefly outlined,[5] are reflected in the territorial situation and in the processes of re-organization of territory. The metropolitan areas of the advanced countries continue to be advantaged as regards the processes of economic growth, above all in terms of strong market economies and better service infrastructures, but they are too congested for the continued installation of industrial enterprises. They are therefore the scene of a process of substitution in the context of a very costly industrial and economic re-organization. The tendency is to decentralize heavy industry and also some light industrial processes to peripheral areas and to replace them, in the cities, with research, management and service-industry installations and, in the urban region, with new residential installations and light industrial productive processes of a more advanced technological level or sensitive to the urban market economy. Naturally this re-organization of territory takes place in extremely contradictory conditions, both from the economic and from the social and political point of view.

The historic centres of the great conurbations tend to become the privileged location of management and service-industry installations. Large urban areas, with considerable infrastructures, are occupied during the day by millions of office and service-industry workers, in the evening by the users of leisure-time services, and at night are almost completely uninhabited. The peripheral part of the regional conurbation is divided into industrial areas and residential areas. Both types of suburban installation are closely controlled from the historic centre. The human and economic costs of administering a regional conurbation increase progressively to the point of becoming prohibitive, but advanced capitalism is unable to do without this type of territorial organization, which is the only one compatible with a very concentrated and centralized capitalistic structure. The fiscal crisis of the large US cities, the continuous increase in commuting distances, the increasing difficulty encountered in controlling the ecological situation of metropolitan areas are the most conspicuous effects of these contradictions. One of the gravest phenomena, to which reference will be made repeatedly in the pages that follow, is the rigidity of the market and labour organization created in the metropolitan areas. A part of the labour-force is continually made redundant, above all by labour-saving investments, which would in fact be useful in other zones, while there is always a demand for new workers, who cannot be brought in from outside owing to the excessively high costs of installation.

The most important change in modern societies is the very differentiated and articulated urban class structure. Both the bourgeoisie and the proletariat are by and large composed of very different strata with different interests. Factory conflict is largely the same, although modified by the new productive organization based on sophisticated labour-saving technologies, by the partial reproduction of the mass assembly-line plants, and by the decentralization and dispersal of production processes in small independent irregular units. Social conflict, however, is becoming more and more important and differentiated. These changes in class structure, in the first instance, cause problems chiefly in the great concentrated metropolitan areas, where all sorts of social groups and cultures are present in some form.[6]

Urban-industrial peripheral areas can be divided schematically into three classes: areas in which specialized industries have long been installed; areas of decentralization of unconcentrated and marginal industry; areas of decentralization of heavy industry and of some partial productive processes of key industrial sectors, in particular the mechanical, electrical and electronic sectors. The first are largely in marked economic and demographic decline, above all when they are not under the direct control of the regional metropolitan area or have not been absorbed by it. In fact these are towns characterized by industrial production based on intermediate-technology. They are susceptible to competition from two quarters, from the emerging industries of the Third World, which benefit from relatively lower labour costs, and from the central industries, which have a much higher degree of capitalistic concentration and productive efficiency. Their only means of survival is by economic rationalization which, on the one hand, places them increasingly under the control of the sources of finance needed for this purpose – the large holding-companies and banks in the metropolitan area – and, on the other, requires a progressive diminution of the labour force (for purposes of labour-saving).

In some cases these areas may regress to a state of marked neo-dualism, shifting to the use of irregular labour, black-market labour, decentralized and home production, thus forming an intermediate class between the first and the second classes. In these cases the economies of the old industrial towns become progressively more integrated into the redevelopment of the informal economy. They end by suffering the same problems (dependence, economic precariousness, marginality) as every other informal industrial sector. The most common examples in Europe of intermediate-technology, mono-industrial towns are the old textile towns.

Industrial areas based on small and medium-sized marginal units and irregular labour are typical of certain forms of neo-dualistic productive re-organization[7] which serve under advanced capitalism as a contingent solution to the economic crisis. In these installations, capital attempts to bring labour costs much lower than the national average and to implement forms of labour exploitation different from those of large factories, while seeking to maintain labour productivity at a sufficiently high level. The advantageousness of this organization of production is founded on a wide-ranging combination of low labour costs: lower wages, less politicized and trade-unionized workers, longer working hours, a more amenable work-force, much higher labour mobility and consequent organization flexibility, the possibility of completely avoiding high insurance and pension charges, etc. Thus, labour costs are lower than those of stable workers in the large industrial complexes, whilst productivity is greater than can be achieved in the Third World countries. The balance between these two factors is likely to survive for only a limited time, for a more advanced productive organization in the Third World or further technological developments in the large factories will eventually render the neo-dualistic industrial installations non-competitive. They are unable either to utilize different technologies, thereby increasing labour productivity, or to reduce the cost of labour further, and thus a crisis is inevitable. An industrial organization of this type may occur in semi-urbanized areas (medium-sized towns) where agricultural activities are still important, possibly in association with a widespread survival of urban and rural handicrafts. In fact in these circumstances there is a considerable supply of irregular labour, moonlighting, part-time agricultural and industrial work, and home-work.

Entire regions of industrialized countries can become involved in a logic of industrialization of this type, subject to a precarious accumulation very often dependent on the interests of the large multinational groups, which, for market reasons or for reasons of financial dominion, appropriate a part of the profits made by the small and medium-sized, decentralized firms. Moreover, in neo-dualistic development regions a very ambiguous relationship is established between industry and agriculture and between town and country; the workers work in both sectors without managing to produce a high income in either, and therefore they are under-employed and underproductive. The crisis of the industrial and agricultural sectors remains latent but tends to become more accentuated. This type of regional articulation of industrial development increases the dependence of the peripheral areas on the central areas and thus gives rise to social tensions which are greater in cases where the populations of the peripheral regions lay claim to a historical and cultural independence of the centre (Scotland, Brittany, the Basque provinces, Friuli, etc.).

The third type of dependent industrial installation is constituted by decentralization of heavy industry or of partial productive processes of oligopolistic industry. The decentralization of the large petro-chemical, steel and mechanical engineering plants fulfils a very important requirement for the expansion and reproduction of advanced capitalism, the need to produce semi-finished goods at decreasing cost. Modern steel and chemical plants occupy large areas, pollute very large regions with slag, semi-toxic fumes and residual liquids, consume enormous quantities of water and energy resources, and require large, private, industrial ports. On the other hand, installations of this type are of very high capital intensity and have a secure place in a logic of the market: they thus do not need a large number of workers in relation to the capital invested or their location in strong market economies. Further they do not give rise to important secondary industrial growth. They can thus be advantageously located at low cost in semi-deserted coastal areas and in underdeveloped regions where there is flat land and available water and energy resources. In view of their very large size, it is advisable for them to be located in the vicinity of a commercial town in order that a new urban centre need not be created. Naturally their degree of interference with the local economy is on the whole fairly low and is mediated by the socio-political structure of the local community.

The decentralization of heavy industry took place on a very considerable scale in the 1960s. In the long-industrialized metropolitan areas, it led to a process of industrial substitution, which, as I have already pointed out, served to avoid an excessively violent crisis of congestion, whilst in underdeveloped areas, it gave rise to a process of dependent industrialization with new characteristics. In some countries this has been demagogically presented as a strategy of development based on various versions of the so-called theory of 'poles of growth'.[8] In reality the decentralization of heavy industry, far from constituting a development strategy, does not even bring about a comprehensive process of industrialization. It is dependent on an external accumulative logic, is extremely partial and gives rise to little secondary growth. It contributes to the devastation of the social and economic structure of the region of installation and to the accentuation of territorial imbalances, increasing the dependence of underdeveloped areas on the large industrial metropoles. Furthermore, industrialization on the basis of poles of growth has no prospect of growth in the medium and long term. In fact the heavy industrial installations find natural limits to continued expansion, and lack flexibility in processes of reconversion or productive restructuring. Further growth requirements of heavy industry must thus be satisfied by means of new installations with different characteristics, which today tend to be located in the countries of the Third World, rich in raw materials, where the demand for industrialization is accompanied by the offer of the financial resources needed to carry it out. But this hypothesis has not yet been fully realized because the recession of the 1970s has placed the heavy industry of the world in a condition of overproduction, which has further weakened the position of the poles of growth that have been established.

ACCUMULATION AND TYPOLOGIES OF UNDERDEVELOPMENT

The non-industrialized or little industrialized peripheral areas undergo, in a complex and differentiated manner, processes of underdevelopment induced by the increasing integration of the world capitalist market. The result is a continuous increase of the relative imbalance between the central areas and the peripheral areas and also a considerable differentiation within the social and economic fabric of the peripheral areas. One should speak first of the great urban areas of the Third World. As administrative and commercial areas, and thus the location of import-export companies, they are the bridgeheads of the penetration of capitalism into the rural periphery of underdeveloped regions.[9] The considerable and progressive urban growth, due in the first place to migrations of increasing numbers of the rural surplus population, and also to increases of population (in some Asiatic countries the second factor is preponderant),[10] is accompanied by only a small and dependent growth of the industrial sector. There is thus a process of urbanization without industrialization and a conversion of rural overpopulation into urban overpopulation. The parasitic development of the service-industry sector, marginal industry and some processes of productive decentralization do not succeed even partially in solving the unemployment problem, which reflects a disastrous social and economic situation. On the other hand, the increase of urban unemployment does not discourage the processes of urbanization, which are the result of the capitalistic penetration of the countryside. The greater the overpopulation of the administrative and commercial metropolis, the greater the penetration of foreign capital in the country and the subordinate integration of the national and regional market in the world market, the greater the increase of urban unemployment, and the larger the migratory flow from the country to the town. The case of Mexico City can be considered emblematic in this sense.[11]

The processes of dependent industrialization that take place in the urban areas of the Third World and in underdeveloped regions are completely complementary to the increase of demographic and territorial imbalances. In fact they induce urbanization in a much greater measure than they increase industrial employment and they destroy the productive capacity of the rural areas to a much greater extent than they develop that of the town.

Rural areas and underdeveloped peripheries are not all affected by the process of monopolistic accumulation in the same way or measure. It is necessary to distinguish between areas of extensive agriculture, generally plantations, and areas of intensive agriculture, in general characterized by direct cultivation by small peasant units, and between fertile areas close to markets and infertile areas far from markets. All the rural and peripheral areas are characterized by considerable and increasing emigration of the peasants, which, in some cases (in infertile zones) amounts to veritable desertion and, in others, gives rise to a considerable increase of dependence on the capitalistic market, and thus to a very rapid development of rural poverty. The increases of productivity achieved in the rural areas, whether in consequence of productive innovations and rationalization of cultivation (mostly the case in plantation economies) or of the diminution of rural overpopulation (principally the case in small farmer economies) are absorbed by continuous deterioration of the terms of exchange between the agriculture of the peripheral areas and the industry of the central areas. In fact urbanization and the penetration of capitalism into the countryside increasingly expose the rural producers to international competition, thus obliging them to sell their produce outside the local markets and to buy the means of production and essential industrial commodities produced by multinational monopolistic industry. Dependence and impoverishment are all the greater to the degree that the agricultural production is of one type or little differentiated, which makes the farmer completely dependent on the fluctuations of world prices.[12] Prices are always fixed according to the requirements of the large monopolistic groups by means of the all-important import/export companies.

Poverty and dependence are relatively greater in rural areas, where the peasants are unable to achieve a sufficient increase of productivity, whether this is because they lack the financial means to make rationalizing investments or because the countryside, despite emigration, remains overpopulated.

The vicious circle of rural poverty is thus not interrupted by monopolistic accumulation but is increased by it. The logic of integration of markets tends to increase the dependence of the rural areas of the Third World on the control of the metropolitan areas. At the same time the desertion of some areas and the process of rationalization of agriculture in others weakens the productive structure of the rural areas of underdeveloped countries. Artisan production and self-sufficiency disappear. The local markets are increasingly subordinated to the logic of the great multinational oligopolies. Neither persistent rural overpopulation nor the growing urban overpopulation finds an adequate productive outlet. In fact in peasant areas necessary rationalization and the purchase of mechanical means and technology, which are always relatively backward, result in less employment for the peasants on their own land. In effect the increase of territorial imbalance is an obvious internal consequence of mechanisms of accumulation which always lead to increases in the total volume of profits made by the large multinational companies and which leave no room for independent processes of decentralized industrialization. Above all, the accumulative cycle continues to multiply and thus is increasingly to the disadvantage of the underdeveloped regions. This is also a result of the increase of urban overpopulation which favours the processes of dependent industrial decentralization, subordinating the markets of the underdeveloped areas and favouring the exploitation of labour by the multinational groups. Major processes of accumulation on the part of the large multinational companies are in fact based on the penetration of the markets of the Third World and on industrial decentralization carried out in underdeveloped urban areas.

OVER-URBANIZATION AND THE UNDERDEVELOPMENT CYCLE

In order to achieve a clearer picture of urbanization and the effects of the present capitalist crisis on the underdeveloped areas, I shall try to synthesize the typical economic cycle characterizing such areas and its territorial patterns.

The three Figures 3.1, 3.2, and 3.3, contribute to the description of the major phenomena characterizing current underdevelopment and its most important territorial patterns. Naturally the specific situations of particular underdeveloped areas are very complex and varied and cannot be included in these figures, nor in this brief piece. However, the underdevelopment cycle can be plotted along general lines, avoiding specific references.

The agricultural and raw materials surplus produced in the underdeveloped regions cannot be accumulated for industrial development within such a region because it has to be used to buy industrial goods and technologies from the more advanced capitalist countries and areas. The very need to increase productivity in agriculture and raw materials production and the exposure to the world market (where the area is not competitive in the production of industrial technologies and goods) forces the area into an underdevelopment and dependence cycle. This process produces overpopulation, either in the countryside or in the city or both. In the majority of recent cases, governments, scared by the danger of a too large urban overpopulation, have tried to slow down rural emigration through an assisted redistribution of resources and through the financial help sent by emigrant workers. Nevertheless the cities represent a growing part of the surplus population which, once urbanized, cannot find a job in the productive sectors. The great difference between the present situation in the underdeveloped areas and the one that obtained in nineteenth-century Europe is that the current urbanized surplus population cannot become an industrial reserve army for a local industrialization process, which will never take place under present conditions, and which in any case offers far fewer jobs, due to the very high average productivity of labour. The ex-peasants find in the cities only difficult ways to survive, through irregular jobs in various kinds of low-income tertiary activities and, to a much lesser extent manufacturing or craft work. In this sense there is a continuous development of urban over-tertiarization, which sooner or later also requires state intervention to assist the poor and contribute to the reproduction of at least a part of the urban population. The only industrial sector able to survive or to grow is a form of very backward craftwork, connected with tourism and the export of handmade objects, and established on the very low cost of the labour-force and on irregular and part-time occupation. In some cases also the building industry absorbs part of the urban overpopulation, though at very low income rates and in irregular jobs, without contributing very much to the long-term solution of the problem of unemployment or to the permanent lack of decent housing for new migrants.

In some countries (Latin America and part of Africa and Asia) the migration flows become concentrated in one or in a few principal cities, the capitals and great ports or commercial centres, which become monstrous conurbations with many million inhabitants, very large slums and diffused urban poverty. In other countries (India) over-urbanization is distributed over a large number of cities, all of which have problems of urban poverty, slums, low productivity, over-tertiarization, etc.

This situation (underdevelopment without any form of decentralized industrialization) is described in Figure 3.1. Some additional explanations are necessary to understand properly the meaning of the various arrows. Foreign exchange is largely unequal both in its terms and in its final effects. For the industrialized countries the possibility of buying agricultural and mineral raw materials from the Third World, and of selling them technologies and industrial goods is one of the principal vehicles for further accumulation, while for the underdeveloped countries this exchange has the very opposite effect, that is to say it prevents any possibility of a local autonomous industrial take-off. For this same reason, in the underdeveloped areas it is very difficult to increase occupation in the productive sectors. The arrow labelled services expresses the demand from the rural areas for services from urban production, and the effective supply of the latter. The relation between the two has great importance in determining the quality of the services, their efficiency and their productive organization. The external (rural) or internal (urban) demand for urban services increases at a much lower rate than the occupational growth determined by the pressure of urban surplus population. This fact produces a deep and permanent distortion in the organization of the tertiary sector. Also, for political reasons, tertiary sector occupation becomes the instrument of controlling the growing urban surplus

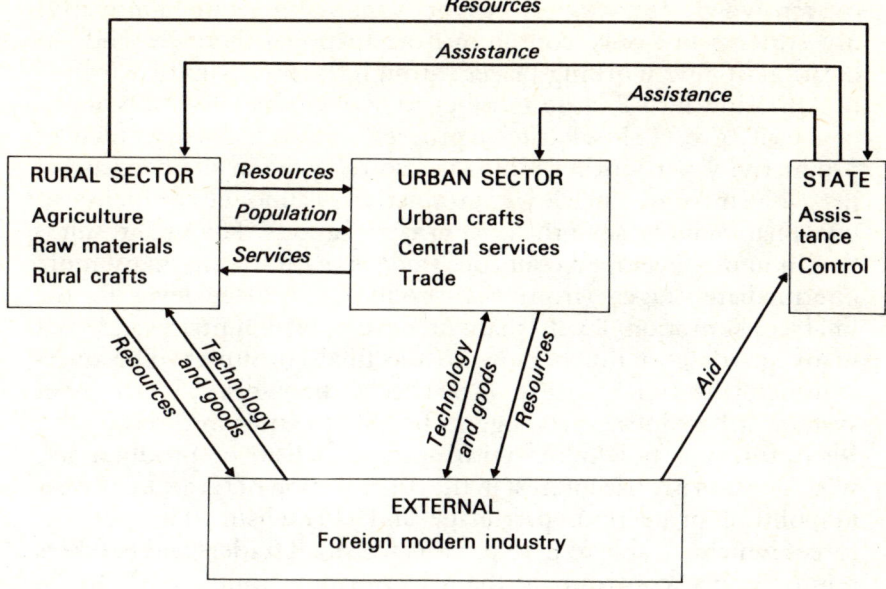

FIGURE 3.1 Over-urbanization and underdevelopment without any dependent industrialization.

population through clientelism and selective job distribution. Pressure from the over-supply of labour, the political manipulation of employment, and the slower increase of demand in relation to supply condemn the tertiary sector of these areas to become the only economic activity whose productivity is regressive (that is to say the more occupation increases the less services are produced by any one worker).[13] This typical phenomenon of urban underdeveloped economies is determined by three factors: a continuous increase in the labour supply which can find only a partial outlet in the tertiary sector; an almost total lack of the financial resources necessary to organize service production at increasing or stable productivity rates; too slow an increase in the rural masses' and the new urbanized population's capacity to buy additional services.

A short general example better explains such phenomena. In this process of over-tertiarization at decreasing productivity the most vulnerable sector is small trade. When urban unemployment increases beyond a certain point, many workers are forced to become small shopkeepers, hawkers, irregular or part-time shop clerks, occasional commercial dealers, and so on. The only resource they put into such low income jobs is their labour. The already overcrowded commercial sector cannot generate innovative investments but only continuous occupational increases and the creation of new working places through the break-up of working organization into a large number of workshops. As the volume of activity grows slowly such a process leads to a sharp decrease of productivity per worker which is also reflected in the decrease of per capita income, since lower productivity cannot be compensated by a relative increase in the final prices of goods. The final result is that in underdeveloped countries trade is organized in many more intermediate stages (from the producer-importer level to the final consumption level) than in developed countries and that many goods cost much more to the final consumer. The overcommercialization process also affects the worker-recruitment system: it becomes a privilege to be able to enter into these jobs. Recruitment is not linked with professionalism or productivity, which results in little interest in the organization of trade, but rather in political protection, patronage and clientelism. The political forces which are able to give permits for small traders and hawkers reinforce their control over the urban surplus population. On the other hand the decreasing productivity of the sector obliges the state and the local authorities to make parallel increases in their supportive intervention to contribute to the reproduction of the urban marginal population.

This cycle, from urban surplus population to over-tertiarization to the necessity of increases in assistance to the urban poor, is an important aspect of the crisis of underdeveloped societies, where increases in the national debt and the inflation rate are unable to contain the continuous growth of urban poverty, social instability, unemployment and the reproduction of economic weaknesses.

Figures 3.2 and 3.3 visualize underdevelopment situations where the different forms of dependent industrialization are present, which is increasingly the case in the current situation. Figure 3.2 hypothesizes that beside the traditional rural and urban economies which characterize Figure 3.1, some large decentralized plants are located in the underdeveloped region or country, dependent upon multinational corporations. They are usually capital intensive petrochemical or steel plants, or in some cases intermediate technology engineering or chemical plants. They are decentralized in the underdeveloped regions to enjoy lower location costs and lower labour costs whilst achieving at the same time a partial decongestion of the industrially developed concentrations. They occupy very large spaces and are dangerous from the ecological point of view. One might even say that, in many of its aspects, this decen-

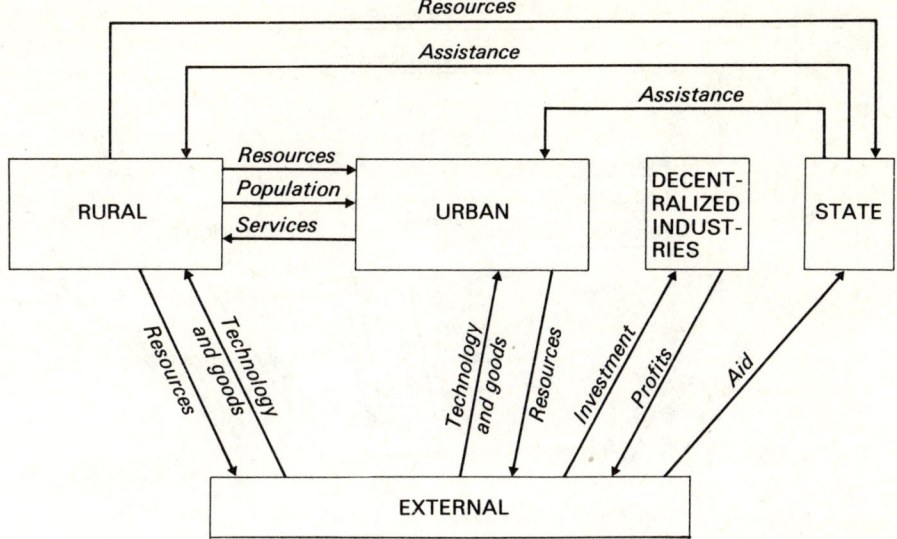

FIGURE 3.2 Over-urbanization and underdevelopment with the addition of large decentralized industries dependent on multinational corporations.

tralization process is even more conducive to underdevelopment than the traditional cycle described above. The capital intensive plants consume a large part of the local resources to the detriment of autonomous development and to the advantage of profits accumulated abroad, while they do not create enough jobs to even partially solve the urban surplus population problem. The only positive aspect of industrial decentralization is the formation in the underdeveloped area of a local, modern working class, quantitatively rather limited but politically important. Another possible positive aspect is the location in these regions of technologically advanced machinery which may afterwards be expropriated by the local government. The main point remains that under this model also, urban surplus population cannot be employed in a development process and grows to become a dramatic social problem. Moreover the decentralized industrial plants always produce only intermediate goods (petro-chemical or steel) or are strongly dependent on the products of the metropolitan, technologically more advanced, industrial centre (engineering and intermediate chemical). So they are insufficient to provide the industrial goods required by the local market and they depend upon an external productive cycle and on external technological research.

142 *Uneven Territorial Development*

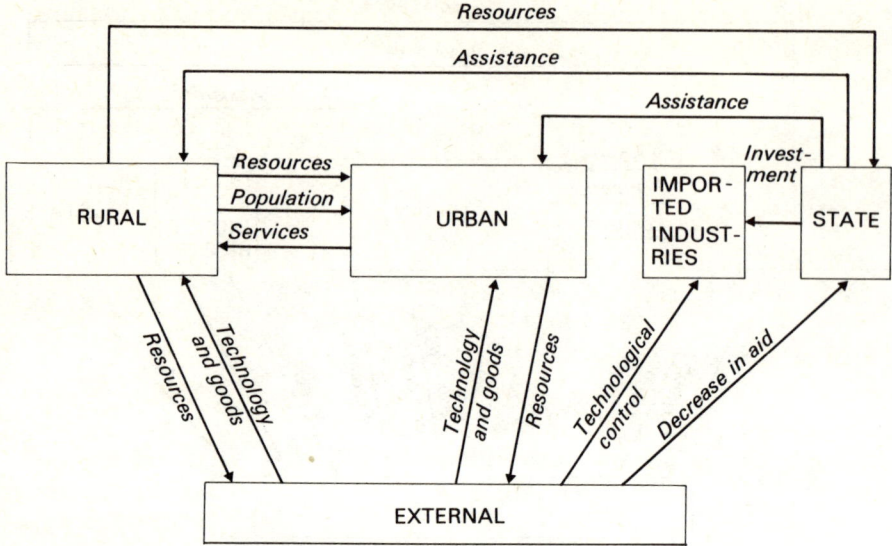

FIGURE 3.3 Over-urbanization and underdevelopment where the state imports whole processes or industries from abroad.

Figure 3.3 illustrates the case of countries which, through the export of large quantities of valuable raw materials (mainly oil), accumulate financial capacities and invest part of this in the purchase from the technologically more advanced countries, of whole plants and productive processes, so as to promote some sort of a partial industrialization process. These cases are more complicated and at the same time very interesting. Independent of whether such countries are connected with the capitalist area or with the self-styled 'socialist' states, imports of industrial productive apparatus do not definitively solve the problem of underdevelopment: they are unable to break the dependence and unequal exchange cycle for several reasons.

(1) Economic dependence is changed into technological dependence, which from the point of view of social development is just as bad. The importing country remains unable to operate the imported technology and is even less able to update it. Technological progress introduces new difficulties as the importing country has to buy innovations at a monopolistic price or become less and less competitive.

(2) The import of productive processes and plants can only break dependence in a limited number of industrial sectors, as no under-

developed country is able to build up a complete industrial system from nothing to compare with that achieved in the industrialized countries over many decades.

(3) The import of technologically advanced industrial plants cannot solve the surplus population problem. Such industries are too capital intensive to employ the number of workers that the very large and growing urban surplus population would require. Moreover the importing country is obliged to undergo a very fast modernization process which often means a sharp increase in its direct dependence and a violent wave of social and cultural conflicts (the case of Iran is rather instructive).

(4) Often this kind of operation involves also the development of local hegemonic and imperialistic tendencies on the part of the industrializing country. The industrializing country tries to impose its control on the surrounding area so that it can buy additional raw materials at cheap prices and sell a part of its specialized industrial production to its neighbours through typical sub-imperialistic strategies. Again the case of Iran under the Shah's rule is a good example. This tendency makes the already severe competition among imperialists, sub-imperialists and underdeveloped countries even more complex and difficult.

(5) This kind of industrialization process accelerates the diffusion of consumption models, which makes the developing country even more dependent upon foreign imports than it was before. Paradoxically the industrialization process establishes an economic cycle through which the more the country imports (irrespective of whether it also imports plants able to produce some final industrial goods) the more it is obliged to import subsequently.

(6) As the countries exporting advanced technologies maintain an almost complete monopolistic control over the market, they impose very high prices and very rigid conditions, which tend to be unfavourable to the importing country, because they cannot be adapted to local conditions. For example, the underpopulated Arab countries have been obliged to buy productive processes and plants inclusive of their industrial workers, so that the immigration of Far Eastern workers has strongly modified the social and demographic balances of many of the Gulf States (Kuwait, the Emirates, Qatar and even Saudi Arabia). For all these reasons, every underdeveloped region, even the less populated, are struck by over-urbanization and over-tertiarization processes, which have contributed significantly to the present situation of economic, social and political crisis.

Dependent industrialization is not only unable to solve the problem of uneven economic development but actually magnifies its disadvantages: on the one hand, it increases the dependence of peripheral regions upon the central ones and, on the other hand, it increases international competition and tendencies to overproduction. The international division of labour is altered in a critical way. The decentralized factories and the factories imported into the underdeveloped regions become competitive with the producers in industrialized countries during periods of reduced growth rate. This new phase of severe competitiveness has modified international relations in favour of a few industrialized countries. These are mainly West Germany and Japan, which enjoy particularly favourable conditions, such as the possibility of reducing industrial occupation at the expense of foreign workers and/or higher investment rates, relatively lower labour costs per unit of production, and so on. At the same time it has increased the crisis and instability of all other countries, which, for one reason or another, are unable to remain competitive with the leading economies.[14]

From the social stratification and social conflict point of view, practically every underdeveloped country is facing widespread changes, different from those associated with the traditional industrialization process. The surplus population moves from the countryside into the cities, but only a very small section becomes an industrial working class. The industrial workers are relatively privileged by their higher income and their working stability in comparison with the rest of the urban, non-bourgeois population. Various strata of under-employed or unemployed urban workers have differentiated interests and tensions, from the hawkers and small shopkeepers to the workers irregularly employed on the building sites and in small local manufacturing and craft industries. In such a situation conflict occurs more often but is more and more dispersed and disunited and decreasingly resembles the traditional class struggle.[15]

THE CRISIS OF CAPITALISM AND TERRITORIAL CONTRADICTIONS

The world recession of the 1970s has been interpreted in various ways.[16] This is not the place to discuss its origins or its prospects but, rather, its effects on the territorial situation and the contribution of territorial imbalances to the crisis itself. The phenomenology of economic recession and the subsequent and persistent period of stagnation can be summarized as follows. The exhaustion of the reserve expansion areas which permitted the post-war boom (penetration of capitalism into the rural areas of central-southern Europe and their integration in the markets of the industrialized countries; the considerable increase in exploitation of the Third World and the opening of enormous new markets in Asia and Africa) tended to reduce the rate of accumulation and the profitability of investment. This led to an increase of inter-capitalistic competition, the subjection of companies to a process of selection, and the failure of the less competitive economic sectors. The recession aggravated the unemployment crisis, which had begun some years previously as a consequence of the introduction of labour-saving processes in agriculture and throughout the industrial sectors. But this increase in unemployment was not accompanied by an adequate reduction in the cost of labour, as it had been in the cyclical recessions of the past. In fact, the division of the labour market[17] and the strength of the trade unions enabled workers in large companies to defend the real value of their wages and to claim increases proportional, if not more than proportional, to increases in productivity. At the same time, in consequence of the employment and social crisis and the parallel danger of an increasing tendency towards overproduction, the unproductive and welfare expenditures of central and local government increased. This factor further increased the tendency towards under-accumulation. The result is a persistent stagnation interrupted by brief periods of slight and partial economic recovery and accompanied by strong waves of inflation and by continuous and irreversible increases in unemployment.

The territorial situation plays a very important contradictory role in the dynamics of production costs and the relationships of labour-markets. In fact both the economic congestion and the territorial dualism of the labour markets are important elements of friction in relation to the need for further expansion of the capitalist economy. In its turn the economic crisis has an unfavourable effect on the situation of territorial imbalance because it affects the developed central areas and the backward peripheral areas differently.

In general, capitalism tries to apply a strategy of sectorialization of the consequences of crisis so that it becomes possible to remain in control of a situation where the living and working standards of the population are worsening. The most dramatic contradictions are pushed towards the various kinds of peripheral areas. The informal economy is developed to provisionally compensate for the severe cut-back in employment in the formal economy. Opposition interests are divided and scattered into various partial and non-simultaneous conflicts. This phenomenon is associated with the new social stratification already outlined.

This progressive social disgregation is very important from the territorial point of view and is in part a consequence of two opposing tendencies of late capitalism: the tendency to increase concentration and social control and the tendency to decentralize productive activities as much as possible for the decongestion of the decision-making centres. Social disgregation develops into a situation full of contradictions but generally still under the control of the capitalist hegemony in the medium and short terms. The class struggle and the working class by and large, suffers widespread disorganization and disunification, which weakens its central force (the only one able to attack the capitalist hegemony) and further disrupts its peripheral forces. The most important example is the difficulty met by trade unions and working class parties, which traditionally represent the workers employed in the large factories of the formal economy, in organizing the struggles and the interests of the under-employed or unemployed population of the peripheral or underdeveloped regions. Examples of this are the revival of autonomistic local and regional movements outside the traditional working class organization or the corporative re-organization of the trade union movement in various European countries.[18]

Territorial concentration is above all a phenomenon associated with inflation and the increase of production costs. I have already mentioned the fact that in advanced capitalism the domination of large oligopolistic industrial-financial groups not only accentuates territorial concentration to the point of notable levels of congestion but leads to the need for very expensive forms of industrial decentralization, with the removal of some installations of heavy industry out of the old industrialized areas and a re-organization of the use of territory into functional modules of territorial division of labour.

The need to proceed with restructuring is in itself very expensive because it necessitates continual destruction and a lot of waste. Industrial investment thus becomes an increasing burden, but market economies for certain productive activities and the need to maintain a centralized direction continue to impose concentration in the large metropolitan areas. Furthermore, the processes of functional re-organization of territory (above all the transfer of the service industries to the historic centres) are encountering increasing resistance from the inhabitants, who must be expelled from the area to allow the re-conversion to take place. In many cases this resistance masks an economic conflict between the needs of concentrated capital and those of certain social sectors which make a living from unconcentrated commercial and artisan activities, a conflict which is growing more serious in view of the employment crisis and the prospects of territorial restructuring leading to considerable increases of unemployment.

The high degree of concentration of advanced capitalism plays a markedly contradictory role in such periods of crisis. Economic recovery is subordinated to a large-scale territorial reconversion to provide new spaces for productive concentration, but this is incompatible with the low level of investments and the scarcity of available resources. The territorial imbalance thus ends up by increasing inflation and diminishing the accumulation rate. The few investments that do find space, in an anarchic manner, contribute to the increase of congestion and ecological devastation, and thus also of the social costs of production. Local government is faced by enormous and progressive increases in the costs of administering an increasingly congested territory, and are thus faced by an increasingly grave fiscal crisis.[19]

As far as the labour market is concerned, advanced capitalism tends to make the employment structure more rigid and to increase regional differences, which play an important contradictory role in the crisis. Relative surplus population, whether urban or rural, is prevalently confined to the peripheral and underdeveloped areas. In the industrial regions residential congestion and the considerable selective processes applied to applicants for industrial work (which discriminate against young people, illiterates, possessors of advanced academic qualifications, women and elderly men) reduce the reserves of 'strong labour' to the minimum and thus reinforce the bargaining position of the labour force. The crisis accentuates the imbalance in the regional distribution of labour reserves. The fundamental problem is that there is an enormous increase of unemployment and under-employment in the backward and peripheral regions, while all the various policies only succeed in creating some labour demand, always insufficient, in the more industrialized areas. This phenomenon is fairly obvious when one considers that such policies can be based at most on a better utilization of existing plants and/or on a diminution of the working hours of the employed in order to increase their number. They are efficacious, therefore, only in those areas where industrial employment is concentrated and where large and efficient plants are located. Moreover, even in these areas the additional labour demand is for a very particular classification of worker (manual, male, literate and without higher education, in other words what has been termed the 'strong' component of the labour market), who is not always available in the area. Since the possibility of the resumption of the migratory flow is excluded, impeded by a concentration which is beyond the possibility of re-conversion and re-organization of the territory, the employment crisis is destined to reproduce itself and to expand on a differentiated regional scale.

The high level of unemployment permits the development of forms of decentralization based on irregular and super-exploited labour and a continuous increase of parasitic employment in the non-productive sectors, which result in the peripheral regions becoming even more dependent on the industrial and political centres. The crisis therefore increases the tendency towards revolt and social conflict in the peripheral regions, where a relatively greater impoverishment and a higher rate of unemployment is registered. The recent resumption of independence movements in many peripheral regions of western Europe (the Basque provinces, Wales, Scotland, Corsica, Sardinia, etc.) should be viewed in this light.

Finally, economic crisis reduces the capacity of governments to make welfare interventions in the underdeveloped areas at the very moment when peripheral and marginal poverty is reaching the limits of toleration. Reductions in government expenditure tend to sacrifice welfare programmes which, even in better times, were the only way of assuring integration and consensus in the underdeveloped areas. The need to reduce public employment discriminates above all against the marginal and peripheral areas which are already the hardest hit by the crisis. In fact, increases of employment in the public service area and further forms of individual welfare assistance (invalid and old-age pensions, unemployment subsidies), served in the past to attenuate the most devastating effects of unemployment, even when they were not strictly necessary from an economic point of view, and could thus be described as parasitic.

UNEVEN DEVELOPMENT WITHIN THE ITALIAN ECONOMIC STRUCTURE

Italy is an industrialized country with a marked, mono-industrial (mechanical engineering), specialized, concentrated economy, which renders it particularly exposed to the vicissitudes of the international market and dependent on general economic cycles and on the policies of the great monopolistic groups. Italian economic expansion has been based mainly on the export of intermediate-technology industrial goods and on the imports of practically all raw materials and the more advanced, control technologies. The expansion crisis of world capitalism struck Italy in a particularly severe way for many reasons. She cannot afford to reduce industrial employment (as Germany has done) because of the already high unemployment rate, further increased by the return of migrants from abroad. At the same time the reduced international competitiveness of Italian industrial production and the decrease in international economic growth cannot be met at a time of economic crisis with a parallel expansion of internal markets in a country so unevenly developed. Moreover the decrease of external resources to sponsor tertiarization and assistance to the depressed regions comes at the same time as an increasing need for such resources. On the other hand the workers employed in large industries are able to resist attacks on their real wages because they are powerfully trade-unionized and no longer competitive with the unemployed (this fact is also due to uneven regional development which has concentrated the employed in a very restricted area to which the unemployed can no longer be moved). The origins of such contradictions are to be found in the specific Italian model of development.[20]

Industrialization has occurred in Italy in a very limited part of the country and in accordance with principles of considerable territorial concentration. At the end of the Second World War, eighty percent of the country had no modern industrial installation, but only agriculture, traditional rural artisan units which had survived and the odd heavy industrial installation, usually hampered by a very low technological level. The absence of industrialization characterized not only the underdeveloped area of the south but also nearly the whole of central and north-eastern Italy and the mountainous and piedmont zones of north-western Italy.

Post-war reconstruction and the economic miracle of the 1960s further increased territorial imbalance and the dependence of the peripheral regions on the metropolitan areas, the industrial triangle (Milan–Turin–Genoa) and Rome. The great private oligopolistic groups, Fiat, Montecatini, Pirelli, etc., were for fifteen years or so able to count on very high accumulation and profit rates, thanks to the complementary nature of the IRI and ENI industries, in which the state was a share-holder, and to the indiscriminate penetration of the country's rural markets. The industrial conurbations of the north underwent an unprecedented increase of population and economic concentration, while almost a third of the population of the south abandoned the countryside to emigrate to the north or to other European countries. The interests of the masses of peasants were subordinated to those of a rapid and unbalanced development of intermediate-technology industry, exporting mass-consumption durable goods, thereby bringing about a profound and structural crisis of agriculture.

These developments were well integrated into the growth of world capitalism. They left room for expansion to foreign capital, mainly American at first and then mainly German: Italian capital was growing but remained non-competitive compared with technologically more advanced producers, and subordinated to a precise role in the international division of labour. But a model of development of this sort is fated to undergo a persistent crisis. The conditions for Italian economic growth, a considerable reserve of cheap labour in the industrial areas of the north and the continuous expansion of exports, had already ceased to exist by the middle of the 1960s. The growing difficulty of installing new workers in the industrial zones of the north and the exhaustion of the local labour reserves added to the bargaining power of the working class. Thus the early 1970s saw the re-emergence of very aggressive trade-union and workers' organization which demanded considerable salary increases. At this point Italian industry began to lose its competitiveness and profitability in the face of the technologically more advanced and less specialized industry of other advanced countries and the industry of some emergent countries. At that time two different unplanned and spontaneous strategies of productive decentralization began to be put into effect, but they were unable to solve the problems of a very weak and unbalanced economy particularly susceptible to the general crisis of capitalism. And, in fact, these strategies of decentraliztion had the effect of increasing the territorial contradictions typical of advanced capitalism. They were the development of medium and small, peripheral manufacturing industries in the north-eastern and central regions and the decentralization of heavy industries in the south through the so-called 'poles of growth' strategy.

I shall briefly consider the results of these two different types of industrial decentralization in the area of maximum concentration and congestion and in the two areas of new industrial installations, some zones of central and north-eastern Italy and some parts of southern Italy.

CONGESTION AND DUALISM IN NORTH AND CENTRAL ITALY

The industrial triangle was already notably congested at the beginning of the 1960s, but market economies and the financial advantages of installing industries producing mass-consumption commodities continued to favour industrial installation in that region. In the Turin area a very articulate complex of industries, in part dependent and in part independent, work for Fiat:[21] a total of more than 135,000 employees, most of them (60,000) are concentrated in the enormous Mirafiori factory, which today is the largest in the world. A further complication is the fact that Fiat has installed in Turin the most technologically advanced car factory in the world, a completely automated line, where one hundred specialized workers produce the same number of cars as many thousands in the nearby Mirafiori plant. This fact threatens the workers with the certainty that any further expansion will not mean an increase in employment.

The Milan area is perhaps even more congested, precisely because its economic fabric is more complex and differentiated. In addition to the mechanical and electrical engineering installations, there are the head-offices of the large chemical industries, factories of practically every industrial sector and the offices of the most important Italian and foreign private financial groups. The decentralization of a part of heavy industry did not free much space in these two areas because the large steel and petro-chemical industries were located in the port zones of Genoa and Venice and in central Italy (Terni). So the progressive decentralization of heavy industry merely resulted in the decline of certain peripheral industrial areas in relation to the great industrial metropolis. Moreover, in the 1960s a notable process of selection of the industrial labour-force in favour of the male intermediate age groups, together with a reorganization of labour to achieve productivity increases without investments, resulted in a considerable increase of congestion, for immigration continued even in the absence of major increases in employment within the industrial triangle. As a consequence of this restructuration of the labour-force, migrations continued when industrial occupation in the area increased very little: local female and old-age workers were replaced by young migrants, who, in addition, took their families to the north, so that the employment rate fell by several points (from nearly forty percent to approximately thirty-four percent).

Since all the available resources were used for financial and industrial accumulation and the realization of maximum short-term profits, there was an almost complete lack of new infrastructures and social investments to bring about an improvement in the living and working conditions of workers in the industrialized areas. This is demonstrated by the data concerning the social services, which reveal shortcomings particularly in the large metropolitan areas.[22] The costs of production in the congested area increased considerably but the north-west metropolitan area remained the only possible location for a number of intermediate- and advanced-technology productive processes because of the high infrastructural level of the market, economies of scale, and the concentration there of the financial decision-making centres.

At the same time a process of retarded industrialization, of dependent, marginal and neo-dualistic character, was established in north-eastern and central Italy. The industrial sectors developed in these regions were mostly traditional ones, such as the textile, garment, footwear, etc., sectors and some branches of the mechanical and electronic industries. This industrial development was founded above all on the low costs of installation and on the exploitation of irregular labour. There was a proliferation of small and medium-sized units which combined relatively advanced technological levels with forms of organization of labour and production different from those of a large factory. Home-work, part-time agricultural-industrial work and various forms of irregular and temporary recruitment of the labour-force permitted production costs to be reduced and notable super-normal profits to be made. At the same time, even the large monopolistic industries decentralized to these regions certain manufacturing processes that could be detached from the large factory, or ordered increasing quantities of semi-finished products from the small concerns already existing there. These forms of industrialization were facilitated by an osmotic relationship with agriculture and by the survival of an archaic family organization. In this way there developed a very complex economic fabric which, however, was capable of producing a good rate of profit.

This form of peripheral economy is very rigid, however, as a productive organization, and precarious in the long-term, as well as being considerably dependent on the central economy. The rigidity of the peripheral economy is due in general to the precarious equilibrium between the costs of labour and the technological and productivity levels. The peripheral economy is subject to increases of production costs imposed from outside (inflation, increased costs of raw materials, etc.) without having sufficient margins to be able to pass them on to the costs or productivity of labour or to the final prices of the goods. The Italian peripheral economy, especially in the traditional exporting sectors (textiles, footwear, clothing, etc.) suffers increasingly from the competition of goods produced in underdeveloped countries, which have much lower relative labour costs and rising productivity levels. In the mechanical and electronic sectors, on the other hand, the peripheral economy is forced, at a certain stage of expansion, to choose between a complete re-organization based on large factories, thereby forgoing the advantage obtainable from super-exploitation of irregular labour, and the maintenance of the existing productive dimensions, which involves exposure to the competition of technologically more advanced and more concentrated economies.

A third possibility is that the decentralization process is further developed through a new division of the production line and the settlement of sub-dependent small plants in even more peripheral areas (the south). But this chain cannot be developed much further, as the possibility of peripheral industrialization of other Italian regions is limited and as the economic structure is already disgregated.

The dependent character of the peripheral economy, on the other hand, is the result both of its lack of control of its own accumulative process (increasing debts to banks, links with commercial and import-export groups of purchaser monopolistic type, the need for state subsidies, etc.) and of the increase of direct decentralizing intervention by the great financial-industrial monopolistic groups. Furthermore, the social situation depending on the peripheral economy of the central and north-eastern regions is continually deteriorating. The super-exploitation of irregular labour, the high inflation rate and a slow but continual increase in unemployment among young people have led to a deterioration of the conditions of life for marginal workers and their families. The limitations of economic expansion of this type of productive structure further increase the problem. At a certain stage in its development a small sectoral crisis is enough to devastate the economy of a whole region. An example of this is the crisis of the footwear industry in the Marche, or of the textile industries in Tuscany and the Veneto. In fact the central and north-eastern regions have benefited from a rapid process of industrialization which, however, offers poor prospects in the long term and is even today fairly precarious, quite apart from having increased the dependence of these areas on the central logic of capitalistic accumulation. To these weaknesses are added the particular precariousness of the Italian economic system as a whole, subordinated as it is to its integration in a very strong market and doubly threatened by industrial decentralizations in the Third World and by the increase of the technological gap separating it from the more advanced capitalist countries (above all the USA,

Germany and Japan). The precariousness of the Italian peripheral economy is thus accentuated, in comparison with other analogous situations, by the fact that Italy itself is in the process of being transformed into an economy which is peripheral and dependent in relation to the major centres of capital accumulation.

THE QUESTION OF THE SOUTH AND THE POLES OF GROWTH

Starting in the late 1950s, a particular process of industrialization took place in southern Italy, which considerably affected its social and economic structure. This was prevalently a case of decentralization of large, heavy-industrial complexes (steel and petro-chemicals) and of some partial production processes of manufacturing industry. The only important exception to the partial character and the complete dependence of industrialization in the south has been the installation of Alfa Sud at Naples, a factory of a state-participation industry which produces the finished product almost completely in the south.

The industrialization of the south had two purposes which were in part incompatible with each other; that of reducing the congestion of the Italian industrial fabric, thereby favouring its continuous expansion at not excessively high cost; and that of reconstructing an economic and occupational fabric in the south to compensate for the great crisis of subsistence agriculture and of a society prevalently founded on agricultural relationships and on very backward extra-agricultural activities.

Right from the start the main, or perhaps the only, protagonist of this process of industrialization was the type of company in which the state had a shareholding. IRI constructed the fourth metallurgical plant at Taranto, which permitted the private mechanical engineering companies to obtain semi-finished products at prices competitive with those of foreign industries. At the same time ENI, and later groups of private oil companies and Montedison, constructed in Sicily (Gela, Ragusa, Augusta-Priolo, Milazzo-Villafranca), Sardinia (Porto Torres, Ottana), Apulia (Brindisi) the enormous petro-chemical installations that permitted the development of the chemical monopolies in Italy and the reinforcement of the whole of the Italian industrial structure (chemical raw materials are used in nearly every sector of the consumer-goods manufacturing industries). Naturally this industrialization had all the characteristics of the dependent decentralization of heavy industry, and thus succeeded only in a very small degree in fulfilling the demagogic purpose of the government projects, which was to boost employment and the economy of the south. Large petrochemical and metallurgical installations do not in themselves have a high power of industrial generation, while they involve the occupation of a very large area, the disruption of ecological balances, and rapid territorial congestion. Furthermore, despite the fact that the poles of growth have been rather ambiguously described as 'cathedrals in the desert', in Italy these large complexes have never been located in uninhabited zones but, rather, in populous areas, in which there was in progress a process of international integration of markets that was having a devastating effect on the local agricultural structure and on the traditional self-sufficient economy. Rather than slowing down or accelerating the decomposition of the traditional society, the 'poles of growth' industrialization have had the effect of altering in a very ambiguous manner the whole social formation of some areas of southern Italy.[23] Islands of factory employment and a large-factory economy, and in consequence nuclei of modern workers, came into being without any prospect of continuing to expand in the long term and, in fact, destined to be reduced during the phases of the crisis, and this in the context of a completely heterogeneous, always underdeveloped and dependent social fabric. The dependence of the southern regions on the logic of central accumulation, whether at world or European level, or that of the industrial triangle, thus became increasingly marked. In the backward agricultural areas this process is mainly due to the progressive integration of local markets in the national and international economic fabric. In the 'poles of growth' areas the dependence is connected with the very nature of the decentralized plants, which rely completely on an external market (the development of car and mechanical industries mainly) and on an external management (as they are part of an industrial organization with directional seats in Rome, Milan, Turin or abroad). The new decentralized capital intensive plants contributed to increasing the average income of the workers in the area of the installation but, at the same time, they gave rise to two very distinct income levels: a higher level deriving from stable employment with the large companies; and a lower level deriving from employment in the complementary industries and in the traditional small industrial, commercial and agricultural units. The resultant consumption model was particularly distorted and was characterized by a rapid change from consumption of local products to that of national and foreign products of the central economy. This, too, contributed to the increase of the dependence of southern society.

The main contradiction of this sort of development in the south lies, however, in the poor economic and employment prospects that this type of industrialization offers. Once the saturation point has been reached, in consequence of a rapid congestion of the industrial area, the employment basis of the 'pole' not only finally ceases to grow but, instead, begins to diminish rapidly because of the closing down of complementary installations or of industrial construction units. The employment expectations that have developed in the meantime are completely unfulfilled and the unemployment of young people becomes one of the more serious local problems. At the same time the inversion of the migratory flows and the continuous aggravation of the agricultural crisis renders the general Italian employment problem even more serious. But here this occurred in an economic context in which the main flows of capitalist investment were destined to cease. In these regions, in fact, the production costs of installations of any industrial sector are relatively high. The cost of labour is much higher than in the countries of the Third World, while the shortage of infrastructures and the poverty of the market economies, as well as the socio-political complications, discourage decentralization even on the part of companies not particularly interested in reducing labour costs.

On the other hand the conditions of the labour market in the south are such as to be no longer compatible with a large-factory economy. The relative overpopulation has three main components and none of them is very interested in, or interesting from the point of view of, stable industrial employment: an increasing proportion of young people with high educational qualifications and expectations of white collar or specialized jobs, who, even if induced by desperation to accept an ordinary workman's job, are not very satisfactory from the point of view of the company (because too susceptible to political influences and resentful of discipline, and also too unstable – if they find another job, they leave); women and older men, more available and suitable for irregular work than for stable and regular work; and chronically unemployed and underemployed persons who are beyond being suitable for the requirements of a factory economy.

The only solution compatible with the conditions of local overpopulation would be the extension to the south of peripheral industry, based on forms of irregular employment. But the degree of industrial dualization attained by the Italian economy is already very high and it is difficult to raise it further. The practice of some clothing and footwear industries of central Italy, which have further decentralized their production procedures to Naples, where they find home-workers at very low salaries, cannot be extended to all the enterprises of the peripheral area or to the whole of the south. And, in any case, a solution of this sort would make the Italian economy even weaker, more dependent and uncontrollable, and would throw the country into absolute chaos.

The employment crisis today in Italy is the greatest multiplier of regional imbalances and social tensions. It is interesting to observe in conclusion that every suggestion for an employment policy, intended to stem the increase of unemployment, is impeded by the unsatisfactory regional distribution both of employment and of industrial activities. In fact, proposals for the restructuring of industry or a reduction in the working hours of the regularly employed would have the result of creating jobs in the industrial regions of the north, where unemployment is less marked and where migratory inflows are no longer possible, while the depressed regions of the country would remain condemned to continual increases in their unemployment rate.

Furthermore, the newly-located southern industries are suffering dramatically from the effects of the economic crisis. They are the first ones to be sacrificed to reduce Italian industrial overproduction. For this reason the petro-chemical plants, both in Sicily and in Sardinia, have been obliged to close sectors and cut back jobs, the Alfa Sud plant in Naples has had to face a growing deficit and never became seriously competitive (it continues to operate only because it gets an increasing subsidy from the state), the steel industries plan, to expand the Taranto settlement and to build a new one in Calabria, has had to be cancelled, the new Calabrian textile and chemical industries had to close, and so on.

The political prospects of this situation are not clear at all. Presumably in the 1980s governments will try to win from the northern workers some sort of control of real wages to promote an increase of profitability of the northern industries and a further expansion of assistance to the depressed areas.

Any economic programme will, however, appear largely inconsequential because the government and the major capitalists will be unable to win substantial control of wages and absolutely unable to cut consumption costs in the poor regions. Workers employed in the large industries will actively resist the prospect of serious cuts in real wages, so that the resources gained by this strategy will never be enough to finance both the re-establishment of accumulation trends and the expansion of the assistance budget. Moreover, the attempt to increase industrial production and competitiveness will mean a parallel increase of unemployment, due to labour-saving investments, of overproduction, due to the incapacity to sell the new production abroad, and of inflation, due to the increased importance of raw material imports in the Italian balance of payments. Under these conditions uneven regional development will further deteriorate and a new wave of peripheral social conflicts will shake consensus in the depressed areas. But only when the interests of the peripheral and marginal masses merge with the interests of the trade-unionized working class into an alternative development-transition project, will peripheral conflict menace the hegemony of conservative political and social forces. Otherwise they will aggravate the progressive disgregation of Italian society towards permanent enlarged reproduction of the social, economic and political crisis.

CHAPTER FOUR
Socialism, Class Conflict and Land-Use

FROM SOCIALIST THEORY TO SOCIALIST EXPERIENCE

I have tried to explain how the late-capitalist social situation, and its territorial consequences, are deeply contradictory. A very severe process of social disgregation is worsening various aspects of the life of both advanced industrialized societies and the poor countries of the Third World. The crisis begun in the late sixties reproduces itself and develops new dangerous aspects every few years. The prospects of this social organization are doubtful: will it survive for some time the contradictions stemming from the crisis or will it be able to ride through the crisis and radically reform social relations although maintaining its essential class-power basis? Will it perhaps be swept out by a new revolutionary alternative social organization? To a Marxist scholar the only possible answer is the third one. But this belief is only a very preliminary and general point in an important, unsettled theoretical debate. The central questions of this fundamental problem are how socialism originates on a world scale (the transition question) and what are the main characteristics of a socialist social organization.[1]

I do not intend to pursue the theoretical debate here; but it seems to me very important to raise a few points about the general theory of socialism and specifically the self-styled socialist societies, so as to be better prepared, at least in part, to defend that third answer. This also applies to territorial questions. The problem should be debated and studied much further. In this chapter I hope to be able to raise some substantial points in favour of the possibility that a radically alternative social organization, and also a radically different socio-territorial system is possible, and will be established as a result of class struggles against the late-capitalist exploitative social organization. However, the contribution of this chapter will remain very partial, incomplete and problematic, due to the enormous complexity of the problem itself and to the confusion which still surrounds the debate on socialism in both the theoretical and political arenas. Nevertheless as a conclusion to this work I shall try to outline possible alternative solutions to the present capitalist crisis.

The crucial problem is no longer one of the lack of empirical knowledge of socialist experiences, as it was for Marx and Lenin. If we omit a few general remarks, nearly all Marx's theoretical approach to socialism is related to the experience of the Paris Commune. The greatest difficulty surrounds the theoretical evaluation of existing socialist experiences. For it seems reasonable to say that, while it is easy to identify most existing capitalist societies, we cannot assume automatically that any self-styled socialist society is such. No actual socialist experiences meet the original conditions foreseen by Marx and other classical Marxist scholars. It has not been the case that:

> At a certain stage of development, the material productive forces of society come into conflict with the existing relations of production . . . within the framework of which they have operated hitherto. From forms of development of the productive forces these relations turn into their fetters. Then begins the era of social revolution . . . No social order is ever destroyed before all the productive forces for which it is sufficient have been developed.[2]

Different forms of self-styled socialist regimes have been established in large areas of the world; yet, at the same time, capitalism has continued to develop. Furthermore, socialism has not yet been established in any country whose productive forces had been already fully developed by capitalism. The existing socialist experiences began mostly in backward capitalist countries, where capitalist hegemony was quite weak. Such countries had therefore to catch up with the capitalist levels of development of the productive forces. The world market has played and continues to play an important role in conditioning the development trends of socialist countries, with two short-term exceptions, the case of the USSR during the immediate post-revolutionary period (war communism 1917-21) and the case of China, after the break with the Soviet bloc until the re-establishment of trade relations with the West (approx. 1960-74). In the main, world market logic has imposed on socialist countries the necessity to achieve as quickly as possible a set of goals delimited by the logic of the general industrialization process. The rate of capital accumulation and of labour productivity, production and consumption technologies, have been by and large the same as in Western industrialization processes. Backward productive forces and market-integration constraints are factors tightly linked together. In fact a country is subordinated in market relations because its backward productive forces put it in a condition of non-competitiveness on the world market so that to become more competitive quickly, the country is forced to adopt a social and productive organization typical of a capitalist order. From the opposite point of view, only a country which, for exceptional reasons, is able to remain isolated from the world market can afford to develop its productive forces with alternative rhythms and character from the capitalist ones.

It is difficult to say how many of the present socialist societies' features are due to 'socialism' and how many have resulted from the existence of still undeveloped productive forces and from the constraints imposed by integration in the international market. Most Marxist socialist theory is abstract and very little of it derives from the actual experience of socialist countries. Most 'socialist' tendencies which Marx identified in the Paris Commune have not fully appeared in any concrete socialist experience. For instance, there has not been a tendency to abolish professional politicians and bureaucrats but the very opposite one of reinforcing the political and bureaucratic professions. The fact that the present socialist order partly derives from market constrictions and 'catch up' programmes and partly from genuine socialist tendencies, explains why socialist experiences are so diverse and why the theoretical debate is so heated. Similarities between capitalist order and development and current socialist experiences result from the constraint of underdeveloped productive forces. However, within the capitalist order, these constraints are the inevitable outcome (i.e. uneven regional development, housing shortage and stratification, massive concentration of population in cities, a fixed hierarchical division of labour and territory, etc.). In a socialist order these should not be the tendencies, but only the constraints of a backward stage of development. Socialist goals and praxis should be very different from those of the capitalist order. I shall try to point out some of these tendencies, as they can be deduced from classical Marxist passages on the theory of socialism.

First, a few points about the nature of socialism and the transition process from capitalism to socialism. Like any other mode of production and social order, socialism is not a fixed condition but a process. In particular, it is the process through which the working class, the very large majority of the population, by developing productive forces and emancipating the population from exploitation in any form, gradually achieves the abolition of any form of division of labour (both between intellectual and manual labour and between countryside and city), and so delivers man from scarcity and want. Socialism itself is a transition stage towards communism, the society in which man is freed from scarcity and want.

The features of a socialist order are: power directly and immediately in the hands of the large majority of the population, i.e. the working class; abolition of private property and of the private ownership of the means of production, abolition of exploitation, of the use of capital for private profit, of the dominance of exchange value over use value; a very high level of development of human productive forces, a very wide diffusion of scientific and technological knowledge; and finally, the progressive abolition of any form of division of labour (including the abolition of technocracy and bureaucracy). As we have already noted, a transition from capitalism to socialism on a worldwide scale is possible, according to Marx, only when the productive forces are so developed as to be in contradiction with the old social order.

I have suggested elsewhere that most contemporary socialist countries arose because of the particularly weak degree of capitalist hegemony in their respective cases,[3] which explains why a self-styled socialist order has been achieved in relatively backward societies and not in advanced capitalist ones, but does not explain the policies of such forms of socialism. The problem should be very carefully looked at not only for this reason but also because we have historical evidence of areas which achieved a capitalist order a few centuries earlier than the worldwide transition, and afterwards lost their advanced character to be re-feudalized (the Russian and Prussian free commercial towns) or to become relative capitalist latecomers (the Italian Milanese, Venetian and Florentine areas). In any case we should reject the Stalinist view that socialism can be achieved in one country only, as any national experience must be interpreted in respect to world-wide processes and no socialist character can be definitively achieved before socialist productive relations become dominant on a world scale. In this sense I do not regard any existing order as a socialist one, but rather as a transitional society on the road to socialism. But this can only explain the persistent lack of some of the theoretical characteristics of socialism in the so-called socialist countries of today. The constraints of a world-wide capitalist-ruled market and of yet undeveloped productive forces still prevent the full achievement of a socialist order. Again an analogy might be made with the capitalist enclaves in feudal society in the fourteenth to the eighteenth centuries (in Lombardy and Tuscany, Germany, Holland, and later, and more conspicuously, England) which were transitional orders and not fully capitalist ones.[4]

I believe that we are, at the moment, in a generalized transitional stage. Some societies have provisionally achieved an anticipated transitional order, but we do not know how and when they will be finally liberated from capitalist constraints. The only point we are theoretically sure of is that such liberation is strongly connected with the more general transitional process on the world scale. In other countries the working class struggles against a capitalist order which is going through its major social crisis. In doing so, the working class in capitalist countries is more or less consciously building an alternative socialist order. This does not necessarily mean that transition to socialism and revolution are gradual and evolutionary processes. On the contrary, they are violent confrontations between classes. But any new social order originates both from the people's consciousness and from the economic structure within the framework of the old social order. The whole history of man (and today's crisis of capitalism) proves this. Socialist trends are detectable in the working class's praxis both in the 'transitional' countries and in the late-capitalist ones. Socialist tendencies can be mentioned only on a theoretically very general ground as follows: the re-appropriation by workers of direct control over their working capacity, tools, organization, and their capacity to master collectively the results of their production in any economic sector; the progressive abolition of the division of labour and the diffusion of knowledge; the progressive abolition of political delegation to parties, bureaucracies, governments, through immediate decision-making by the whole population and the building of a directly democratic system; the achievement of very advanced socio-productive capacities and organizations, incompatible with capitalist order (in this sense it is correct to say that socialism cannot be based on backward productive forces and poverty but rather on their opposites).

The fact that these tendencies have appeared only occasionally and very poorly in some self-styled 'socialist' societies proves two points. First, how far the present stage of world history is from a world scale transition to socialism. Second, the fact that the present 'socialist' countries are very minimally socialist and still dominantly capitalist in their fundamental character, which also means that they cannot be taken as models of socialism and that they have no priority within the world scale transition process.

THE THEORETICAL DEBATE ON SOCIALIST TERRITORIAL DEVELOPMENT

The debate on socialist territorial development is characterized by two opposite views. On one side there is a hard, anti-urbanization position, which argues that socialism should develop an even distribution of population and resources and destroy the large concentrations and the cities. This view has been inherited from the Utopian socialists of the last century and claims an implicit (and sometimes also explicit) basis in Marx and Engels' writings. On the opposite side, there is the view that socialism should develop urbanism, but in a form which differs from capitalist urban and territorial concentration.

When, during the thirties in the USSR, an important controversy began about the process of urbanization, Marxist theoreticians who opposed territorial concentration were able to found their view on a single passage of Engels' writings:

Civilization has undoubtedly, with its cities, left us a heritage which will take much time and effort to eliminate; but they must and will be eliminated even if this process of elimination will be a laborious one.[5]

But Stalin and those responsible for Soviet territorial planning held opposite views. They argued that the development of socialism in the USSR should be based on the development and growth of socialist towns, as is shown by the following remarks of Stalin himself:

The problem of the elimination of the conflict between town and country, between industry and agriculture, is a well-known problem which both Marx and Engels have posed. The economic basis of this conflict is the exploitation of the countryside by the towns, the expropriation of the peasants and ruining of the majority of the rural population following the course of the development of industry, commerce and the capitalist system of credit. The conflict between town and country in capitalism must, therefore, be considered as a conflict of interests. On these grounds arose a hostile attitude of the countryside toward town dwellers. This does not of course mean that the elimination of the conflict between town and countryside necessarily leads to the downfall of large towns and cities. [Note the explicit opposition to the quotation by Engels.] Cities will not be destroyed, but new cities will arise and these cities will be centres of greater cultural development, centres not only of big industries but also of the processing of agricultural products, of great developments of all branches of the food industry. This will encourage the cultural growth of the country and will determine a levelling out of living conditions in town and country.[6]

Despite the immediate and specific considerations which could make it more convenient from a political point of view to urbanize the country (urbanization and concentration may be the only means of developing productive forces at certain stages of history), I believe that Stalin's position can be seriously questioned. For example, capitalist urbanization concentrated the processing of agricultural foods and industrial food production in the cities and promoted the cultural growth of all capitalist countries (such as the development of higher education, research and cultural centres); but because of this very concentration process, it has never achieved equality between living conditions in the town and the country, nor even between large and small towns or between peripheral and central regions. Stalin's view is still widely accepted and is sustained by further arguments. For example, Nekrasov recently maintained that:

> ... the territorial division of social labour is an objective economic law. ... Urbanization is the most significant social and economic process at the present time. ... The high level of concentration of material production, the ongoing improvements in technology and engineering, the rapid growth of labour productivity, combine to bring into being a new form of population distribution. Contemporary civilization is linked with urban growth as the highest form of the organization of production and other activities carried out by the population.[7]

Further, the French, Marxist sociologist Henri Lefebvre, although in different terms, views urban concentration as the starting point of socialist revolution and the sole foundation of socialist development, contrasting this with the backward countryside where both capitalism and pre-capitalist forms still survive and hinder the growth of the new society.[8]

The opposite view, anti-urban socialist development, is perhaps more widely held; mainly by Western Marxist scholars and trade union movements, but is less explicitly stated. China is the only socialist country which has partially supported this position through its planning and development process in the sixties, only to abandon it again more recently when the integration of China in the world market imposed different trends of socio-economic development to the ones adopted in the previous decade.

I believe that we should first consider the theoretical problems surrounding this question separately from the concrete experience of the development of existing socialist societies. From this strictly theoretical point of view, both Nekrasov's and Lefebvre's claims are highly questionable. The territorial division of labour is not an objective historical law, nor a definitive achievement of humanity. It is the territorial expression of capitalist social order at a specific stage of its development. A territorially divided, concentrated and highly urbanized society reflects the more developed and advanced productive forces of society in comparison to pre-capitalist societies which are founded on rural communities and dispersed populations. It is not an invariable attribute of society. This point can also be made in a criticism of anti-urbanism, which is often based on a nostalgia for the pre-capitalist order, for example, as occurs in Utopian socialism, and in most British anti-urbanism.[9]

The productive forces of capitalism have developed to a level at which they come into contradiction with the territorially, highly-concentrated order. Socialism is supposed to further develop productive forces and to establish the alternative territorial order by solving this very contradiction. In an era of fast and cheap communication, of computers and electronics, territorial concentration is no longer a condition for the development of productive forces. Decentralization, dispersion and undivided territorial development have become possible, and necessary, without negative effects. Electronic technology, ever cheaper and more accessible computer terminals and rapid transport, if run directly by the people, could equalize the quality of life independently of geographical location, permit global collaboration and communication of the most sophisticated kind whatever the size of the human communities involved. It could also maximize the utilization of local resources in a very differentiated way, so as to promote further developments of the productive forces. We can imagine without any great effort, an era of cheap decision-making, constantly consulting the people by computers. This would tend to abolish the division between the political rulers and ruled. This equalization could also apply to the diffusion of knowledge, artistic expression and professional skills, resulting in a progressive abolition of the division of labour *tout court*. Moreover, territorial dispersion enables territorial and human resources to be fully used, decreases the high costs of congestion created by late capitalism in large cities and the dreadful social and human stress connected with such highly concentrated and divided societies.

Late capitalism uses this very growth of productive forces and of modern technology to increase concentration, exploitation, division and control over the large majority of the population, and this is the territorial expression of the final contradiction between the development of productive forces and the current social order foreseen by Marx more than a century ago. Hierarchical, class-based suburbanization, the abuse of technology to increase control over living standards, the continuous increase of the vertical concentration of knowledge and professionalism, and uneven regional and national development, are examples of how capitalist development frustrates the productive forces by using new achievements in an exactly opposite manner to the way in which liberated productive forces would use them. (Marx's writings about machines and technological innovations explain this process clearly.)[10]

The working class is engaged in reversing the capitalist territorial order. I have given some examples of class struggles in capitalist countries which show socialist or transitional trends with regard to the use of land. Even though I disagree with Lefebvre's position, i.e. socialist order and socialist issues as urban ones, I also disagree that socialist movements can be based on a nostalgia for rural and pre-capitalist community life. Lefebvre is right when he states that no pre-capitalist territorial order based on the rural community should be salvaged by socialism.

The socialist territorial order will not only be against the forms of concentration and division of labour developed by capitalism, but will also oppose any form of regression to the old, agricultural, rural and pre-capitalist community. It is a totally new order, neither urban nor rural, based on undivided, polyvalent productive unities.

The reality of current self-styled socialist experiences is, however, complicated by the need to stimulate the growth of productive forces which are still backward, and to respect world market constraints. Very often this means concentration, urbanization, territorial division of labour and specialization as well as uneven regional development. Due to these factors it may appear difficult to distinguish between a capitalist country and a society which is genuinely progressing on the road of transition to socialism, although meeting difficulties and conflicts. Specific cases of policy evaluation do not concern us here. In general, we can establish two principles, and one practical rule. First, socialist planning and policies are characterized by a class methodology content opposite to capitalist ones. In the case of socialism, planning is not only in the interests of the large majority of the population (a reactionary policy can easily be masked as 'revolutionary' populism), but is also directed by the large majority of the population – not a bureaucratic process, but a popular one. At the beginning the popular planning process may present difficulties which are progressively overcome with the raising of socialist awareness and abolition of the division of labour.

The second principle is the acceptance of the long term aim of socialist territorial development referred to above (i.e. to build a new territorial order based on non-urban and non-rural, diffused, undivided, polyvalent, and highly technologically orientated, territorial productive unities). The policies of transitional concentration must be consciously understood as provisional ones, not intended to prevent the necessary further development of socialism. Hence, in general terms it is possible and necessary for societies in transition to begin to establish counter-trends (at least experimentally). As soon as possible, new polyvalent communities must be created with a high degree of socialist decentralization and development of uninhabited regions (which, in the first case, is not just suburbanization and in the second case should not be a 'poles of growth' policy), industrialization of the countryside should be pursued by means of new small-scale technology, and diffusion of equal levels of services and knowledge.

One finds these characteristics only in short term 'socialist' experiences, when a society for special reasons can afford to be isolated from the world market: in the Soviet Union during the civil-war period (1917-22); in China for a longer period (1959-72), when the isolation from the Soviet block and from the West was nearly total; in other countries (Cuba, Kampuchea, Vietnam, etc.) for much shorter periods (one-two years) in immediate post-revolutionary periods. By contrast the state-centralized development of 'socialist' experiences in the long term have been severely influenced by world market conditions and by 'gap filling' restrictions.

Under these conditions it is not surprising that urbanization processes have been very similar both in the West and in the East. In fact the state, while promoting accelerated industrialization has also stimulated a high degree of urban concentration, the fast growth of enormous metropolitan areas, the decadence of peripheral rural economies, a 'poles of growth' strategy in the desert regions and so on. The territorial and productive structure of socialist countries is not particularly different from that of capitalist countries; it is characterized by a persistent uneven distribution of resources in space, by gigantic urbanization and by regional underdevelopment, though social contradictions have not yet reached the stage achieved in Western capitalism because they are usually mediated by more intensive intervention by the state. Yet important conflicts and incongruencies can be found: from the lack of homes in the large cities to the inefficiency of service industries, from the economic depression of peripheral regions to the dependence of vast suburban regions upon central urban activities.

On the contrary, the main point of the alternative experiences is that, being free from market conditioning, they can stress long-term and social investments against short-term productivity and profitability-raising investments. This may mean a vast decentralization of the development priorities to the periphery, a de-urbanization process and a struggle against the division of labour. In fact the division of labour is, at the same time, the only way to achieve a higher short-term productivity per worker and the main factor of centralization and uneven development. An isolated country will be able to produce different goods in a different production organization and to achieve different social goals. Compared with a capitalist country such socialist experiences will look, in the short term, largely irrational, from a purely economic point of view, mainly because productivity will be lower, employment of labour higher, technology and factory organization totally inconvenient and unprofitable and so on. Such criticisms have been made by Western economists against the cottage-commune-industrialization of the countryside in China in the sixties. Although more expensive and non-profitable from the capitalist point of view such development meant a rapid diffusion of industrial production throughout the whole country, the reinforcement of peripheral economies, a process of industrialization in parallel with de-urbanization and the limitation of rural-urban migration, a better environmental balance and the achievement of permanent full employment.

In the medium term even Western economists had to recognize that this alternative model presented some advantages. I believe that if such a process could have been kept working for a much longer period, it would have shown other important advantages from the general social point of view, like the progressive abolition of the division of labour and of professional elites, a better utilization of the productive capacities of man, an improved consumption pattern and way of life, the birth of a completely new technology, etc.

It is clear that industrialization and economic growth can be achieved by various different means and at different rates but that the position of each country in the international capitalist market and the stage of general world economic development play a very important role. An alternative socialist experience is not achievable in only one country as a permanent long-term process. But it can be part of a process of capitalist crisis either by the short-term isolation from the market of a single but large country or, and we have not yet faced this hypothesis, as a more general phenomenon of the defeat of capitalism in various parts of the world.

I believe that recently, within the capitalist crisis, some alternative socialist goals and issues have been discovered and pursued, although in a very confused way, on a world scale. The peripheral revolt, the regional and ecological movements, the new local dimension of various problems are examples of such tendencies in many capitalist, developed countries. On a world scale the power achieved by Third World raw material producers and the success of revolutionary movements in Indo-China and in some African countries provide the bases for different development trends in conjunction with the competitive pressures by the capitalist trade crisis. From this fact I argue that integration conditions in the world market are now much more negotiable than before. Even small countries can take the opportunity of developing an alternative industrialization process even over quite a long period. This possibility is certainly contrary to the capitalist necessity to keep the market as large as possible, that is, the desperate need advanced capitalist countries have to keep selling their goods and technologies to Third World countries. But the fact that their bargaining position has grown weaker will certainly mean that in the future such contradiction will become dramatic and that peripheral countries and regions will gain more opportunities to control their development trends themselves. So within the present capitalist and world market crisis many Third World countries enjoy the possibility of bargaining for better market conditions and can try to invest resources for development strategies. The OPEC countries' experience is the most important example. But it is clear that the additional wealth accumulated by some raw-material-rich countries is not a sufficient condition to translate underdevelopment into development. In fact it is very difficult to break an underdevelopment cycle based on a deep technological and productive gap (see Chapter 3). So in most cases the developing countries remain completely dependent on foreign technology and find it hard even to invest their own resources in their own countries.

There are two different development alternatives which can be chosen from either the economic or the territorial point of view. The first one is centralized; it is easier and more familiar; it has been chosen by practically every country to various degrees. It is mainly based on state intervention and on centralized planning. In my opinion this alternative has largely failed everywhere to achieve permanent socialist goals and trends. The second alternative is more difficult and still confused and it is based on socialist decentralization. I will return briefly to this possibility in the last paragraph of this book.

State intervention, through economic and physical planning, has been considered in many countries, although in very different terms, as the only possible solution to uneven development's contradictions. But planning experiences have not been satisfactory for various reasons, which I shall try to schematize here.[11] Central issues and goals have been preferred and at the expense of local ones, with the result that social conflicts and uneven distribution of resources have not been avoided but in many cases even increased; planning activity has been particularly unable to foresee and keep in mind long-term development issues and needs, so that the conflicts and contradictions have only been postponed; neither the 'socialist' model of planning nor the capitalist one has been able to develop planning as an instrument for popular democratic participation; it has been more sensitive to the needs of ruling classes than to those of the large majority of the population. In general we can say that planning processes have worked mainly as transfer instruments of various social contradictions in the sense that they have often postponed conflicts from the medium to the long term; they have transformed immediate economic contradictions into political struggles; they have decentralized the dialectical focus from the centre to the peripheries in various different ways, thus contributing to the transformation of unmanageable contradictions into manageable ones.

The point is that planning, as a centralization policy and methodology, is absolutely unable to manage the class contradictions created by the industrialization processes. In fact by definition, planning has in any case been an authoritarian undemocratic mechanism which has tried to limit the anarchist multi-directional tendencies of economic and social movements into a single direction guided by a political elite. In capitalist countries most of the goals fixed by planners have not been achieved, since market forces have not been controlled. Only goals compatible with market conditions have been finally achieved. This has meant that the planning process in general has been complementary to and subordinated to the capital accumulation one, and thus unable to solve contradictions raised by the capitalist development and market. In the 'socialist' countries, the planning process has served mainly to transmit from the centre to the peripheries the goals imposed by world market competition. Thus planning became the main vehicle for centralization, division of labour, urbanization, peripheral dependence, uneven exchange and so on.

On the other hand we cannot exclude an alternative path of planning and development as impossible. It should be principally based on the valorization of local and peripheral forces from either the political or economic point of view. The central authorities should bargain with world market forces for the opportunity of protecting local economies and promoting local development, thus deriving some benefit from the general capitalist crisis. This model should be based on the maximum peripheral autonomy and on the possibility that industrialization can be built on a diffused and small-scale basis. Agricultural, industrial and service industry activities should be combined and cross-fertilized on the local, decentralized scale. The productive potentialities of the peripheries should be developed in various directions mainly by stimulating agricultural producers to build an alternative technology for simultaneous development of agriculture, industry and services. In this sense neither urbanization nor persistent ruralism should be stimulated, but, on the other hand, the formation of decentralized settlements largely autonomous and able to promote their development independently, should be encouraged.

I turn now to the analysis of such alternative characteristics as obtained in the development of People's China in the isolation period, the longest socialist experience to enjoy the particular conditions mentioned above.

THE SOCIALIST CHARACTERISTICS OF THE CHINESE EXPERIENCE

The period between the crisis of the early 1960s and the Cultural Revolution saw the spread of alternative experiments in development.[12] In particular, the new-style industrial-agricultural settlement of Taching was begun during this period, as well as the experiment of the Tachai agricultural brigade. However, these experiments remained of secondary importance until the Cultural Revolution, when they became a fundamental part of the Maoist line and spread rapidly. They began a phase of socialist development which is completely different from any other experience of development – whether capitalist, Third World, or other socialist type.

The fundamental points of this Chinese alternative territorial development, to be analysed briefly in this section, are as follows. First, the development of the countryside has been directed towards optimal utilization of all productive resources – mainly peasant labour together with modern technology – and has depended on the political activation of the peasants and on the industrialization of rural areas rather than on migration and urbanization. Widespread industrial growth throughout the whole country in various spheres, instead of specialization by region, has favoured the development of small and medium-sized towns and peripheral areas rather than a concentration in the traditional, large Chinese cities of the coast. Through a civil and political struggle, millions of people living in urban slums and shanty towns and millions of peasants living in huts or shacks in the countryside have been rehoused. During this period China seems to have succeeded in shifting the axis of industrial development from the coastal strip, where the majority of the population and practically all of the industrial productive capacity of the country were previously concentrated, and has spread this development more evenly throughout the country.

In 1949, the urban population of China was approximately 58 million; by 1957 it had passed 100 million, representing 15.4 percent of the total. After several fluctuations the urban population stabilized in the 1970s at about eighteen percent of the total, i.e. 140–150 million. Big cities such as Shanghai and Peking have grown relatively little in terms of population and have been radically re-shaped in terms of land use. Shanghai now has a population of 10 million (as compared to 5 million in 1959), but it is no longer a city in the strict sense of the term, because a third of the active population is engaged in agriculture, and the increased area covered by the city includes a considerable number of popular communes, which make the inhabitants of urban districts self-sufficient as far as food is concerned.

The main elements of the Chinese, alternative, socialist territorial development have been the following: to choose agriculture as the basis for development; to diffuse the industrialization process instead of concentrating it; to adopt a much more decentralized model of planning than in other developments. The whole process was made possible by a continuous political mobilization of the population, which re-created conflicts and tensions but involved the larger part of these Chinese people in the development process.

(1) Agriculture as the basis of development. It is not difficult to explain from an economic point of view the significance of the phrase 'make agriculture the basic factor'. Difficulties begin when one attempts to explain the political implications of this slogan. After the revolution, China was mainly an agricultural country (over ninety percent of the population was engaged in agriculture) and a process of economic development could be carried out only through an increase in agricultural production and the consequent accumulation of an agricultural surplus that could be used to build up modern industry.

The Chinese aimed, therefore, at consolidating the production structures of the countryside, making sure that this did not at the same time lead to too great an expulsion of the labour force towards towns and industry, since Chinese industry was too weak at this stage to absorb the surplus labour. A policy of labour-intensive agricultural development was therefore stressed. The increases in productivity were to be achieved through greater and better utilization of the vast existing agricultural population. This type of policy is not in itself new nor typical only of Chinese socialist development. Both Japan over a long period and India today, followed or are following economic policies based on labour-intensive agricultural development. The crucial difference is in the destination of the agricultural surplus realized in this way and its subsequent utilization. If the agricultural surplus is systematically taken away from the agricultural sector in order to support the indiscriminate growth of capitalist industrial production, as was true in Japan, it is inevitable that things become difficult for the poorer peasants and eventually the process of abandonment of the countryside and the impoverishment of agriculture, typical of capitalist development, gets under way on a large scale. If, on the other hand, the surplus is taken over systematically by a class of rich peasants and by the state in order to maintain a strong bureaucracy and substantial urban overpopulation, as is happening in India, without even starting a process of industrialization, the weaker peasants are ruined and urban and rural poverty are constantly reinforced.

However, in China most of the agricultural surplus has been managed, in the main, by the peasants themselves and has been used to advance agricultural development, to improve production and the standard of living of the peasants and, therefore, ultimately to strengthen peasant demand for industrial products. The remainder of the agricultural surplus has been utilized for industrial accumulation. Industry and agriculture were then able to expand in a co-ordinated manner and make mutual use of each other. The process is not quite as simple as I have described it, but it seems clear that it is the political implications of appropriation of the surplus which define the difference between capitalist and socialist development.

This type of development has not been possible without contradictions in China, even from a strictly economic point of view. The increase in agricultural production and the simultaneous increase in demand from the peasants for industrial goods could lead (and certainly has done in capitalist development) to a scissors-like relationship of agricultural prices compared with industrial prices. If this is not controlled and limited, it rapidly leads to impoverishment of the countryside. If agricultural prices tend to drop while industrial prices rise, the peasants pay more and more while receiving less and less; this process ruins weaker agriculture, which has a lower productivity rate. In China, had there not been a centralized policy of maintaining agricultural prices, the peasants of the poorer areas would have been forced to abandon their work and emigrate to the towns, thus triggering again the mechanism of territorial inequality.

Secondly, at a certain stage of development, the mechanism of industrial accumulation entered into competition with agriculture for the utilization of resources. Any further expansion of industrial activity meant the concentration of a new labour force and of raw materials in factories located in towns, and therefore a process of urbanization. Neither could the growing demand originating in the countryside for industrial products be ignored. The answer given to this problem by the Chinese is the industrialization of the countryside. An increasingly large part of industrial demand generated in the countryside has been satisfied by the small industries of the communes springing up all over China. The mechanized workshop of the commune was no longer used just to mend broken machinery or carry out routine maintenance; it now supplied spare parts, produced new agricultural equipment, and had its own foundry. Small chemical plants produced fertilizers needed for local agriculture. Building materials were generally produced locally. Although the rate of productivity of these small decentralized industries was lower than that of the large urban manufacturing plants, real production costs were more or less similar if not lower, since the small units utilized residual labour that otherwise might have been wasted, new methods were discovered to use raw materials that otherwise would have been overlooked, and a saving was made on the economic and social costs of transport. All this meant a tendency to overcome, in the long run, the division of labour between industry and agriculture and the territorial inequality between town and country, thus sparing China a rapid process of concentration of the population in big cities.

Another aspect of the solution was the administrative and political decentralization of the country and the tendency to lessen the administrative dependence of the peasants on centralized bureaucracy located in cities. An increase in employment in public services and in the number of bureaucrats who could control and oppress was a typical tendency of development, both in developed countries and in most underdeveloped ones. In China there was an attempt to control this tendency through the creation of popular communes. The peasants administered themselves directly, at the levels of the popular communes and brigades, deciding how much to produce and how to co-ordinate their plans with the demands of regional and national planning. The leaders of the communes and brigades were peasants, who carried on with their jobs.

(2) Diffused industrialization. The principal elements of the process of Chinese industrialization in my view, are:

(a) the attempt to make each region self-sufficient with respect to basic industry;
(b) the attempt to overcome the division of labour and specialization between industry, agriculture and public services in the new territorial units;
(c) maximum utilization of territorial infrastructures already in existence (towns, transportation, large factories, etc.) and the further development of these to meet the immediate needs of the population.

The autonomous development of each region inverted the tendency towards specialization typical of capitalist industrial development, a tendency which eventually causes the underdevelopment of large areas and transforms the interdependence of modern economies into dependence upon a centre. The Chinese aimed to make every region autonomous, within the limits of natural resources, at least as far as basic iron and steel, mechanical and chemical industries are concerned. This involved stressing the development of peripheral and depopulated areas by decentralizing capital investments and manpower and encouraging local socialist accumulation through the modernization of agriculture and the creation of basic industries connected with growing agricultural demand and the availability of local raw materials. The old capitals of outlying provinces and the parasitic administrative towns – whose old purpose had been to guarantee capitalist-feudal control of the region – were thereby transformed into industrial centres linked to the local economy. New settlements integrating farming, industry, and public services were established which permitted exploitation of local resources without recreating the division of labour and a contradiction within the surrounding countryside. Regions such as Sinkiang and Tibet were administered in such a way as to be less subject to centralized development, and to progressively overcome their relative poverty without paying the social costs of massive emigration, without suffering from imposed 'poles of growth' which uproot local activities, and without the growth of parasitic public employment designed to compensate for the lack of dynamic industrial growth.

On the other hand, in this period the Chinese tried to reduce the economic division of labour (and as a consequence also the territorial one) by promoting the establishment of new productive unities, where manpower could be utilized in parallel developments in industry, agriculture and services. The example of Taching, which served as a model for other new settlements, illustrates the policies designed to overcome the division of labour and thereby reduce the contradiction between town and country. This territorial experiment, in which light and heavy industry, agriculture and public services are integrated, and where the concentration of population creates neither town nor countryside (in our sense of the terms), is extremely complex: I shall describe it briefly.

Taching originated in 1960, when China, isolated internationally, was stressing self-sufficiency. Geologists maintained that below the frozen surface of the plain of Taching were considerable oil deposits. Numerous teams of workers with their families went to this desolate area to begin drilling. Within a few years, the settlers had established a completely new kind of community. The houses were built directly by groups of industrial workers who followed the solid and inexpensive methods of local tradition. The land was gradually ploughed and the workers took turns at farming, especially during the sowing and harvesting seasons when demand for labour went up. Women worked in farming, workshops, and small factories engaged in light industry which were set up. Families of the workers established social services, schools, hospitals, a cinema and a theatre, and are now running them. Through job rotation the division of labour has been reduced to a minimum. This is reflected in spatial organization; the community is a non-centralized but cohesive settlement in which factories, houses, public buildings and farm lands are mixed in an orderly manner. Meanwhile, the production of oil has been increasing at an annual average of thirty-one percent and a modern refinery and pipeline to link the area to the industrial coastal zone several hundred miles away has been built. In the late sixties this example was followed by various other new industrial settlements and soon became one of the outstanding features of Chinese industrial development. During this same period the Chinese tried to maximize the utilization of local resources and to avoid waste, so often a product of late-capitalist industrialization processes. This aspect is particularly interesting now when capitalist countries too are obliged to revise their policies to face the energy and resources crisis.

The policy of avoiding waste has had two very different territorial effects. First of all, it has required the preservation of large territorial concentrations and large-scale productive structures created earlier under capitalism, although it has sought to transform them. The parasitic cities that had become bloated with excess population under the capitalist-feudal system were transformed into centres of modern, heavy-industrial production. Similarly, the few, already existing, heavy industries, which had formerly been almost entirely dependent on foreign capital, together with the mining centres, were further developed and not destroyed, even if this did strengthen the tendency towards concentration and the division of labour. But this conservation and use of existing structures did not start irreversible and progressive urban concentration because it was balanced by parallel processes of decentralization. As we have already seen, Chinese development favoured the birth of local industries, especially in less densely populated rural and peripheral areas and in underdeveloped regions. This second policy resulted logically from the principle of keeping waste to a minimum, just as the policy of integrating existing resources into the system followed from it.

The combined result of these two processes has been that in China, unlike other cases of rapid industrial development, the large cities retained their population and their dimensions but, at the same time, rural and peripheral areas, small towns, and economically and demographically underdeveloped regions have had, in general, much higher rates of growth than the large urban concentrations. On the whole, therefore, a process of decentralized industrialization was set in motion which spared China the problems of urban overdevelopment and metropolitanization typical of Western countries as of many underdeveloped countries, especially in Latin America.

(3) Decentralized planning.[13] The planning system of this period in China, both in socio-economic and territorial terms, was rather different from that of other 'socialist' countries. The final goals of planning were to be fixed by the basic and local units, even in contradiction of the opinion of the central authorities. The planning process was established in China as a complex compromise between democracy and central co-ordination, in which decision-making involves the whole population and requires careful attention to local-peripheral needs and opinions.

The fact that the Chinese process of planning worked upwards, rather than being imposed by central power, is extremely important. Only through a decentralized process can one put to maximum use local manpower, raw materials, and traditional knowledge and skills. In China it has been the peasants of a brigade or the local housewives who set up a new industry in order to produce what they needed and in order to utilize manpower that might otherwise be wasted. It has been the workers of the individual factories who, within certain limits, of course, decided to expand production or to modify the product manufactured, especially when they were in direct contact with the consumer. State and central planning intervened to co-ordinate or to press for changes which the central administration believed important, but the local unit had the final say in the matter. This allowed the productive apparatus to adapt to changing social relations and to particular needs of the masses in a manner that is not possible in a highly centralized system of planning. As agricultural production increased and the amount of labour required diminished, the peasants could devote more time to industrial and social service activities without needing to emigrate or to wait for the creation of a new large factory in the neighbourhood. Industry permeated the countryside without upsetting agriculture and without ruining masses of peasants. Modern technology and higher rates of productivity did not cause the total disappearance of traditional industry and craftsmanship nor did improvement bring about the terrible disruptions typical of the countryside surrounding the European or South American 'poles of growth', because modern industry created by the masses established a complementary and functional relationship with local traditions and needs. To sum up, industrialization planned by the masses is a process that reduces to a minimum the inevitable contradictions connected with growth.

In conclusion it is important to stress that the Chinese development, although it has been recently reshuffled by the integration of China into the world market and by new international relations, showed some signs of the progressive realization of what has been called socialist transitional tendencies. In my opinion this proves that an alternative economic, social and territorial development is possible when the transition to socialism is more advanced on a world scale and when the capitalist crisis has reached its peak, in the near future.

DECENTRALIZATION AS A SOCIALIST ISSUE

As a conclusion to this book I should like to analyse very briefly the possible socialist characteristics of industrial decentralization through a short comparison of an Italian experience (the growth pole of Augusta-Priolo near Syracuse in Sicily) and a Chinese one (the Taching new settlement, already mentioned in the previous section). I have chosen those two examples because I know them better than others, although I would have liked to consider also the experience of one of the new industrial peripheral settlements in the Soviet Union, so as to understand better the general phenomenon and the characteristics of Soviet development. But I am obliged to skip this attempt as I have only very general empirical evidence on the decentralization experiences in the Eastern European countries.

Decentralization tendencies, even in late-capitalist societies, may be features of a transition to a socialist society. Without any doubt, de-urbanization, a better use of the peripheral productive forces, a less conflictual territorial structure, and a progressive increase of popular political participation, i.e. various forms of decentralization, are socialist goals.

From our territorial point of view, some of the theoretically identified socialist trends could be described in this way:

(a) The progressive re-appropriation of the workers' control over their own production capacities, means freedom from territorial dependency and hierarchies and the end of the domination of the centres over the peripheries.

(b) A valorization of the productive forces and a new socialist scale of production mean rapid independent economic and social development of peripheral areas, both from the socio-economic and technological point of view.

(c) The progressive abolition of the division of labour means the building of a completely new territorial structure within an alternative organization of production, i.e. de-urbanization; co-ordination of agricultural, manufacturing and service industries within a socialist productive collectivity.

(d) The power of the large majority of workers and new forms of socialist participatory democracy mean a new decentralized territorial distribution of power.

However, these goals cannot be fully achieved when productive forces are still under the developmental restraints of capitalism[14] and capital is still dominant on a world scale. They can appear, as trends, both in self-styled socialist societies and within the crisis of late-capitalist societies. So it is very difficult to understand the true nature of a decentralization process, present both in 'socialist' and in capitalist societies. When territorial developments are very similar in different societies[15] we cannot say 'a priori', without referring to our theoretical background, whether this is due to a common socialist character or to a common capitalist character, which is still much more likely. In any case, current societies show a relatively similar pattern of territorial development, although with many peculiarities due to particular historical, social, economic and cultural conditions. Such similarities apply both to concentration processes, like urbanization or the more rapid development of industrial regions, and to decentralization processes. The Siberian new industrial settlements are very similar to Western 'poles of growth' and new towns. The regional suburbanized structure of Moscow or East Berlin is practically the same as that of London, Paris or New York.

Again, some of the positive aspects of decentralization are common to many different current societies. Advanced rural communities, based on a non-specialized production and on common land ownership, can be found in the USA, in China, Italy or Tanzania. The limited and experimental nature of these forms of decentralization, is again a consequence of capital and market economy domination over any alternative form of production. This control over socialist trends may be direct, i.e. capital accumulation attacks the peripheral alternative units, or indirect, i.e. general market mechanisms alter the revenue and the development prospects of socialist unities. The former conditions are usually found in capitalist countries; the latter in so-called socialist countries.

In both cases the problem is how long and how much a decentralized, alternative village economy – although protected by a socialist state or by the organized working class and although characterized by a not-too-backward technological background – can resist market competition with very concentrated capitalist units. This question is further complicated by the crisis of the market-capitalist economy. From the seventies onwards, a very slow growth-rate, increasing unemployment and inflation have strongly and persistently affected the world economy. In this situation economic competition is both increased and decreased: capitalism has become more aggressive against competitors because of its survival problems but competition is less effective because of the low accumulation rate. In a normal rapid development period capitalist competition would be able to crush decentralized village economies quickly, at least when they are exposed to competition (only large and isolated countries, like People's China in the sixties, could resist this kind of attack). In this persistent crisis period any solution to the problem is extremely elusive. Decentralized economies could survive, improve and become one of the most important elements of the transition process to socialism on a world scale. On the other hand they could be crushed by an (unlikely)[16] new phase of fast capital accumulation and a new concentration process.

The following comparative analysis aims to point out the differences between a strictly capitalist form of decentralization and one which is relatively very close to a transition to socialist experience. Although set in different contexts, the two examples have some important similarities. Both are petro-chemical plants, developed in the sixties, and both symptomatic. In fact, the industrial new settlement of Taching in China has been taken as the example and model of socialist development by the Chinese leaders themselves. The Augusta-Priolo[17] petro-chemical complex is the largest new industrial settlement of its kind realized by late capitalism in Europe, and is perhaps the best example of the 'poles of growth' failure to bring about fast, complete and persistent economic growth in a backward region. The most important natural difference is that while Taching is a completely new settlement in a desert region, Augusta-Priolo is in the Syracuse region close to a relatively large town (Syracuse, more than 100,000 inhabitants in 1971) and surrounded by an overpopulated agricultural area. The second important difference is that while Taching is predominantly an oil-extracting area, Augusta-Priolo is only a petro-chemical refining plant. The Italian petro-chemical pole[18] is part of a more general development strategy which is trying to isolate in the two large islands (Sicily and Sardinia) the large majority of the ecologically destructive and land-hungry petro-chemical plants. Moreover, recently, the development plan for the Italian Chemical Industries tried to link the three most important Sicilian petro-chemical areas – Syracuse–Ragusa–Gela – to create a large mono-industrial integrated region.

The industrial location process began in the early fifties – with the decentralization of small refineries belonging to multinational Esso. Later on, the Italian Chemical monopoly, Montecatini, decided to build a plant in the area, in order to utilize locally refined oil and profit from the low costs of settlement as well as state subventions. This industrial settlement grew very rapidly in the sixties. The Italian Chemical monopoly – now called Montedison due to the concentration of various large chemical companies under the financial group Edison – enlarged the plant to enormous dimensions – more than 6,000 workers, over seventy miles of internal roads, the occupation of nearly five miles of shoreline and of a very large area north of Syracuse. Finally, in 1974, the largest refinery in Europe (ISAB) was built in the same area, occupying the only space left north of Syracuse and destroying a village of more than a thousand inhabitants. At present the whole plain north of Syracuse, including twenty miles of coast, described some forty years ago by Tommasi di Lampedusa as 'the only coast in the world where mermaids still survive' (now the sea and the shore are heavily oil-polluted), has become the location of the largest petro-chemical complex in southern Europe.

The level of employment in these plants is relatively low, less than 10,000 workers have a job in the petro-chemical industries and another 10,000 have a much more unstable and badly paid job in complementary, medium-sized mechanical, building and chemical industries. The workers were recruited mainly in the early sixties from the large surplus population of the surrounding rural area. The workers of the petro-chemical plants were trained in the factory itself and quickly reached the necessary competence. Moreover, work is very strictly divided, and characterized by low mobility. This situation has determined a strict tri-partition of the local labour market and working class: the stable workers of the large petro-chemical plants, the marginal workers of the medium-small complementary plants, and the agricultural workers. Different tensions and prospects characterize these three job sectors. The workers of the large plants have relatively very high salaries, practically no ties with the local social background, are highly trade-unionized and very difficult to fire. Starting from the middle seventies the development prospects of the large petro-chemical industries have been totally stopped. In part this is due to the chemical crisis and to the present overproduction of various products in the area, in part to the heavy industrial congestion of the area (there is no room left for further development). The rate of unemployment, already rather high, has become almost intolerable (more than fifteen percent of the working population), mainly because young men, trained to work in the chemical plants, are now out of a job. In the complementary industrial and commercial sectors, occupation is very irregular and salaries are extremely low. Many workers have two or three part-time jobs and seasonally return to agricultural activities. They are very often out of a job, and their gross income is not sufficient to survive, so that the migration rate has been relatively high. In the countryside, the situation is much worse. Small firms cannot survive because of low productivity and

TABLE 4.1 Comparison of the industrial settlements in Syracuse and Taching.

	Syracuse–Augusta–Priolo	Taching
Natural Historical Differences	1 Settlement in an inhabited area. Agriculturally overpopulated.	1 Settlement in a desert region.
	2 Petro-chemical plants receiving oil from outside.	2 Oil extracting industries and refineries.
Economic Organization	3 Domination of large external monopolies and complementary, often also external, industries.	3 Small local industries.
	4 Very specialized.	4 Undivided and less specialized economic activities.
Labour Market and Organization	5 Increasingly divided labour market with three different sectors: petro-chemical large plants; complementary industries; agriculture.	5 Progressive abolition of labour division. Everybody works on very different initiatives through job rotation.
Local Market Organization	6 Increasingly dependent upon externally produced goods. No promotion and valorization of local activities.	6 Progressively less dependent upon external production through a very differentiated economy.
Decision Making Processes	7 Totally centralized. The local community is expropriated of any decision making by monopolies and/or central state.	7 Partially decentralized. The local community takes the large majority of decisions on local development in every sector.
Territorial Features	8 Concentrated, polluting and congested industrialization.	8 Spread-out and uncongested industrialization surrounded by agricultural settlements.

	9 Strong urbanization processes.	9 Diffusion of the population over a large area.
Prospects	10 Sectorial crisis and increasing unemployment.	10 High rate of industrial development and persistent full employment.
	11 No further industrialization is possible in the area.	11 New development is still possible due to small scale and high flexibility.

market competition. Only medium-large firms, utilizing advanced technology and a small work-force, survive relatively well. But, due to the lack of alternative opportunities, agricultural overpopulation and crisis are persistent and without solutions. The rural population thus depends more and more on state assistance.

I have already mentioned in the previous section some of the characteristics of the Taching experience. Taching is a new settlement in an oil-rich desert area, established through family migration in the sixties (by 1966 Taching was already taken as a model for socialist industrial development by the Chinese leadership). The settlers were organized into autonomous teams which, in a very few years, established a completely new kind of community through a tremendously comprehensive programme of drilling the oil, building houses and the urban infrastructures, cultivating the surrounding land, administering the collective through direct assembly democracy, and so on.

The houses were built directly by groups of industrial workers who followed the solid and inexpensive methods of local tradition. At the same time they built various theatres, shops, meeting rooms and other collective services, controlled by the community itself. The land has been gradually ploughed and the workers take turns at farming, especially during the sowing and harvesting seasons when demand for labour goes up. Workshops and light industry plants have been set up to tap the full employment potential of the growing local community and to respond to an increasing and diversified demand for goods. Although the human settlement has grown to become a middle-sized town (at least as large as Syracuse

– 100,000 population), division of labour has been reduced to a minimum through job rotation. Further, the territorial organization differs from other petro-chemical industrial towns. To avoid urban concentration and industrial congestion, residences, service industries and other manufacturing industries are spread over a very large region. The refinery and the extractive plants are not large scale and are unconcentrated. Cultivated land surrounds every human and industrial settlement. Ecological problems are under strict observation and control by the community itself. Although the settlement has grown very rapidly to become a developed, highly populated area, it has not yet reached the concentration diseconomies of other industrial cities. On the contrary, Taching apparently presents prospects for further development.

The Chinese, in this case, have carefully avoided mono-industrial specialized development, which is particularly dangerous because, although at first more productive in comparison with a differentiated economy, in the long run it is very vulnerable to overproduction and industrial crisis. At the same time the Taching settlement seems less rigidly organized and less dependent upon the outside in comparison with the Syracuse industrial area. The small size factories can be easily converted, avoiding high costs. Local production, although oriented to the national oil market, is also able to produce different goods for the local market. At Taching petrochemical industrialization has been the basis for a general industrial development, while in every case of southern Italian industrialization the local activities have not been valorized by decentralization.

Certainly Taching, from a purely economic point of view, enjoyed the advantage of not being exposed to external market competition, for historical reasons. At that time, China was isolated internationally and had a very backward national economy: no external manufacturing industry was able to compete with the new, low productivity, Taching cottage unit. But, on the other hand, up to very recently, the Chinese regarded some social and human aspects of economic development as more important than the brute calculation of productivity alone.

Some of the positive aspects of the Chinese experience are also due to the large degree of freedom left to the peripheral population in determining social and economic trends. Direct control by the local population of the development rate, the size and quality of settlements, the location and quality of housing, the development of complementary industries and parallel agricultural units has certainly been the most important element of success, while the enormous repression of local interests and initiative in the Italian experience has been among the principal reasons for their failure. In fact the increasingly divided labour market and the unavoidable crisis of traditional and complementary economic activities have totally expropriated the local population from any possibility of creating new development prospects. Again the industrial decentralization process has only allowed petro-chemical monopolies to accumulate large profits as a consequence of low production costs, the occupation and pollution of an industrially virgin region, the exploitation of a backward market. The centralization – exploitation – dependence elements have strongly prevailed over decentralization and development.

NOTES TO CHAPTER ONE
A Marxist Critical Approach to Urban and Regional Development

1. This methodological approach is very similar to that of the classical historicist scholars which I shall try to criticize later in this chapter. The most sophisticated contribution to this approach is M. Weber, *The City*, 1921, D. Martindale & G. Neuwirth (trans. & ed.), Glencoe, Ill., Free Press, 1958.
2. Marx believes that while use-values remain essential to determine the possibility that a commodity is sold and consumed, exchange values are the ones which count in a market-based economy. Every commodity or service should have a precise use-value to become marketable, but its concrete value is established according to its exchange value, independently of whether it is more or less useful to the final consumer.
3. The Marxist approach is based on a progressive level of abstraction from the concrete reality which makes it possible to undertake a very comprehensive class analysis. The very best example is the concept of social class, which reflects a precise reality but is determined at such a high level of abstraction that it cannot be an instrument of micro-sociological analysis. The workers of a specific factory or community cannot be described purely as 'the working class': they are only the starting point for the construction of an analysis of class relations in a specific situation. This means one must reduce the micro- and macro-economical data (quantitative) to well determinated qualitative meanings if they are to be of use in class analysis.
4. J. Habermas, *Legitimation Crisis*, London & Boston, 1976 (Original German edition, 1973); C. Offe, *Strukturprobleme des kapitalistichen Staates*, Frankfurt, 1972; J. Holloway & S. Picciotto (eds.), *State and Capital*, Arnold, London, 1978.
5. P. M. Sweezy, *The Theory of Capitalist Development*, Monthly Review Press, New York, 1942; P. A. Baran & M. Sweezy, *Monopoly Capital*, Monthly Review Press, New York, 1966; P. A. Baran, *The Political Economy of Growth*, Monthly Review Press, New York, 1957.
6. M. Castells, *La question urbaine* (English edition: *The Urban Question*, Arnold, London, 1976); D. Harvey, *Social Justice and the City*, Arnold, London, 1978; M. Castells & F. Godard, *Monopolville*, Mouton, Paris & The Hague, 1974; M. Harloe (ed.), *Captive Cities*, Wiley, Chichester

& New York, 1977; C. Pickvance (ed.), *Urban Sociology: Critical Essays,* Tavistock, London, 1976; J. Lojkine, *Le Marxisme, l'état et la question urbaine,* Presses Universitaires de France, Paris, 1977.
7. As an example one might quote the theory of social reproduction and of the relation between productive and unproductive workers developed by Karl Marx in *Capital,* in *Grundrisse,* and in *Theories of Surplus Value.*
8. This process can be called the decreasing of the productive basis, as the number of workers employed in directly productive activities decreases.
9. Cf. J. O'Connor, *The Fiscal Crisis of the State,* St. Martin's Press, New York, 1973.
10. See M. Harloe (ed.), *Captive Cities,* p. 91.
11. The debate on unequal exchange and surplus profits is too vast to be extensively reported here. We can only mention that when goods are exchanged they should theoretically contain the same quantity of value. But commodities produced in different situations, more or less capital concentrated or technologically advanced or where the cost of labour subsistence is relatively lower, may be exchanged at the same price although they contain different quantities of value. In these cases the producers in countries where labour costs are higher, capital is more concentrated and technology more advanced, exchange goods which contain less value for goods containing more value. In doing so, they realize surplus profits.
12. This approach to the class analysis of urban and regional conflict is different from the one proposed by the most important contemporary neo-Marxist sociologists and geographers. For example, according to Castells and Harvey, the working class struggles only to get a less expensive and less exploitative reproduction of the labour force as such, while capital is trying to impose the optimal utilization of land in order to reproduce fixed capital. The incompatibility between these two different sets of interests generates urban class struggles. In fact, capital reproduction is a much more complex and controversial phenomenon, seeking both the reproduction of living capital (the working class) and of dead capital (accumulated or fixed capital) at minimal costs. The impossibility of achieving both of these goals at the same time is an internal contradiction of capitalism.

The working class is not struggling for better standards of self-propagation as a working class; this is an absurd idea; it does not struggle to be better exploited by capitalism. On the contrary, the working class movement aims at changing the social relations of production. In doing so, it challenges both the reproduction of fixed capital and the standards of reproduction of the labour force as such. It opposes the possibility that capital should continue and develop exploitation through its optimal, but in any case controversial, utilization of land.
13. For an excellent comprehensive criticism of English anti-urbanism see

R. Glass, 'Urban Sociology in Great Britain', *Current Sociology* 4, 1955, pp. 5-19. The worsening living conditions of the British urban population in the nineteenth century are well documented in various Parliamentary inquests (Blue Books), and in the accounts of philanthropists, physicians and travellers, as reported in some recent essays by social historians quoted in Chapter 2 of this book.
14. On the contrary, Marxist structuralists have a very different position, since they distinguish economic social relations from political ones. It seems to me that we enter the superstructural sector only when we decodify the production-class consciousness relations into political institutions or specific political forms of domination and confrontation. Cf. N. Poulantzas, *Political Power and Social Classes,* New Left Books, London, 1973; N. Poulantzas, *Classes in Contemporary Capitalism,* New Left Books, London, 1975.
15. For an idea of the contemporary historicist approach there is a very clearcut essay by W. G. Runciman, 'Towards a theory of social stratification', in F. Parkin (ed.), *The Social Analysis of Class Structure,* Tavistock, London, 1974.
16. Cf. K. Marx, *Class Struggles in France, 1848-50,* in K. Marx & F. Engels, *Selected Works,* Progress Publishers, Moscow 1973; and K. Marx, *The 18th Brumaire of Louis Bonaparte,* in K. Marx & F. Engels, *op. cit.*
17. Antonio Gramsci, *The Prison Notebooks,* Q. Hoare & G. N. Smith, (eds.) Lawrence & Wishart, London, 1973. For the concept of hegemony the most important passages are in *The Risorgimento* and *Notes on Macchiavelli.*
18. Cf. A. Gramsci, *The Risorgimento.*
19. Cf. N. Poulantzas, *Political Power;* and N. Poulantzas, *Contemporary Capitalism.*
20. I shall consider only some selected works which are particularly interesting because they remain within the Marxist methodological approach and, at the same time, discuss the problems inherent in the application of this methodological approach to the analysis of late-capitalist societies.
21. For an Italian example cf. M. Boffi, S. Cofini, A. Giasanti & E. Mingione, *Città e conflitto sociale,* Feltrinelli, Milan, 1972, which shows that public authorities discriminate in the distribution of public housing between manual and non-manual workers. The latter get better flats for only slightly higher rents.
22. Cf. N. Ginatempo, *La casa in Italia,* Mazzotta, Milan, 1976, and the very large bibliography on the problem there appended. See also the more recent article by the same author in *International Journal of Urban and Regional Research,* III (4) 1979.
23. The Italian case has given rise to a very important and interesting debate. Various analyses have been produced, from the early seventies, giving different interpretations of the decreasing official occupation rate and of the development of a very diffused informal

economy. The most important contributions are, in my opinion: M. Paci, *Mercato del lavoro e classi sociali,* Il Mulino, Bologna, 1973; S. Vinci (ed.), *Il mercato del lavoro in Italia,* Franco Angeli, Milan, 1974; M. Salvati, *Sviluppo economico, domanda di lavoro e struttura dell'occupazione,* Il Mulino, Bologna, 1976; G. Fuà, *Occupazione e capacità produttive: la realtà Italiana,* Il Mulino, Bologna, 1976.

24. Cf. H. Braverman, *Labor and Monopoly Capital,* Monthly Review Press, New York & London, 1974.
25. The problem is whether or not the planning process can be a democratic one. Both capitalist planning and east European planning processes appear very centralized and authoritarian. As I shall try to argue in the last chapter of this book, a successful planning process should be based on democratic decision making and on very decentralized processes of economic and social organization.
26. Cf. mainly R. E. Park *et al., The City,* University of Chicago Press, 1925; and E. W. Burgess & D. J. Bogue (eds.), *Contributions to Urban Sociology,* University of Chicago Press, 1964.
27. Apart from the already quoted contribution of Max Weber, various other social studies are important for the understanding of the urbanization process. These include the contribution of F. Engels, *The Condition of the Working Class in England,* and *The Housing Question;* the study by A. Weber, *The Growth of Cities in the Nineteenth Century: a Study in Statistics,* Cornell University Press, New York, 1899; the relatively very old study of F. Tönnies, *Community and Association,* 1877 (reprinted by Routledge and Kegan Paul, London, 1955); the works of the German geographer W. Christaller; the contribution of P. Geddes, *Cities in Evolution,* William and Norgate, London 1915, and many others.
28. Cf. mainly R. E. Park *et al. The City.*
29. The major contributions to the structural-functionalist theory of society are the following: T. Parsons, *The Structure of Social Action,* (Free Press, Glencoe, Ill. 1937; R. K. Merton, *Social Theory and Social Structure,* Glencoe Ill. Free Press, 1949; T. Parsons, *The Social System,* Free Press, Glencoe, Ill., 1952.
30. Among the vast production and contribution of C. Mills I believe the most important for this purpose is: *The Sociological Imagination,* Oxford University Press, New York and Oxford, 1959.
31. Cf. R. E. Pahl, 'Castells and collective consumption: a critical note', *Sociology,* xii (2) 1978.
32. M. Castells, *La question urbaine (The Urban Question).* This approach is rather diffused in Western Marxism, which is fundamentally based on a rationalist and positivist interpretation of the dialectic processes. The most important theoretical essay on contradiction, with a genuine, non-rationalist approach, remains Mao Tse Tung, 'On contradiction', 1937, in *Selected works of Mao Tse Tung,* vol. I, Foreign Languages Press, Peking, 1967, pp. 311-47.
33. Cf. M. Castells & F. Godard, *Monopolville.*

34. Cf. D. Harvey, *Social Justice and the City*.
35. See mainly M. Weber, *The City*.
36. See E. Mingione, 'Pahl and Lojkine on the state: a critical comment', *International Journal of Urban and Regional Research*, I (1) 1977, pp. 24–36.

NOTES TO CHAPTER TWO
Territorial Division of Labour and Capitalist Development

1. Where ultimate means the fundamental cause, not the only one.
2. The level of productivity and the development of productive forces have an important influence but are always subordinated to the respective socio-productive relations.
3. 'Capitalist monopoly becomes a fetter upon the method of production which has flourished with it and under it. The concentration of the means of production and socialization of labour reach a point where they prove incompatible with their capitalist husk. This bursts out.' K. Marx, *Capital*, vol. 1, Everyman, London, 1972, p. 846.
4. Absolute rent – which is fundamental to territorial structure – is one of the social relations typical of pre-capitalist society which is absorbed and survives, however partially and in a contradictory way, in most capitalist societies.
5. Marxists have carried on a long and controversial dispute over the concepts of 'transition' and 'transitional society'. Sweezy for example, believes that Europe went through a transitional stage between feudalism and capitalism which he defines as 'pre-capitalist mercantile society' (in M. Dobb (ed.), *The Transition from Feudalism to Capitalism*, Science and Society, New York, 1954). Other authors do not share this view at all. There is no agreement on the idea of a transitional society between capitalism and socialism; the most widespread opinion is that rather than a transitional society one should talk about forms of transition. Cf. on this point C. Bettelheim, *Calcul économique et formes de propriété*, Maspero, Paris, 1971 (English edn.: *Economic Calculation and Forms of Property*, New Left Books, London, 1976); C. Bettelheim, *La transition vers l'économie socialiste*, Maspero, Paris, 1968; M. Kalecki, *Introduction to the Theory of Growth in a Socialist Economy*, Blackwell, Oxford, 1969.
6. Cf. especially G. Bolaffi (ed.), *La transizione del feudalismo al capitalismo*, Savelli, Rome, 1974, which reports a recent and interesting debate ensuing from the essential text on the topic, i.e. M. Dobb, *Studies in the Development of Capitalism*, Routledge & Kegan, London, 1951. While writing this chapter I was not able to take into account the recent contribution of I. Wallerstein, *The Capitalist World-Economy*, Cambridge University Press, 1979. I particularly agree with this author's thesis of a world scale transition and on the necessity of a

Notes to Chapter Two

comprehensive analysis of world processes at various points in history.

7. Cf. E. Mingione (ed.), *L'uso del territorio in Cina*, Mazzotta, Milan, 1977.
8. K. Marx, *Capital*, Vol. 1, pp. 844-55. We have quoted the definition from *Capital*, vol. 1, because here primary accumulation is better presented than in vol. 3, *Grundrisse* or *Theories of Surplus Value*.
9. A Gerschenkron's three alternative definitions of primary accumulation (in A. Caracciolo (ed.), *La formazione dell'Italia industriale*, Laterza, Bari, 1969, pp. 53-81) are reductionist in relation to Marxian typology. He argues that primary accumulation is a financial mechanism through which resources are sieved to the industrial sector from extra-industrial ones, as a prerequisite to the process of industrialization. W. Rostow's conception is very evolutionist and deterministic, since for him industrial take-off is based upon the maturation of preconditions (cf. *The Stages of Economic Growth*, Cambridge University Press, 1960, p. 17 and ff.).
10. T. Kemp, *Industrialization in Nineteenth-Century Europe*, Longman, London, 1969, pp. 50-1.
11. M. Dobb, *Development of Capitalism*, p. 37.
12. M. Dobb, p. 70.
13. Cf. mainly: T. Kemp, *Industrialization*, pp. 1-51; B. Moore Jr., *Social Origins of Dictatorship and Democracy*, Penguin, 1967 (Beacon Press, 1966), pp. 3-39; J. H. Clapham, *An Economic History of Modern Britain*, Cambridge University Press, 1950-52; G. Mori, *La rivoluzione industriale*, Feltrinelli, Milan, 1972.
14. Cf. T. Kemp, *Industrialization*, pp. 81-118, H. Böhme, *Deutschlands Weg zur Grossmacht*, Köln, 1966; K. Borchardt, 'The Industrial Revolution in Germany', in Carlo M. Cipolla (ed.), *Fontana Economic History of Europe*, Collins, Glasgow, 1972, vol. 4; Gordon A. Craig, *Germany 1866-1945*, Clarendon Press, Oxford, 1978.
15. Cf. T. Kemp, *Industrialization*, pp. 52-80; B. Moore Jr. *Social Origins*, pp. 40-110; J. H. Clapham, *The Economic Development of France and Germany*, London, 1945; R. Cameron, *France and the Economic Development of Europe*, Princeton, 1945. In general also B. W. Slicher van Bath, *The Agrarian History of Western Europe (500-1850)*, London, 1963; E. L. Jones & S. J. Woolf (eds.), *Agrarian Change and Economic Development: the Historical problems*, Methuen, London, 1969.
16. Cf. T. Kemp, *Industrialization*, pp. 70-80.
17. Cf. T. Kemp, pp. 172-8.
18. These are the most important studies on Italian industrialization and the *Risorgimento*: A. Gramsci, *Il Risorgimento*, Einaudi, Turin, 1949; Rosario Romeo, *Risorgimento e Capitalismo*, Laterza, Bari, 1959; A. Gerschenkron, *Economic Backwardness in Historical Perspective*, Belknapp Press of Harvard University Press, Harvard, 1962; A. Caracciolo (ed.), *La formazione dell'Italia industriale*, Laterza, Bari, 1969; G. Luzzatto, *L'economia italiano dal 1861 al 1894*, Einaudi, Turin,

1968; E. Sereni, *Il capitalismo nelle campagne* (1860-1900), Einaudi, Turin, 1968; G. Toniolo (ed.), *Lo sviluppo economico italiano 1861-1940*, Laterza, Bari, 1973; V. Castronovo, 'La storia economica', in *Storia d'Italia*, Vol. 4. 1, 1975. Specifically on the southern question cf. R. Villari's (ed.) anthology, *Il sud nella storia d'Italia*, Laterza, Bari, 1966, and the most recent original opinion (which I personally do not share) by E. M. Capecelatro and A. Carlo, *Contro la 'questione meridionale'*, Savelli, Rome, 1972.
19. For thirteenth-century rationalization of agriculture in Lombardy cf. the essay by R. Zangheri, '*I rapporti storici tra progresso agricolo e sviluppo economico in Italia*', in E. L. Jones and J. S. Woolf (eds.), *Agrarian Change*.
20. Cf. E. Sereni, *Il capitalismo nelle campagne*, pp. 145-200.
21. All data are taken from V. Castronovo's essay, 'La storia economica', p. 48. The gap between northern and southern agriculture has been amply demonstrated. E. Sereni convincingly argues that such a gap is the basic cause of the north-south dichotomy; this thesis is demonstrated in detail by R. S. Eckaus, 'Il divario nord-sud nei primi decenni dell'unità', in A. Caracciolo (ed.), *La formazione dell'Italia industriale*, pp. 223-43 (also in English, 'The North-South Dichotomy in the First Ten Years of Unity', *Journal of Economic History*, XXI (3), Sept. 1961).
22. Cf. in particular E. Sori's essay, 'Assetto e redistribuzione della popolazione italiana', in G. Toniolo (ed.), *Lo sviluppo economico*, pp. 299-301.
23. Cf. E. Sori, ibid., p. 300.
24. Concerning Italian industrialization cf. also T. Kemp, *Industrialization*, pp. 159-78; L. Cafagna, 'The Industrialization of Italy', in *Fontana Economic History of Europe*; B. Caizzi, *Storia dell' industria italiana dal XVIII secolo ai giorni nostri*, Einaudi, Turin, 1946; R. Morandi, *Storia della grande industria in Italia*, Einaudi, Turin, 1966; L. Rosa, *La rivoluzione industriale in Italia e nel Mezzogiorno*, Laterza, Bari, 1974.
25. Cf. E. Sereni, *Il capitalismo nelle campagne*, p. 143. The table on the redistribution of mortmain land given by Sereni is:

Church property	hectares 750,000	divided in 170,000 plots
Church property in Sicily	hectares 190,000	divided in 23,000 plots
Ancient state land property	hectares 300,000	divided in 97,990 plots
Property with communal rights	hectares 370,000	divided in ? plots
'Conciliated' state land	hectares 393,957	divided in 600,000 plots
Allotted state land	hectares 461,296	
	Total hectares 2,465,253	

My own belief is that most of this vast booty – amounting to more than two and a half million hectares – directly or indirectly (after resale or bankruptcy) accrued to medium and large bourgeois landowners.
26. Cf. Gerschenkron, *Economic Backwardness*, pp. 72-6.
27. Cf. especially: L. Mumford, *The City in History*, Penguin Books, Harmondsworth, 1966, p. 515 and ff.; A. Briggs, *Victorian Cities*, Penguin Books, Harmondsworth, 1968. Some of the principal English industrial cities were no more than small villages in the

seventeenth century. This applies in particular to Manchester and Birmingham which, according to Mumford (p. 518), had a population of 6,000 and 4,000 respectively, in the seventeenth century.
28. Cf. A. Weber, *The Growth of Cities in the Nineteenth Century: A Study in Statistics,* Cornell University Press, New York, 1899.
29. Cf. C. Carozzi and A. Mioni, *L'Italia in formazione,* De Donato, Bari, 1970, p. 33.
30. Cf. E. J. Hobsbawm, *Industry and Empire,* Penguin Books, Harmondsworth, 1969, diagrams 4 (p. 327), 13 & 14 (p. 335).
31. This thesis is accepted by A. Briggs, *Victorian Cities,* and J. R. Mellor, *Urban Sociology in an Urbanized Society,* Routledge & Kegan Paul, 1977.
32. There are many texts on this point; it is enough to remember the existence of Parliamentary inquests (Blue Books) and the famous study by Engels, *The Condition of the Working Class in England.*
33. On London's comeback Asa Briggs writes that 'During the early nineteenth century London had declined in industrial importance in relation to the provinces . . . During the late nineteenth century London's numbers rose rapidly, from three million in 1860 to four and a half million by the beginning of the new century. However, there was also an impressive increase of 'the outer ring' from 414,000 in 1861 to 2,045,000 in 1901. London had become a gigantic metropolis with its seven million inhabitants, if one includes suburban population (A. Briggs, *Victorian Cities*).
34. For Asia cf. especially T. G. McGee's works *The South-East Asian City,* London, 1961, and *The Urbanization Process in the Third World,* G. Bell & Sons, London, 1971. For Latin America I recommend the anthology, *Imperialismo e urbanizzazione in America Latina,* Mazzotta, Milan, 1972. See also J. Abu-Lughod & R. Hay Jr. (eds.), *Third World Urbanization,* Maaroufa Press, Chicago, 1977.
35. This is not the place to enter into the complex and extended debate on imperialism: it must suffice to mention the most recent work which I think well summarizes the debate, i.e. M. Baratt-Brown, *The Economics of Imperialism,* Penguin Books, Harmondsworth, 1974.
36. Cf. M. de Cecco, 'Lo sviluppo dell'economia italiana e la sua collocazione internazionale', *Rivista Internazionale di Scienze Economiche e Commerciali,* October 1971, pp. 973-93.
37. Cf. A. Gerschenkron, *Economic Backwardness,* p. 76.
38. Cf. E. Sereni, *Il Capitalismo nelle campagne,* and G. Luzzatto, *L'economia italiana.*
39. Gerschenkron places the Italian industrial take-off at the end of the last century; whereas R. Romeo places the take-off in the 1880s. Economic historians by and large agree with Gerschenkron; so do I.
40. According to data established by T. Kemp, *Industrialization,* pp. 202-3, in 1910 per head consumption of raw cotton was kg. 5.4 for Italy, 6.0 for France, 6.8 for Germany and 19.8 for UK; cast-iron consumption

was kg. 8 for Italy, 100 for France, 200 for Germany and 210 for UK; coal consumption was kg. 150 for Italy, 1,200 for France, 2,650 for Germany and 4,070 for UK. One can see that Italy was relatively backward even after its first rapid growth and despite being considered one of the great industrial powers.

41. Cf. F. Colletti, 'Zone grige della popolazione di Milano', in Carozzi and Mioni, L'Italia in formazione pp. 107-8.
42. Cf. Castronovo, 'La storia economica', p. 168.
43. Cf. Castronovo, *op. cit.*, p. 189.
44. In relation to Fascist economic policy and in particular for agriculture cf. G. Tattara, 'Cerealicoltura e politica agraria durante il fascismo' and G. S. Cohen, 'Un esame statistico delle opere di bonifica intraprese durante il regime fascista', in G. Toniolo (ed.), *Lo sviluppo economico*; L. Villari, *Il capitalismo italiano del '900*, Laterza, Bari, 1972.
45. Cf. L. Villari, op. cit., p. 230 and ff.
46. Particularly useful on reconstruction is the 'Introduction' by A. Graziani in *L'economia italiana 1945-1970,* Il Mulino, Bologna, 1972; P. Saraceno, *Ricostruzione e pianificazione* (1943-1949), Laterza, Bari, 1969; B. Manzocchi, *Lineamenti di politica economica in Italia 1945-1949*, Editori Riuniti, Rome, 1960.
47. For the 1951 agrarian reform see especially the anthology, *Riforma agraria e azione meridionalista,* Il Mulino, Bologna, 1956, particularly M. Rossi-Doria's contribution; G. Barbera, *Riforma agraria italiana, risultati e prospettive,* Editori Riuniti, Rome, 1960.
48. Cf. G. Orlando, 'Progressi e difficoltà in agricoltura', in G. Fuà (ed.)., *Lo sviluppo economico in Italia,* vol III, Angeli Editore, Milan, 1969, pp. 35-7.
49. Cf. C. Daneo, *Agricoltura e sviluppo capitalistico in Italia,* Einaudi, Turin, 1971.
50. There are many interpretations of the 'economic miracle' but they all centre around the two factors which I consider to be the basic motors of development. There is, however, no agreement on the extent to which exports and low wages have helped promote development. There are also other elements that have contributed towards the Italian economic boom, such as the positive balance of payments due to money sent back home by emigrants and to the growth of the tourist industry. Cf. besides A. Graziani, *L'economia italiana,* also M. d'Antonio, *Sviluppo e crisi del capitalismo italiano,* 1951-72, Laterza, Bari, 1973.
51. Studies of development, to date, are more or less agreed in denying the existence of any desire for mushrooming of local and autonomous industrial initiatives. Cf. E. Hytten and M. Marchioni, *Industrializzazione senza sviluppo,* Angeli, Milan, 1960; E. Peggio, M. Mazzarino, V. Parlato, *Industrializzazione e sottosviluppo,* Einaudi, Turin, 1960; M. Lelli, *Il proletariato e ceti medi in Sardegna,* De Donato, Bari, 1975.
52. It is impossible to list the numerous studies on concentration, polar-

ized development, industrial decentralization and cottage industry. Only the work of the French geographer E. Dalmasso – *Milan, capitale économique de l'Italie,* Faculté de Lettres de Strasbourg, 1970 *(Milano capitale economica d'Italia,* Angeli, Milano, 1972) – is mentioned here for its monumental research on the process of economic concentration in Milan and the interesting analysis by the Italian social geographer L. Gambi on the Italian historical urbanization processes. Cf. L. Gambi, 'I valori storici de quadri ambientali', in *Storia d'Italia,* I, and L. Gambi, 'Da città ad area metropolitana', in *Storia d'Italia*.

53. Cf. particularly the works mentioned in the previous note.
54. Cf. The anthology, *Piccola industria grande sfruttamento,* Bertani, Verona, 1974.
55. The analysed municipalities are the following (in brackets are, first the population in 1951 and then the population in 1971 taking the figure for 1951 as being 100): Cinisello Balsamo (15,336-504), Cologno Monzese (8,584-553), Cesano Maderno (16,830-196), Corsico (9,060-413), Bollate (11,932-358), Cusano Milanino (8,621-238), Desio (16,824-181), Paderno Dugnano (14,218-247), Pioltello (6,401-446), San Donato Milanese (2,667-1,006), Cesano Boscone (3,688-575), Bresso (4,575-700), Limbiate (9,087-352).
56. Cf. E. Dalmasso, *Milano,* pp. 235-39.
57. Cf. especially M. Paci, *Mercato del lavoro e class social,* Il Mulino, Bologna, 1974; L. Melodesi, *Disoccupazione ad esercito industriale di riserva,* Laterza, Bari, 1972.
58. Cf. V. Lutz, *Italy: A Study in Economic Development,* Oxford, 1962; Istituto Gramsci, *Tendenze del capitalismo italiano,* Editori Riuniti, Rome, 1964; G. H. Hildebrand, *Growth and Structure in the Economy of Modern Italy,* Harvard University Press, Cambridge, Mass., 1965; as well as d'Antonio, *Sviluppo e crisi,* and A. Graziani, *L'economia italiana.* On the reshaping of the Italian economy after the 1963 crisis see mainly A. Graziani (ed.), *Crisi e ristruttuzazione nell' economia italiana,* Einaudi Torino, 1975; and M. Salvati, *Il sistema economico italiano: analisi di una crisi,* Il Mulino, Bologna, 1975.
59. Apart from the works mentioned in note 57, there are many research projects under way on developments in Italy. One being conducted at Messina University under my supervision concerns Taranto, Gioia Tauro and Augusta Priolo. Also important are the Intersind research on Taranto, Ottana, Cassino and Gela together with the COSPOS-ISVI researches on Naples, plus various other studies undertaken by Formez, Rome.

NOTES TO CHAPTER THREE
Uneven Territorial Development and the Crisis of Advanced Capitalism

1. On the territorial aspects of capital accumulation the theoretical basis was dealt with in Chapter 1 and the historical process in Chapter 2.
2. J. G. Williamson, 'Regional inequality and the process of national development: a description of patterns', *Economic Development and Cultural Change,* 13 (4), 1965, pp. 3-84. A critique to Williamson's law and an alternative approach are found in B. Secchi, *Squilibri regionali e sviluppo economico,* Marsilio, Padua, 1974. Holland's approach is also critical and opposed to the neo-classical and neo-Keynesian analysis. See S. Holland, *Capital versus the Regions,* Macmillan, London, 1976; *The Regional Problem,* Macmillan, London, 1976.
3. Bureaucratization is a parallel phenomenon to urbanization. It is likely that the economic crisis and increased state intervention in the economy have accelerated this process in the last few years. For the Italian situation, see E. Mingione, *Impiegati, lotta di classe e sviluppo capitalistico,* Savelli, Rome, 1973; S. Caruso, *Burocrazia e capitale in Italia,* Bertani, Verona, 1974.
4. The internal division of the various social classes is determined in large part by the neo-dualist organization of late-capitalist economies and by various processes of marginalization. See E. Mingione, 'Capitalist crisis, neo-dualism, and marginalization', *International Journal of Urban and Regional Research,* 2 (2), 1978.
5. I have expressed elsewhere in a more detailed way my interpretation of the accumulation process in late capitalism; see E. Mingione, 'Capitalist Crisis' and E. Mingione, *La società in frantumi,* Feltrinelli, Milan, forthcoming.
6. The most important recent essays on the class structure in Italy are collected in the two following readers: M. Paci (ed.), *Capitalismo e classi sociali in Italia,* Il Mulino, Bologna, 1978; C. Ragone & C. Scrocca (eds.), *La sociologia delle classi in Italia,* Liguori, Naples, 1978.
7. Various works have been published recently concerning the peripheral neo-dualistic organization of late capitalism. Among them see mainly: S. Amin, *Le Développement inégal,* Editions de Minuit, Paris, 1973; H. Braverman, *Labor and Monopoly Capital,* Monthly Review Press, New York & London 1974; J. O'Connor, *The Fiscal Crisis of the State,* St. Martin's Press, New York, 1973. On Italy see: P. Calzabini, *Economia periferica e classi sociali,* Liguori, Naples, 1976; A. Bagnasco, *Le tre Italie,* Il Mulino, Bologna, 1977.

200 Notes to Chapter Three

8. For a critical analysis of the different growth poles theories see mainly S. Holland, *Capital versus the Regions*.
9. I agree only partially with Gunder-Frank's theory on domination hierarchies in the underdeveloped countries. It applies correctly only to the Latin American cases. I want here to underline the importance of the large administrative cities as penetration platform for imperialistic capital.
10. In many Asian countries migrations from the countryside to large cities are contained by the absolute lack of perspective of the urban economies. Strong urbanization processes often arise for historical reasons like the concentration in Calcutta of the Indo-Pakistani refugees, and cannot be generalized.
11. Among various studies on urban development in Mexico I would particularly recommend the following one: J. Montaño, *Los pobres de la ciudad en los asentamientos espontaneos*, Siglo Veintiuno, Mexico, 1976.
12. The point is that many ex-colonial countries have inherited a strongly mono-cultural or mono-industrial economic structure. Sugar, coffee, tea, rubber, copper, bananas, guano and others are practically the only exportation wealth of most Third World countries. These goods are exported through foreign multinational corporations which are able to impose their prices and exercise a strong political control. The multi-national import corporations have thus been able to condition the economic development and political character of many monocultural Third World countries through their hold on the international prices of exported goods.
13. On the Asian experience, which, so far, has been more fully analysed, see mainly T. G. McGee, *The South-East Asian City*, G. Bell & Sons, London, 1967; T. G. McGee, *Hawkers in Hong Kong*, University of Hong Kong, Centre of Asian Studies, 1973.
14. The debate among economists about the present economic crisis is too vast and articulated to be quoted here. In a study I am publishing in Italian, I include a select bibliography of the most important recent works on the problem. See E. Mingione, *La società in frantumi*.
15. In this sense also the territorial phenomenology of class struggles is rapidly changing. Regional and local struggles are becoming relatively more important than general national problems, like the housing one, which nourished social conflict in the past.
16. The various interpretations of the crisis can be reduced to two classical hypotheses: the gradual decrease of the profit rate and overproduction. Recently many authors (principally scholars from the Frankfurt school – see the works by Habermas & Offe) have underlined and re-evaluated the importance of extra-economic factors in the determination of the crisis.
17. By balcanization of the labour market we mean the progressive division of the market into many different sectors not communicating one with the other.

18. In the Italian case this phenomenon has been reflected in two important events: divisions and competitiveness among the national trade unions to get better and better conditions for their own workers, and even more, the successes of the new, independent union organizations (*sindicati autonomi*).
19. See J. L. O'Connor, *The Fiscal Crisis of the State* and R. C. Hill, 'State capitalism and the urban fiscal crisis in the United States', *International Journal of Urban and Regional Research*, 1 (1), 1977, London.
20. Cf. A. Graziani (ed.), *Lo sviluppo economico italiano 1945-1970*, Il Mulino, Bologna, 1974; M. Paci (ed.), *Capitalismo e classi sociali in Italia*, Il Mulino, Bologna, 1978; M. Salvati, *Il sistema economico italiano: problemi di una crisi*, Il Mulino, Bologna, 1975. On uneven territorial development: B. Secchi, *Squilibri regionali;* P. Calzabini, *Economia periferica e classi sociali*, Liguori, Naples, 1976; A. Bagnasco, *Le tre Italie*.
21. See: E. Deaglio (ed.), *La Fiat com'é*, Feltrinelli, Milan, 1975.
22. Some of the data reproduced here and the terminology used are taken from A. Bagnasco, *Le tre Italie*.
23. On the recent problems of the southern Italian question see mainly: A. Graziani, 'Il mezzogiorno nella economia Italiana oggi', *Inchiesta*, VII (29), pp. 3-18 and A. Bagnasco, *Le tre Italie*. Specifically on the Italian poles of growth, I have mainly referred to a research project I have directed for the University of Messina: E. Mingione (ed.), *Ricerca sociologica sui Poli di Sviluppo*, 12 volumes, duplicated for the Formez, Rome, 1977.

NOTES TO CHAPTER FOUR
Socialism, Class Conflict, and Land-Use

1. Apart from the contributions already quoted in Chapter 2, Note 5, see also: O. Lange, *Socialism and Socialist Economy*, Warsaw, 1966; M. Dobb, *Welfare Economics and the Economics of Socialism*, Cambridge University Press, 1969; C. Bettelheim, *Problèmes théoriques et pratiques de la planification*, Maspero, Paris 1966.
2. K. Marx, *A Contribution to the Critique of Political Economy*, reprinted, London, 1971, p. 21.
3. Cf. E. Mingione, 'Pahl and Lojkine on the state: a critical comment', *International Journal of Urban and Regional Research*, I (1) (1977).
4. Apart from very general similarities, the transition processes should be considered very different from one another. The feudal social and economic system was not very progressive or dynamic; it was based on an unstable equilibrium with the progressive force of international trade. After a very short period of 'pure feudalism' (the Carolingian Empire), the Western world entered a very long and slow process of transition which lasted overall at least seven centuries. It is likely that transitions to socialism will be a much shorter process, because capitalism is a very dynamic social organization and because class consciousness is now more diffused.
5. Cf. F. Engels, *Anti-Duhring*, in K. Marx & F. Engels, *Selected works*, Progress Publishers, Moscow, 1973.
6. G. Stalin, *Economic Problems of Socialism in the USSR*. Moscow, 1952.
7. V. Nekrasov, *The Territorial Organization of the Soviet Economy*, Progress Publishers, Moscow, 1974, p. 143.
8. H. Lefebvre, *La révolution urbaine*, Gallimard, Paris, 1970.
9. Cf. R. Glass, Urban Sociology in Great Britain, *Current Sociology* 4, 1955, pp. 5-19.
    In the works of Marx and Engels too, there are some interesting pieces of criticism against the early anti-urbanism of Utopian socialists (Fourier, Saint-Simon, Proudhon, etc.).
10. Marx argues that, while the technological progress could, in theory, bestow an easier life upon humanity, the specific capitalist use of any technological innovation means a worsening of the working and living conditions of the large majority of the workers. Cf. R. Panzieri, 'Sull'uso capitalistico delle maccine nel neo-capitalismo', in *La ripresa del marxismo-leninismo in Italia*, Sapere, Milan, 1972.
11. Cf. C. Bettelheim, *La planification soviétique*, Marcel Rivière, Paris,

1948, and more recently, *Les luttes de class en URSS*, Maspero, Paris, 1975.
12. On the study of the Chinese case I have adopted a particular methodology. I have relied minimally on macro-economic and macro-social data, which appear very controversial because they can be interpreted in different ways; they require a very detailed knowledge of their precise meaning. I have referred only to a few selected Western studies on Chinese development. The study chiefly makes use of the vast Chinese documentation published in *Peking Review*, *China Quarterly*, and other Chinese publications, plus personal observation during a thirty-five-days' study visit to China. This information was discussed in a permanent seminar held at the Centro di Ricêrche sui Modi di Produzione (CRMP) in Milan between 1972 and 1976. See C. Bettelheim, J. Charrière, H. Marchisio, *La construction du socialisme en Chine*, Maspero, Paris, 1965; K. Buchanan, *The Transformation of the Chinese Earth*, Bell & Sons, London, 1970; *Aperçus Géographiques de la Chine nouvelle,* Association des Amitiés Franco-Chinoises, Paris, 1975; E. Mingione (ed.), *L'uso del territorio in Cina,* Mazzotta, Milan, 1977.
13. There is very little material on the organization of public administration and planning in China. Spazzali has written a very interesting short essay on the subject, to which I mainly refer, in E. Mingione (ed.), *L'uso del territorio in Cina*, pp. 146-58.
14. I believe that only very recently has capitalism reached the maximum possible development of its productive forces. The present crisis is thus a general social crisis due to the contradiction between the dominant capitalist form of production and the pressure of productive forces for further development, no longer compatible with capitalism itself.
15. See mainly R. Pahl, 'Stratification, the relation between states and urban and regional development', *International Journal of Urban and Regional Research,* 1 (1) 1977, pp. 6-18.
16. I do not believe in the capacity of capitalism to revive the accumulation process. See E. Mingione, 'Capitalist crisis, neo-dualism, and marginalization', *International Journal of Urban and Regional Research,* 2 (2) 1978.
17. All the information on the Syracuse 'pole' comes from a research project I directed for the CES-CNR-FORMEZ in 1973-76. See E. Mingione, *Ricerca sociologica sugli effetti della pianificazione industriale nel Mezzogiorno (Poli di Sviluppo)*, FORMEZ – Rome 1-9.
18. See also E. Mingione (ed.), *L'uso del territorio in Cina*. The last chapter is totally devoted to Taching.

Name Index

Abu-Lughod, J. 196
Amin, S. 199

Bagnasco, A. 199, 201
Baran, P. A. 188
Baratt-Brown, M. 196
Barbera, G. 197
Bettelheim, C. 193, 202, 203
Boffi, M. 190
Bogue, D. J. 191
Böhme, H. 194
Bolaffi, G. 193
Borchardt, K. 194
Braverman, H. 191, 199
Briggs, A. 195, 196
Burgess, E. W. 191

Cafagna, L. 195
Caizzi, B. 195
Calzabini, P. 199, 201
Capecelatro, E. M. 195
Caracciolo, A. 194, 195
Carlo, A. 195
Carozzi, C. 196, 197
Caruso, S. 199
Castells, Manuel 68, 188, 191
Castronovo, Valerio 109, 195, 197
Charrière, J. 203
Christaller, W. 191
Cipolla, C. 194
Clapham, J. H. 194
Cofini, S. 190
Cohen, G. S. 197
Colletti, F. 197
Craig, Gordon, A. 194

Dalmasso, E. 198
Daneo, C. 197
D'Antonio, M. 197, 198
Deaglio, E. 201
De Cecco, M. 196
Dobb, Maurice 77, 193, 194, 202

Eckaus, R. S. 195
Engels, Friedrich 164, 191, 196, 202

Fuà, G. 191, 197

Gambi, L. 198
Geddes, P. 191
Gerschenkron, A. 86, 108, 194, 195, 196
Giasanti, A. 190
Ginatempo, N. 190
Glass, Ruth 190, 202
Godard, F. 188, 191
Gramsci, Antonio 7, 41, 42, 45, 190, 194
Graziani, A. 197, 198, 201
Gunder-Frank, A. 200

Habermas, Jurgen 15, 188, 200
Harloe, M. 188
Harvey, David 68, 69, 70, 188, 192
Hay, Jr., R. 196
Hildebrand, G. M. 198
Hill, R. C. 201
Hobsbawm, E. J. 196
Holland, S. 199, 200
Hytten, E. 197

Jones, E. L. 194, 195

Kalecki, M. 193
Kemp, Thomas 77, 79, 80, 89, 194, 195, 196

Lange, Oscar 202
Lefebvre, Henry 165, 167, 202
Lelli, M. 197
Lenin, Vladimir Ilich 160
Lojkine, J. 189, 192, 202
Lutz, Vera 121, 198
Luzzatto, E. 194

McGee, T. G. 196, 200
Manzocchi, B. 197
Mao Tse Tung 191
Marchioni, M. 197
Marchisio, M. 203

Marx, Karl 12, 14, 15, 22, 41, 45, 72, 75, 91, 160, 161, 162, 164, 166, 167, 188, 189, 190, 193, 194, 202
Mazzarino, M. 197
Meldolesi, L. 198
Mellor, J. R. 196
Merton, R. K. 191
Mills, C. Wright 65, 191
Mingione, E. 190, 192, 194, 199, 200, 201, 202, 203
Mioni, A. 196, 197
Montaño, J. 200
Moore Jr., Barrington 194
Morandi, R. 195
Mori, G. 194
Mumford, L. 195, 196

Nekrasov, I. 165, 202

O'Connor, James 45, 189, 199, 201
Offe, Klaus 45, 188, 200
Orlando, G. 197

Paci, M. 191, 198, 199, 201
Pahl, Ray 67, 191, 192, 202, 203
Park, R. E. 191
Parlato, V. 197
Parsons, Talcott 64, 191
Peggio, E. 197
Pickvance, C. 189
Poulantzas, Nico 45, 190

Ragone, C. 199
Romeo, R. 194
Rosa, L. 195
Rossi-Doria, M. 197
Rostow, W. 194
Runciman, W. G. 190

Salvati, M. 191, 198, 201
Saraceno, P. 197

Scrocca, C. 199
Secchi, B. 199, 201
Sereni, Emilio 86, 195, 196
Slicher van Bath, B. W. 194
Sori, E. 195
Spazzali, S. 203
Stalin, G. 162, 164, 165, 202

Sweezy, P. M. 188, 193

Tattara, G. 197
Toniolo, G. 195, 197
Tönnies, F. 191

Villari, L. 197
Villari, R. 195
Vinci, S. 191

Wallerstein, Immanuel 193
Weber, A. 191, 196
Weber, Max 71, 188, 191, 192
Williamson, J. G. 125, 199
Woolf, S. J. 194, 195

Zangheri, R. 195

SUBJECT INDEX

built environment 68–70

capital accumulation
  current crisis of 144–8
  industrial take-off: comparative synthesis 89–95; England 75–9; France 79–81; Germany 79; Italy 81–9, 106–8
  monopolistic 128–30
  primitive/primary/original 22, 25–8, 46, 73–81
  stages of 96–9
  territorial features of primitive 25–8
  territorial logic of 126–8
  theoretical basis of 14–18
class consciousness 31–2, 43–4
Chicago school 64
collective consumption 66–8

decentralization 62–3, 104–5, 115–16, 122, 133–4
  comparative Italy and China 180–7
  Italy 150–6

fiscal crisis of cities 30, 38, 51–2, 130–31
functionalism 64

hegemony 7, 33–4, 41–4, 55, 162
housing question 27–8

industrial reserve army 56–7
informal economy 9, 11, 51, 129, *see also* neo-dualism
Italy
  economic structure 148–50
  south, problem of the 50–51, 112–13, 118–22, 154–8

labour market 55–9
  Italian south 156–7
labour-value, theory of 12–14
large corporations 45–8

metropolitan areas 104–5, 130–32
migration
  general 126–7
  international from Italy 86–7, 107–8
  Italy, from the south (1945–75) 113
mode of production 72–6

neo-dualism 46, 132–4
  Italy 115–18, 152–4

opposition between city and countryside 22–3, 36, 164–6
over-urbanization 21, 59, 137–44

regional economic theories 124–6
regional policies 48
  Italy 50–1; poles of growth in 154–8
  USA 48–50
rent and land speculations 36–7
Risorgimento 42–3, 81–9
rural classes in transition 76–89

social conflicts and movements 23–4, 31–3, 38–40
  ecological 60
social disgregation 11, 30, 59, 146–7
social margination 11, 16, 30, 61
social restratification 16, 18, 131–2
socialism
  bureaucracy 10, 61–2
  experiences 7–8, 10, 61–3; in China 172–9
  territorial structure 63, 163–72
  theory of 74, 158–63
state and political organizations
  fiscal crisis of 17
  housing 53–4
  intervention in the economy 10, 16, 17, 45–55, 128
  theory of 34, 40–55
suburbanization 21, 28–30, 59

Taching experiment 177, 180–7
technology
  and territorial imbalances 124–8
tertiarization 47, 56, 58–60
Third World
  large cities in 134–5
  rural areas in 135–7
transport policies 54–5

under-accumulation 47, 48, 145–8
underdevelopment cycle 137–44
unemployment 56–7, 60–1
unequal exchange 10, 31, 58, 135–44, 189

urban problems
    conflicts 24–5, 38–40
    congestion 21, 28–9, 145–6; in Italy 150–4
    diseconomies 21, 60–61
    poverty 30, 103–4
urbanization
    England 99–103
    factory-city to metropolis 99–105
    general 27–8
    Italy 106–23
    and primary accumulation 89–95
    Third World 105, 137–44

White collar workers 58–60
working class 14–18, 32–40, 60–1